MICROSOFT FLIGHT SIMULATOR 2024 TRAINING GUIDE

A Practical Manual to Realistic Flying, Procedures, and Aircraft Control for PS5 Users, PC Users, and Other Users

KENNETH RADNOR

TABLE OF CONTENTS

INTRODUCTION

Welcome to **Microsoft Flight Simulator 2024**, the most advanced and immersive flight simulator to date. This guide covers everything you need to master flying on **PC, Xbox, or PlayStation**, from basic flight and landing techniques to advanced aircraft systems and mission-based careers.

Experience a **digital twin of the entire planet**, with realistic weather, day-night cycles, and thousands of airports. Fly a wide range of aircraft — from light planes to airliners and helicopters — while exploring career missions, multiplayer events, and community content.

Whether you are a beginner or a seasoned virtual pilot, this guide will help you **take off, navigate, and land confidently** in a fully-realized world of flight simulation.

HISTORY OF THE FLIGHT SIMULATOR FRANCHISE

The **Microsoft Flight Simulator** franchise began as a passion project by **Bruce Artwick** in the late 1970s and grew into one of the longest-running and most influential simulation series in gaming history. What started as a simple wireframe flight model has evolved into a **near-photorealistic, planet-wide simulation**, powered by satellite imagery, cloud computing, and artificial intelligence.

Early Foundations: subLOGIC and Microsoft (1970s–1980s)

In the mid-1970s, Bruce Artwick developed a flight simulation program as part of his graduate studies. Recognizing its potential, he founded **subLOGIC Corporation** in 1977 and began distributing the software by mail order.

In **1979**, subLOGIC released **FS1 Flight Simulator** for the **Apple II**, followed by versions for systems such as the **TRS-80**. These early releases laid the groundwork for personal computer flight simulation.

Microsoft entered the picture in **1982**, licensing the software and releasing **Microsoft Flight Simulator 1.0** for the **IBM PC**. This version introduced major improvements, including **color graphics, variable weather, and time-of-day settings**, bringing the simulator to a wider audience.

Between **1983 and 1986**, subLOGIC continued developing **Flight Simulator II** across multiple platforms, adding features such as **multiple 3D viewpoints and expanded airport coverage**.

The Microsoft Era: Innovation and Expansion (Late 1980s–2000s)

In **1988**, Bruce Artwick formed the **Bruce Artwick Organization (BAO)** to work directly with Microsoft on future releases, beginning with **Microsoft Flight Simulator 3.0**.

The 1990s marked a period of rapid technical progress:

- **Flight Simulator 5.0 (1993)** introduced textured terrain, significantly improving realism.
- **Flight Simulator 5.1 (1995)** added satellite imagery and became the first version distributed on **CD-ROM**.
- Later in 1995, Microsoft acquired BAO, bringing development fully in-house.

With **Flight Simulator 98**, the franchise embraced **DirectX**, enabling hardware-accelerated 3D graphics and introducing **helicopter flight**.

Throughout the 2000s, releases expanded realism and scope:

- **Flight Simulator 2000** introduced downloadable real-world weather
- **Flight Simulator 2002** added AI aircraft and air traffic control
- **Flight Simulator 2004: A Century of Flight** celebrated aviation history with historical aircraft
- **Flight Simulator X (2006)** delivered major graphical upgrades, multiplayer features, and DirectX 10 support

Hiatus and Modern Revival (2009–Present)

In **2009**, Microsoft closed **Aces Game Studio**, casting uncertainty over the franchise's future. During this period, third parties kept the ecosystem alive:

- **Lockheed Martin** adapted the codebase for professional training as **Prepar3D**
- **Dovetail Games** re-released **Flight Simulator X: Steam Edition**, extending its lifespan

Microsoft attempted a reboot with **Microsoft Flight (2012)**, but its simplified design and lack of add-on support led to an early shutdown.

The franchise returned in spectacular fashion with **Microsoft Flight Simulator (2020)**, announced at E3 2019 and released on PC in 2020 and Xbox in 2021. Using **Bing Maps satellite imagery, Azure cloud computing, and AI**, it recreated the entire Earth with unprecedented realism.

Microsoft Flight Simulator 2024

Released in **November 2024**, **Microsoft Flight Simulator 2024** builds upon the 2020 foundation by introducing **structured career modes**, expanded activities, and deeper simulation systems. It represents the next evolution of a franchise that has continually redefined what flight simulation can be.

MICROSOFT FLIGHT SIMULATOR 2024: INSTALLATION & SETUP

Microsoft Flight Simulator 2024 is installed in two stages: an initial base download through **Steam, the Microsoft Store, or Xbox**, followed by an **in-game download of core data** and setup of graphics and controls. A **stable internet connection** is essential, as the simulator streams global scenery, weather, and live data in real time.

The simulator is available on **PC**, **Xbox Series X|S**, and **PlayStation 5**.

System Requirements (PC)

Ensure your system meets the following specifications for optimal performance:

Component	Minimum Requirements	Recommended Requirements
CPU	AMD Ryzen 5 2600X / Intel Core i7-6800K	AMD Ryzen 7 2700X / Intel Core i7-10700K
Graphics	AMD Radeon RX 5700 / NVIDIA GTX 970	AMD Radeon RX 5700 XT / NVIDIA RTX 2080
RAM	16 GB	32 GB
Storage	50 GB (base install)	50 GB+ (add-ons & cache recommended)
OS	Windows 10 (latest update)	Windows 10 (latest update)
Internet	10 Mbps	50 Mbps

Installation Process (PC)

The installation consists of two main steps:

1. Install the Launcher

- **Microsoft Store / Xbox App:** Sign in with your Microsoft account and install the base game from your library or via a redeemed code.
- **Steam:** Open Steam, go to your **Library**, locate *Microsoft Flight Simulator 2024*, and click **Install** to download the launcher.

2. Launch and Download Game Content

- Start the game and sign in with your **Microsoft account or Gamertag**.
- The simulator will prompt you to download the main content packages.
- MSFS 2024 uses a **thin-client architecture**, keeping the initial download around **50 GB**, with most world data streamed from the cloud.
- Optional Deluxe or Premium content can be downloaded immediately or installed later.

Initial Setup & Configuration

Once installation is complete, the simulator will guide you through first-time setup:

Startup Configuration

- **Graphics Settings:** Automatically detected (e.g., Medium or High-End). These can be fine-tuned later under **Options > Graphics**.
- **Language & Subtitles:** Select your preferred language and subtitle settings.
- **Pilot Identity:** Customize your in-game avatar.

Controls & Hardware

- The simulator automatically detects connected devices such as **yokes, joysticks, throttles, and gamepads**, assigning default profiles.
- If controls feel overly sensitive, reduce input sensitivity (recommended **–30% to –50%**) under **Controls > Hardware**.
- Confirm essential controls—**pitch trim, flaps, rudder, and brakes**—are mapped to accessible inputs.

Assistance Settings

- Go to **Options > Assistance** to adjust realism.
- Beginners should start with **Default or All Assists**, with crash damage disabled.
- Assists can be gradually reduced as skill and confidence improve.

BEST GENERAL SETTINGS FOR SMOOTH FLIGHT PERFORMANCE

A smooth and enjoyable experience in **Microsoft Flight Simulator 2024** depends heavily on your **General Settings**, especially graphics, flight modeling, and interface options. While some choices—like camera motion and audio—are purely personal, the settings below provide consistent performance and visual clarity for most players, regardless of hardware.

Graphics Settings (Recommended)

These settings balance visual quality with stable performance.

Setting	Recommended Value	Description
Display Mode	Full Screen	Ensures optimal performance and stability
HDR10	On (if supported)	Improves brightness and contrast
Full Screen Resolution	Native / Highest	Match your monitor's resolution
Anti-Aliasing	AMD FSR 2 (Quality) / DLSS (RTX)	Smooths jagged edges
Render Scaling	100	Maintains native internal resolution
FidelityFX Sharpening	100	Improves clarity with minimal performance cost
V-Sync	On	Prevents screen tearing
NVIDIA Reflex Low Latency	On + Boost	Reduces input lag (NVIDIA GPUs)
Frame Rate Limit	100%	Caps FPS to maintain consistency
Dynamic Settings	Off	Prevents automatic quality shifts
Global Rendering Quality	Custom	Enables manual fine-tuning

Global Rendering Quality (Custom Preset)

These options are only adjustable when **Global Rendering Quality** is set to *Custom*.

Setting	Value	FPS Impact
Terrain Level of Detail	160	High
Objects Level of Detail	80	Medium
Volumetric Clouds	Ultra	High
Texture Resolution	High	High
Buildings	High	Medium
Trees	Medium	High
Grass	High	Medium
Shadow Maps	1536	Medium
Ambient Occlusion	High	Low
Motion Blur	Off	Low
Ray-Traced Shadows	Off	High
Glass Cockpit Refresh Rate	Medium	Medium
Traffic (Road/Air/Sea)	Low–Off	Medium–High
Characters Quality	Low	Low

These selections prioritize smoothness during takeoff, landing, and low-altitude flying—where performance matters most.

Flight Model Settings

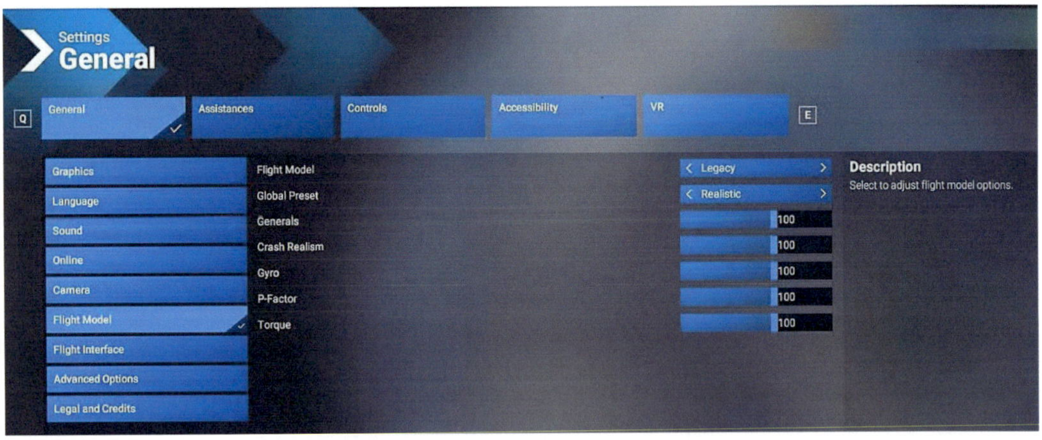

For realistic yet controllable aircraft behavior:

Setting	Value	Purpose
Flight Model	Modern	Enables advanced physics and add-ons
Global Preset	Realistic	Balanced realism
General Flight Dynamics	80	Controls inertia and drag
Crash Realism	65	Realistic without punishing errors
Gyro Effect	100	Improves controller-based tilt control

P-Factor	100	Simulates propeller effects
Torque	100	Adds realistic engine behavior

Flight Interface Settings (Recommended)

These settings balance clarity and immersion by keeping essential information visible while reducing unnecessary on-screen clutter.

Setting	Recommended Value	Purpose
Aerodynamic Visualization	Off	Disables airflow overlays to keep the screen clean
White Dot Cursor (Freelook)	Off	Removes the cursor while freelooking
Landmark Markers	On	Highlights major landmarks for navigation
City Markers	On	Displays nearby cities
Airport Markers	On	Shows nearby airports
Preflight Pins	On	Highlights inspection points during walkarounds
POI Labels	Off	Prevents excessive on-screen labels
Traffic Nameplates	Off	Removes aircraft name tags
HUD in Cockpit View	Yes	Displays key flight data inside the cockpit
HUD in External View	Off	Keeps external views distraction-free
Cockpit Interaction System	Lock	Prevents accidental cockpit inputs
Instrument Name Tooltips	Delayed	Shows instrument names after a brief hover
Instrument Instruction Tooltips	Delayed	Displays descriptions without clutter

Best Assistance Settings for a Balanced Experience

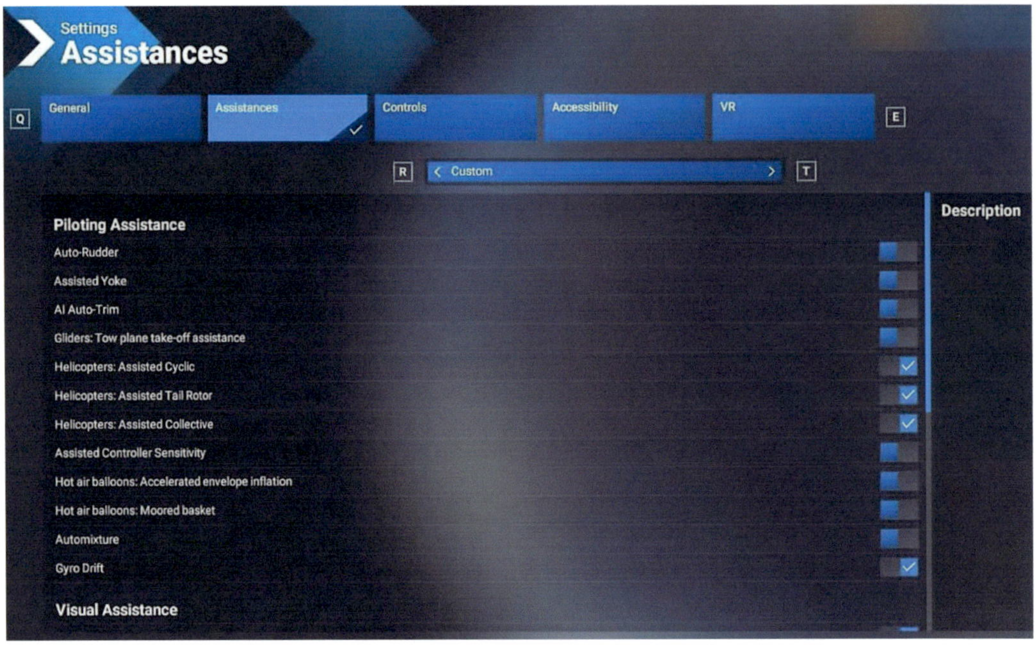

Assistance settings control how much the simulator helps you fly. These recommendations provide stability without removing learning opportunities.

Piloting Assistance

Setting	Recommended Value	Purpose
Auto-Rudder	On	Helps maintain coordination, especially without pedals
Assisted Yoke	Off	Encourages manual control
AI Auto-Trim	Off	Promotes proper trim management
Glider Tow Assistance	On	Stabilizes glider takeoffs
Helicopter Assisted Cyclic	Off	Preserves realistic rotorcraft handling
Helicopter Assisted Tail Rotor	Off	Manual yaw control
Helicopter Assisted Collective	On	Eases power control
Assisted Controller Sensitivity	On	Smooths controller inputs

Auto-Mixture	On	Automatically manages fuel mixture
Gyro Drift	On	Simulates realistic instrument behavior
Hot Air Balloon Inflation	Off	Requires manual envelope control
Hot Air Balloon Moored Basket	Off	Enables realistic ground handling

Visual Assistance

Setting	Recommended Value	Purpose
Active Waypoint Marker	On	Displays the next waypoint
Flight Path Gates	Off	Disables arcade-style guidance
Taxi Ribbon	Off	Encourages real-world taxi awareness
Control Notifications	Off	Removes constant pop-up reminders

Realism Settings

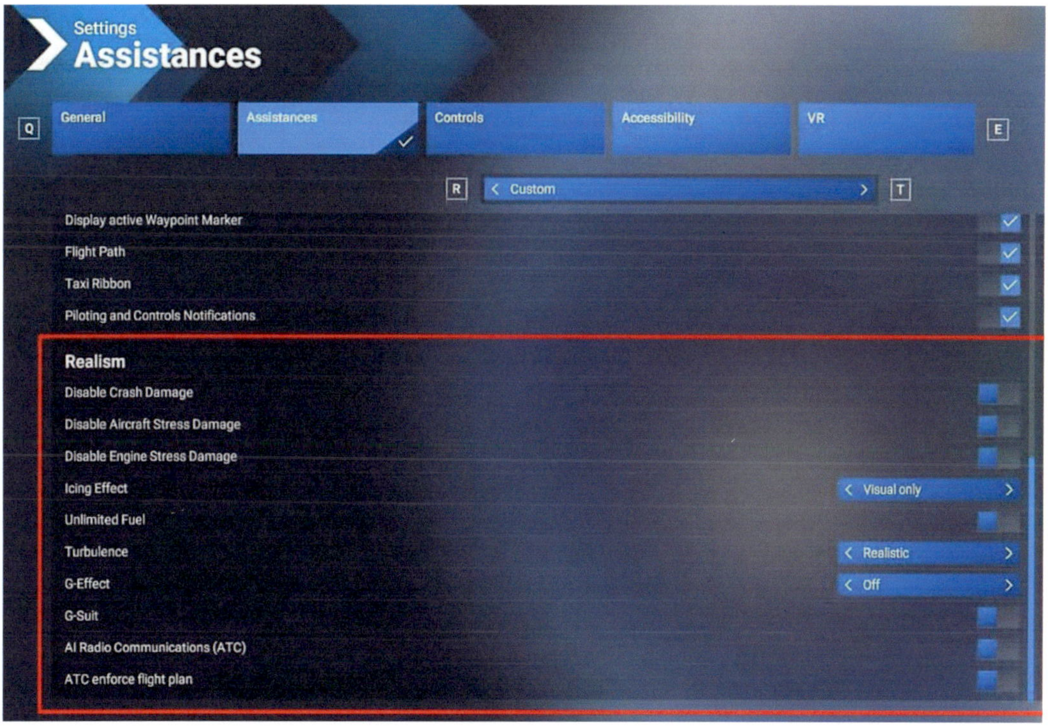

These options add authenticity while keeping gameplay forgiving enough for learning.

Setting	Recommended Value	Purpose
Crash Damage	Off	Prevents flight-ending crashes
Aircraft Stress Damage	Off	Avoids damage from high G-forces
Engine Stress Damage	Off	Protects engines during learning
Icing Effects	Visuals Only	Shows icing without performance penalties
Unlimited Fuel	Off	Encourages fuel planning
Turbulence	Realistic	Adds immersion
G-Effects	Off	Prevents blackout
G-Suit	On	Simulates protection at high G
AI ATC Communications	On	Handles radio calls automatically
ATC Enforce Flight Plan	Off	Allows flexibility in departures and arrivals

KEYBOARD SHORTCUTS

Cockpit Camera and Instrument View Controls

These keyboard commands control cockpit views, instrument focus, and pilot positioning within the aircraft.

Instrument View Navigation

- **Previous Instrument View:** SHIFT + F
- **Next Instrument View:** SHIFT + H
- **Toggle Instrument Views:**
  - View 1: SHIFT + NUM 1
  - View 2: SHIFT + NUM 2
  - View 3: SHIFT + NUM 3
  - View 4: SHIFT + NUM 4
  - View 5: SHIFT + NUM 5
  - View 6: SHIFT + NUM 6
  - View 7: SHIFT + NUM 7
  - View 8: SHIFT + NUM 8
  - View 9: SHIFT + NUM 9
  - View 10: SHIFT + NUM 0

Cockpit Look Directions

- **Look Left:** SHIFT + J
- **Look Right:** SHIFT + L
- **Look Up:** SHIFT + I
- **Look Down:** SHIFT + K

Zoom and View Height

- **Zoom In:** SHIFT + O
- **Zoom Out:** SHIFT + U
- **Increase View Height:** SHIFT + E
- **Decrease View Height:** SHIFT + Q

Cockpit Camera Movement

- **Move Forward:** SHIFT + W
- **Move Backward:** SHIFT + S
- **Move Left:** SHIFT + A
- **Move Right:** SHIFT + D

Pilot Position Selection

- **Previous Pilot Position:** SHIFT + G
- **Next Pilot Position:** SHIFT + T

Quick Views and Reset

- **QuickView Left:** SHIFT + F
- **QuickView Right:** SHIFT + H
- **Reset Cockpit View:** SHIFT + SPACE

Drone Camera Controls

These keyboard shortcuts allow precise movement, rotation, focus, and tracking control while using the Drone Camera.

Drone Translation (Movement)

- **Move Forward:** W
- **Move Backward:** S
- **Move Up:** E
- **Move Down:** Q
- **Move Left:** A

- **Move Right:** D

Drone Orientation (Rotation)

- **Pitch Up:** I
- **Pitch Down:** K
- **Yaw Left:** J
- **Yaw Right:** L
- **Roll Left:** U
- **Roll Right:** O

Zoom and Focus Controls

- **Increase Zoom:** SHIFT + O
- **Decrease Zoom:** SHIFT + U
- **Increase Depth of Field:** Y
- **Decrease Depth of Field:** H
- **Toggle Depth of Field:** 3
- **Toggle Foreground Blur:** 4

Exposure and Auto Controls

- **Increase Exposure:** T
- **Decrease Exposure:** G
- **Toggle Auto Exposure:** 2
- **Toggle Auto Focus:** 1

Speed Adjustments

- **Increase Rotation Speed:** SHIFT + R
- **Decrease Rotation Speed:** SHIFT + F
- **Increase Translation Speed:** SHIFT + T
- **Decrease Translation Speed:** SHIFT + G

Target Lock and Tracking

- **Lock to Next Target:** M
- **Lock to Previous Target:** N
- **Attach to Next Target:** B
- **Attach to Previous Target:** V
- **Toggle Follow Mode:** 5
- **Toggle Lock Mode:** 6

Presets and Reset Options

- **Top-Down View:** F
- **Reset Drone Roll:** SHIFT + SPACE
- **Reset Target Offset:** R

External Camera Quick Controls

These shortcuts allow fast adjustments to the external camera view for better situational awareness and cinematic angles.

- **QuickView Right:** SHIFT + F (Instantly switches the external camera to the right-side view)
- **QuickView Top:** SHIFT + G (Displays a top-down external view of the aircraft)
- **Zoom In:** SHIFT + O (Zooms closer to the aircraft in External View)
- **Zoom Out:** SHIFT + U (Pulls the camera back for a wider external view)

Photo Mode Camera Controls

Photo Mode allows precise camera positioning and fine visual adjustments for capturing high-quality screenshots and cinematic shots.

Camera Movement

- **Move Forward:** W
- **Move Backward:** S
- **Move Left:** A
- **Move Right:** D
- **Move Up:** E
- **Move Down:** Q

Zoom Controls

- **Zoom In:** SHIFT + O
- **Zoom Out:** SHIFT + U

Camera Orientation

- **Pan Left:** J
- **Pan Right:** L
- **Pitch Up:** I
- **Pitch Down:** K
- **Roll Left:** U
- **Roll Right:** O

- **Reset Horizon:** SHIFT + SPACE

Photo Mode Actions

- **Toggle Photo Mode:** SHIFT + V
- **Take Picture:** SPACE

Exposure & Focus Controls

- **Toggle Auto Focus:** 1
- **Toggle Auto Exposure:** 2
- **Increase Exposure:** T
- **Decrease Exposure:** G
- **Increase Focus:** R
- **Decrease Focus:** F

Autopilot Controls & Keyboard Shortcuts

These controls manage aircraft automation, including speed, altitude, navigation, and engine thrust modes. They are essential for efficient cruise, climb, descent, and approach operations.

Autopilot Master Controls

- **Toggle Autopilot Master:** CTRL + 1
- **Disengage Autopilot:** CTRL + 2

Throttle & Engine Automation

- **Arm Auto Throttle:** CTRL + [
- **Disconnect Autothrottle:** CTRL + '
- **Auto Throttle to Go-Around (GA):** CTRL +]
- **Autopilot N1 Hold:** CTRL + F6
- **Set Autopilot N1 Reference:** CTRL + 8
- **Increase N1 Reference:** CTRL + HOME
- **Decrease N1 Reference:** CTRL + END

Airspeed & Mach Control

- **Autopilot Airspeed Hold:** CTRL + F1
- **Increase Reference Airspeed:** CTRL + INSERT
- **Decrease Reference Airspeed:** CTRL + DEL
- **Autopilot Mach Hold:** CTRL + F11

Altitude & Vertical Control

- **Toggle Altitude Hold:** CTRL + F2
- **Increase Reference Altitude:** CTRL + PAGE UP
- **Decrease Reference Altitude:** CTRL + PAGE DOWN
- **Toggle Vertical Speed (VS) Hold:** CTRL + F8
- **Increase VS Reference:** CTRL + HOME
- **Decrease VS Reference:** CTRL + END
- **Toggle Flight Level Change (FLC):** CTRL + F9

Navigation & Lateral Guidance

- **Heading Hold:** CTRL + F5
- **NAV1 Hold:** CTRL + F7
- **Localizer Hold:** CTRL + F10
- **Approach Hold:** CTRL + F3
- **Wing Leveler:** CTRL + F12

Attitude Control

- **Toggle Attitude Hold:** CTRL + F4

Banner Towing Controls

These controls are used for banner towing operations, allowing you to deploy or retract towing equipment during flight.

- **Toggle Grapple Hook:** Z (Deploys or retracts the banner grapple hook)
- **Toggle Lead Pole:** X (Raises or lowers the banner lead pole for banner attachment)

Braking Controls

These controls manage ground stopping power and directional braking while taxiing, landing, or parking.

- **Toggle Parking Brakes:** CTRL + SPACE (Engages or releases the aircraft's parking brakes)
- **Apply Brakes:** SPACE (Applies wheel brakes simultaneously)
- **Left Brake:** NUM / (Applies braking force to the left wheel only, useful for tight ground turns)
- **Right Brake:** NUM *(Applies braking force to the right wheel only, allowing precise steering control)

Camera & SmartCam Controls

These commands let you switch views, manage Smart Camera targets, and quickly save or load custom camera angles.

Smart Camera

- **Toggle Smart Camera:** CTRL + B (Enables or disables the Smart Camera system)
- **Next SmartCam Target:** SHIFT + Y (Cycles to the next available SmartCam focus target)
- **Previous SmartCam Target:** SHIFT + R (Cycles to the previous SmartCam focus target)

View Switching

- **Cockpit / External View Toggle:** BACKSPACE (Switches between cockpit and external camera views)
- **Toggle Drone Camera:** SHIFT + X (Activates or deactivates the drone camera)

External Camera Navigation

- **Reset External View:** SHIFT + SPACE (Resets the external camera to its default position)
- **Look Up:** SHIFT + K
- **Look Down:** SHIFT + I
- **Look Left:** SHIFT + L
- **Look Right:** SHIFT + J

External Quick Views

- **QuickView Left:** SHIFT + H (Instantly snaps the camera to the left external view)
- **QuickView Rear:** SHIFT + T (Instantly snaps the camera to the rear external view)

Custom Camera Presets

Use these shortcuts to save and recall personalized camera angles.

Load Custom Cameras

- **Load Camera 1**: SHIFT + F1

- **Load Camera 2**: SHIFT + F2
- **Load Camera 3**: SHIFT + F3
- **Load Camera 4**: SHIFT + F4

Save Custom Cameras

- **Save Camera 1**: SHIFT + F5
- **Save Camera 2**: SHIFT + F6
- **Save Camera 3**: SHIFT + F7
- **Save Camera 4**: SHIFT + F8

Slew Mode Camera Controls

Slew Mode allows free movement of the aircraft for repositioning, photo setups, or practice without engine power. Use these shortcuts to navigate and orient the aircraft in 3D space.

Activating Slew Mode

- **Toggle Slew Mode:** SHIFT + Z (Enter or exit Slew Mode)
- **Reset Slew Mode:** SHIFT + SPACE (Returns the aircraft to default position and orientation)

Translating the Aircraft

- **Forward / Backward:** W / S
- **Left / Right:** A / D
- **Up / Down:** E / Q

Fine adjustments (speed modifiers)

- **Move Up / Down Fast**: SHIFT + E / SHIFT + Q
- **Move Up / Down Slow**: CTRL + E / CTRL + Q

Rotating the Aircraft

- **Pitch Up / Down:** I / K
- **Roll Left / Right:** U / O
- **Yaw Left / Right:** J / L

Pitch Speed Modifiers

- **Pitch Up / Down Fast:** SHIFT + I / SHIFT + K
- **Pitch Up / Down Slow:** CTRL + I / CTRL + K

Freezing Movement

- **Freeze X-Axis Translation:** 1
- **Freeze Y-Axis Translation:** 2
- **Freeze Pitch:** 3

ATC (Air Traffic Control) Controls

Use these shortcuts to manage communications with air traffic control efficiently during your flight.

Accessing ATC Panels

- **Open Communications Panel:** \
- **Select ATC Panel Choice 0–9:** 0 → 9 (Quickly switch between different ATC options)

Sending Responses

- **Quick Reply:** ENTER (Sends a predefined response to ATC prompts)

MSFS 2024 – Developer Mode Shortcuts

Document Management

- **New Document:** ALT + N
- **Open Document:** ALT + O
- **Save Document:** CTRL + S
- **Save As Document:** CTRL + SHIFT + S
- **Close Document:** CTRL + Z
- **Rename Document/Object:** CTRL + R
- **Validate Document:** ENTER

Undo / Redo / Edit

- **Undo:** CTRL + W
- **Redo:** CTRL + Y
- **Cut Selection:** CTRL + X
- **Copy Selection:** CTRL + C
- **Paste Selection:** CTRL + V
- **Duplicate Selection:** CTRL + D
- **Split Edge:** SHIFT + S
- **Ungroup:** CTRL + SHIFT + G
- **Find / Focus Object:** CTRL + F

Object Management

- **Hide Selected:** CTRL + H
- **Hide Selected Edition:** CTRL + SHIFT + H
- **Hide All Objects:** ALT + H
- **Hide All Edition:** ALT + SHIFT + H
- **Lock Selected:** CTRL + L
- **Lock Object:** ALT + L
- **Range Selection:** SHIFT
- **New Group:** CTRL + G

Gizmo Controls

- **Gizmo Translate:** Z
- **Gizmo Rotate:** E
- **Gizmo Scale:** R

Add / Place World Elements

- **Add Apron:** SHIFT + Q
- **Add Painted Line:** SHIFT + L
- **Add Parking:** SHIFT + ,
- **Add Taxiway Point:** SHIFT + P
- **Add Runway:** SHIFT + R

Camera & Tools

- **Developer Camera Look At:** ALT
- **Toggle Sim Pause:** SPACE
- **Hide Lock Window:** F2
- **Toggle Console:** '

Navigation

- **Move Up:** ↑
- **Move Down:** ↓

Firefighting Controls

- **Toggle Spray:** Z – Activates or deactivates the water/foam spray system.
- **Mission: Toggle Scoops/Doors:** Z – Opens or closes the firefighting aircraft's water scoops or doors during missions.

Player Character Controls

Movement

- **Move Forward:** W
- **Move Backward:** S
- **Strafe Left:** A
- **Strafe Right:** D
- **Toggle Run:** SPACE
- **Toggle Crouch:** C

Looking / Camera

- **Look Up:** I
- **Look Down:** K
- **Look Left:** J
- **Look Right:** L
- **Camera Reset:** SHIFT + SPACE

Interaction

- **Take Control of Character:** SHIFT + C
- **Interact / Use:** E

Power Management Controls

Engine Start / Stop

- **Auto Start Engine:** CTRL + E
- **Engine Autostop:** CTRL + SHIFT + E

Condition Lever (Throttle / Engine Power for piston/turboprop)

- **Decrease Condition Lever:** H
- **Increase Condition Lever:** Y
- **Condition Lever Cut Off:** CTRL + H
- **Condition Lever High Idle:** CTRL + Y

Mixture (Fuel-Air Ratio)

- **Decrease Mixture:** H
- **Increase Mixture:** Y
- **Set Mixture Lean:** CTRL + H
- **Set Mixture Rich:** CTRL + Y

Propeller Pitch / RPM

- **Decrease Propeller Pitch:** G
- **Increase Propeller Pitch:** T
- **Propeller Pitch Low:** CTRL + T
- **Propeller Pitch High:** CTRL + G

Throttle Control

- **Decrease Throttle:** F
- **Increase Throttle:** R
- **Throttle Previous Detent:** CTRL + F
- **Throttle Next Detent:** CTRL + R

Skydive System Controls

Door Lights Switch:

- **Get Ready:** C
- **Jump:** Z
- **Turn Off:** X

Tools Controls

- **Toggle Active Pause:** P
- **Toggle Pause / Set Pause Off:** ESC
- **Skip RTC:** ESC
- **Toggle EFB (Electronic Flight Bag):** TAB
- **Toggle Pushback:** ALT + P
- **Back to Fly:** ALT + SPACE
- **Sim Rate (Speed up/slow time):** ALT + R
- **Toggle CFD (Computational Fluid Dynamics):** ALT + 5
- **Toggle Landing Ribbon:** ALT + 4
- **Toggle Nameplates:** ALT + 2
- **Toggle Taxi Ribbon:** ALT + 3
- **Toggle 3D Thermals Display:** ALT + 6
- **Toggle Flight Assistant:** ALT + 1
- **New UI Window Mode:** RIGHT ALT
- **Toggle Screen Narrator:** ALT + BACKSPACE
- **Toggle Headphone Simulation:** ALT + H
- **Next Flight Phase:** ALT + N
- **Back on Track:** SHIFT + B

VR Controls

- **Camera Reset (VR):** SHIFT
- **Activate / Deactivate VR Mode:** CTRL + TAB
- **Toggle VR Toolbar:** ALT + T
- **Eye Tracking Reset:** ALT + 8
- **Toggle Head Tracking:** ALT + 7

Flight Control Surfaces

Ailerons (Roll):

- **Roll Left:** A
- **Roll Right:** D
- **Center Ailer/Rudder:** NUM 5
- **Trim Left:** J
- **Trim Right:** L

Elevator (Pitch):

- **Pitch Up:** S
- **Pitch Down:** W
- **Trim Nose Up:** K
- **Trim Nose Down:** I

Rudder (Yaw):

- **Yaw Left:** Q
- **Yaw Right:** E
- **Center Rudder:** CTRL + Q
- **Trim Left:** U
- **Trim Right:** O

Flaps:

- **Increase Flaps:** B
- **Decrease Flaps:** V
- **Extend Flaps:** CTRL + B
- **Retract Flaps:** CTRL + V

Spoilers:

- **Toggle Arm Spoilers:** CTRL + \
- **Increment Spoilers:** N
- **Decrement Spoilers:** M

- **Extend Spoilers:** CTRL + M
- **Retract Spoilers:** CTRL + N

Other Controls:

- **Toggle Water Rudder:** CTRL + /
- **Toggle AutoRudder:** CTRL + P

Instruments

Navigation & Radios:

- **Set Altimeter**: ,
- **Set NAV1**: CTRL + D
- **ADF**: CTRL + 9
- **VOR OBS**: CTRL + 0

Transponder & Bugs:

- **Transponder**: .
- **Select Airspeed Bug**: CTRL + 3
- **Select Altitude Bug**: CTRL + 4
- **Select Heading Bug**: CTRL + 5
- **Select VSI Bug**: CTRL + 6

Cockpit Modes:

- **Toggle IFR Mode**: SHIFT + F9
- **Toggle VFR Mode**: SHIFT + F10
- **Toggle Landing Mode**: SHIFT + F11

Electrical & Engine Systems:

- **Toggle Master Battery & Alternator**: CTRL + Z
- **Toggle Avionics Master**: CTRL + X
- **Set Magnetos**: CTRL + C
- **Toggle Anti-Ice**: *(no default key assigned)*

Copilot & Flight Limiter:

- **Toggle Delegate Control to Copilot**: ALT + C
- **Toggle G Limiter**: Z

Miscellaneous:

- **Plus (=) & Minus (-):** Adjust instrument values

Landing Gear

- **Toggle Landing Gear**: /

Miscellaneous

- **Toggle Tail Hook Handle**: CTRL + /

Lights

- **Toggle All Lights**: ;
- **Toggle Flashlight**: ALT + F

CHAPTER ONE

HOW TO PLAY & USE MICROSOFT FLIGHT SIMULATOR 2024

Microsoft Flight Simulator 2024 (MSFS 2024) is one of the most realistic and immersive flight simulators ever created. Whether you're a complete beginner, a student pilot learning procedure, a licensed pilot staying proficient, or simply someone who wants to explore the world from the cockpit, MSFS 2024 offers an exceptional blend of education and entertainment.

That said, your first launch can feel overwhelming—almost like stepping into a real aircraft for the first time. This guide is designed to ease you in and help you get flying with confidence.

CHOOSING YOUR EDITION & PLATFORM

MSFS 2024 is available in multiple editions and runs on **PC, PlayStation, and Xbox Series X/S**.

Editions

The simulator is offered in **Standard, Deluxe, Premium Deluxe, and Aviator Editions**. The primary differences are the number of **handcrafted airports** and **highly detailed aircraft** included. All editions share the same core simulation features.

Platform Options

- **PC:** Offers the greatest flexibility, including advanced graphics settings, external flight hardware, and extensive third-party add-ons. Best suited for serious simulation, training, and long-term use. Requires a capable PC that meets the official system requirements.
- **Xbox Series X/S:** A streamlined, console-optimized experience. Easy to use and visually impressive, but with fewer customization options and limited add-on support compared to PC.
- **PlayStation:** Designed for plug-and-play accessibility with smooth performance and strong visuals. Ideal for casual and intermediate pilots using a controller, though it offers less hardware support and fewer advanced customization options than PC.

GAME PASS & CLOUD GAMING

MSFS 2024 is included with **Xbox Game Pass Ultimate**, allowing you to play on Xbox, PC, or via **Xbox Cloud Gaming**. Cloud gaming lets you stream the simulator without installing it, even on lower-end devices such as tablets or phones—provided you have a fast, stable internet connection. This is an excellent way to try the simulator before investing in storage space or hardware.

INSTALLATION: STEAM VS. MICROSOFT STORE (PC)

On PC, MSFS 2024 can be purchased through **Steam** or the **Microsoft Store** (and is included with PC Game Pass).

- **Microsoft Store / Game Pass:** Often receives updates slightly earlier and is required for Xbox cross-buy and cross-play.
- **Steam:** Offers simpler folder management and a more flexible refund process, though updates may arrive slightly later.

Tip: The full installation can exceed **100 GB** and may take several hours. Start the download well in advance of your first flight.

FIRST LAUNCH: ESSENTIAL SETTINGS FOR BEGINNERS

Before taking off, adjusting a few key settings can dramatically improve your early experience.

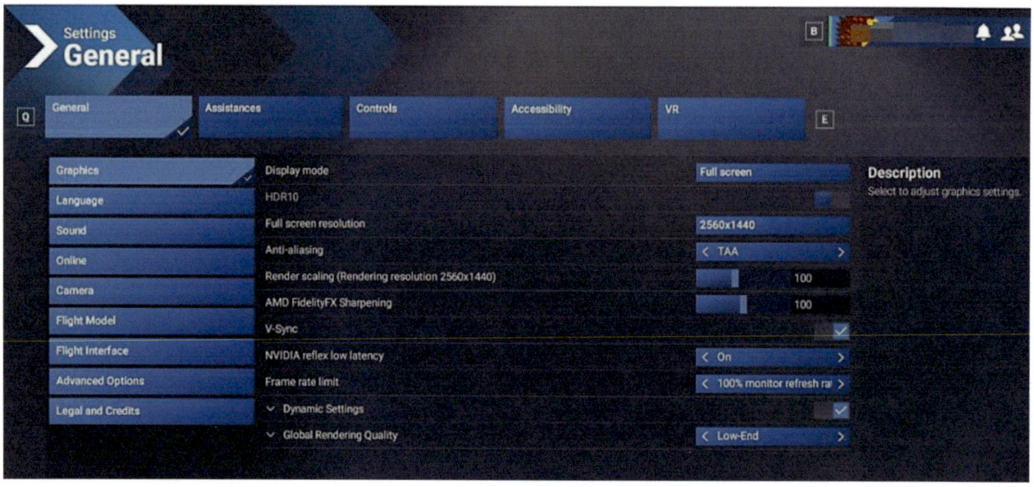

Assistance Options

(Options > Assistance)

- **New players or casual flyers:** Start with **All Assists** enabled to simplify aircraft handling, navigation, and systems.

- **Student or licensed pilots:** Use **Default Assists** and disable visual aids for a more realistic experience.
- Consider turning **Crash Damage OFF** at first. This allows you to learn without abruptly ending flights.
- Gradually reduce assists as your skills improve.

Control Sensitivity

(Options > Controls > Select Device > Hardware Settings)

- If the aircraft feels overly sensitive, reduce control sensitivity to around **–30% to –50%** as a starting point.

Graphics Settings

(Options > Graphics)

- Begin with **Medium** or **High-End** presets, depending on your system.
- If performance drops—especially near large airports—lower graphics settings until you achieve smooth frame rates.

Audio Settings

- Confirm that the correct audio output device is selected for clear engine sounds, ATC, and cockpit alerts.

UNDERSTANDING THE INTERFACE: MENUS & VIEWS

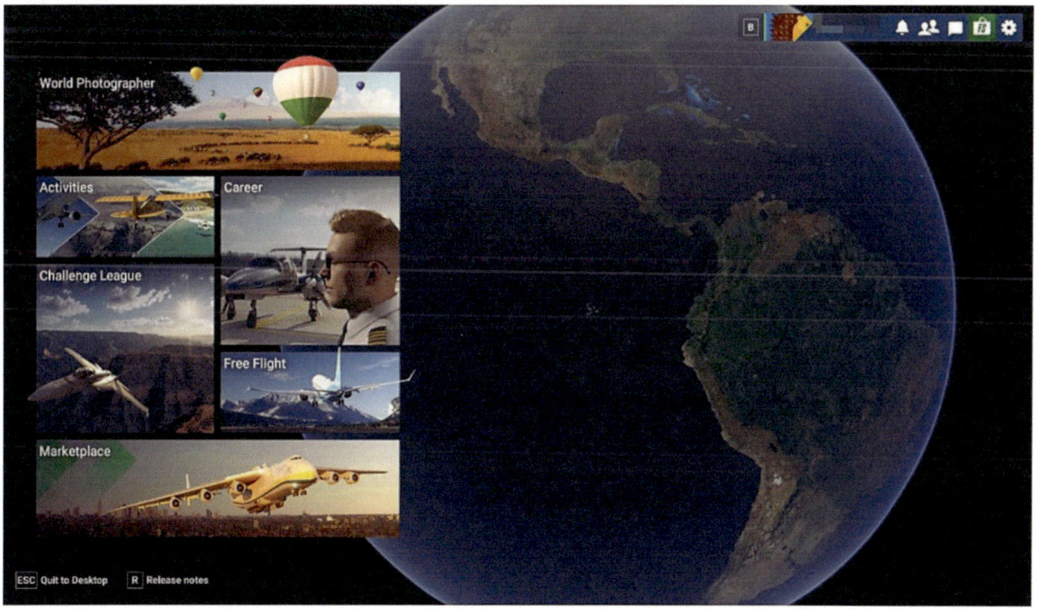

Main Menu Overview

The main menu uses large, easy-to-navigate tiles that give quick access to every major feature:

- **Free Flight:** Create fully customized flights anywhere in the world. This is the best mode for open-ended practice and learning.
- **Activities:** Pre-built experiences such as training lessons, landing challenges, bush trips, and special flights. These are fun and structured but often lock aircraft and weather settings.
- **Career:** New to MSFS 2024, this mode lets you progress through aviation missions, earn certifications, and build a virtual flying career.
- **World Photographer:** Travel to scenic locations and complete photography challenges by capturing specific in-game shots.
- **Marketplace:** Browse and download aircraft, airports, and other add-ons.
- **Profile:** View your pilot logbook, achievements, and statistics.
- **Options (Gear Icon):** Access all simulator settings, including graphics, controls, and assistance options.

Menu Navigation Tips

- **Bottom Buttons:** Most screens display context-sensitive buttons at the bottom with shortcut keys shown for quick access.
- **Fullscreen vs. Windowed Mode:** Press **Alt + Enter** to switch between fullscreen and windowed mode. Windowed mode is useful if you want to view charts, checklists, or guides alongside the simulator.

In-Flight Toolbar

While flying, move your mouse to the **top-center of the screen** to reveal the in-flight toolbar. This provides quick access to essential tools, including:

- Camera controls (cockpit and external views)
- Weather settings
- Assistance options
- Air Traffic Control (ATC)
- Additional utilities and panels

You can customize which icons appear by clicking the **gear icon** on the toolbar.

CONTROLS EXPLAINED: YOKES, JOYSTICKS & KEYBOARDS

MSFS 2024 supports a wide range of control methods, including **keyboard and mouse, gamepads, and dedicated flight hardware** such as yokes, joysticks, throttles, and rudder pedals.

Basic Control Setup

1. Go to **Options > Controls**.
2. Select your input device (for example, a joystick or yoke).
3. Use the **Filter** at the bottom of the screen and set it to **Assigned** to view current button and axis mappings.

Most popular devices come with default profiles that work well out of the box.

Assigning or Changing Controls

If a function such as flaps or trim is missing:

1. Change the filter to **All**, or search for the desired control.
2. Click the empty input box next to the function.
3. Move the button or axis you want to assign.
4. Confirm and save the assignment.

Axis Sensitivity

Use the **Sensitivity** menu to fine-tune control response and eliminate overly sensitive or sluggish handling.

YOUR FIRST FLIGHT: FREE FLIGHT VS. OTHER MODES

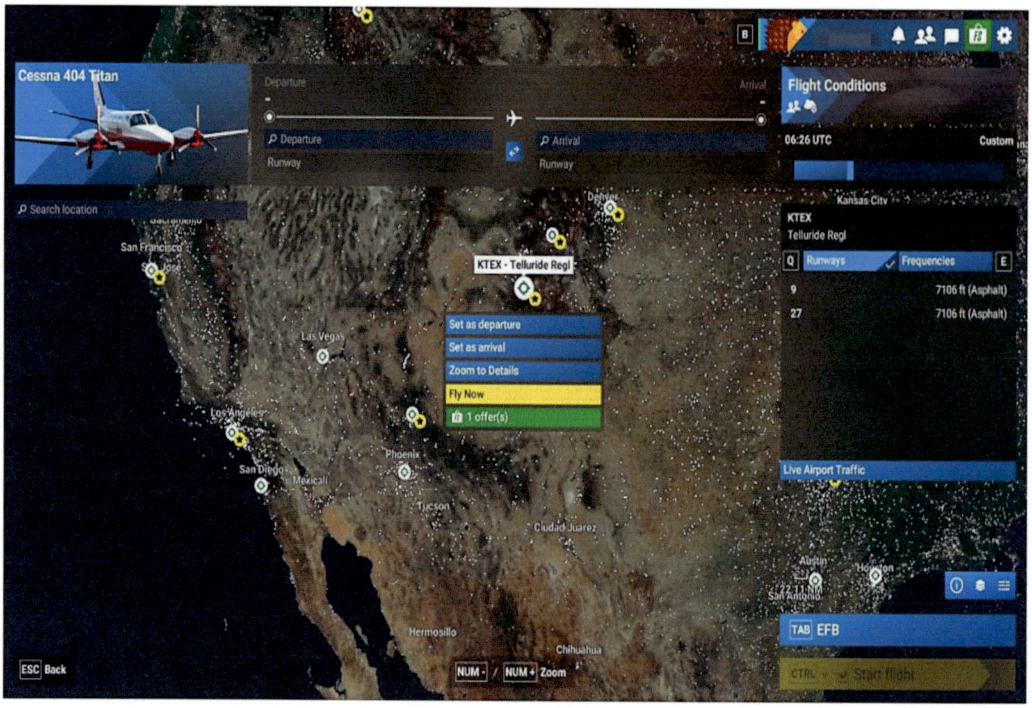

While Activities and training missions are excellent learning tools, **Free Flight** offers complete control and is ideal for structured practice.

Setting Up a Free Flight

1. Select **Free Flight** to open the World Map.
2. **Choose an Aircraft:** Click the aircraft icon (top left) and select a beginner-friendly trainer such as the **Cessna 152** or **Cessna 172**. Choose between glass cockpit (G1000) or classic gauges if available.
3. **Select a Departure Airport:** Click on the map or search using an airport code. Choose either a runway or parking spot.
4. **Set Flight Conditions:** Select the **Clear Skies** preset and daytime lighting. Disable live traffic and multiplayer for a distraction-free experience.
5. Click **Save and Back**, then **Start Flight**.

STARTING OPTIONS: RUNWAY VS. PARKING SPOT

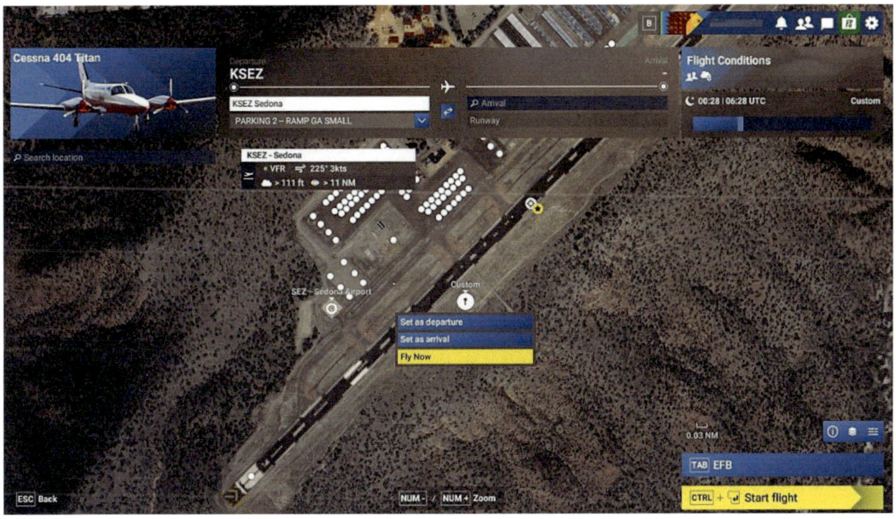

Your starting location determines how the flight begins:

Runway Start

- Aircraft is already lined up for takeoff
- Engine running and avionics powered
- Fastest way to get airborne and practice flying

Parking Spot (Gate or Ramp)

- Aircraft starts cold and dark
- Engine off, systems powered down
- Requires startup, taxi, and checklist procedures
- Best for realism and procedural training

THE WALKAROUND: STARTING FROM A PARKING SPOT

When you begin a flight from a parking spot, MSFS 2024 introduces **Character Mode**, allowing you to perform a realistic preflight walkaround. Certain items must be checked or removed before you can enter the cockpit and start the engine.

Moving Around (Character Mode Controls)

- **W / A / S / D:** Walk forward, left, backward, and right
- **Mouse Movement:** Look around
    - You may need to click the **middle mouse button (scroll wheel)** once to unlock the cursor for interacting with objects. Press it again to return to free look.
- **Right Mouse Button + Drag:** Pan the camera without moving
- **C:** Crouch (useful for inspecting lower areas)

Required Preflight Items

You must approach and interact with the following items to remove or inspect them:

- Wheel chocks
- Pitot tube cover
- Engine inlet and exhaust covers
- Static port covers
- Control surface locks (such as rudder gust locks)
- Tie-downs

Failing to remove these can cause serious issues, such as **no airspeed indication**, **restricted control movement**, or **inability to taxi**.

Entering the Cockpit

- Walk up to the aircraft door and click it to enter
- **Quick Entry:** Press **Shift + C** at any time during the walkaround to jump directly into the pilot's seat

Quick Engine Start (Optional)

If you want to skip the full startup checklist:

- Press **Ctrl + E** to auto-start the engine (works on most default piston aircraft)

INTERACTING WITH THE COCKPIT

Once seated, you can freely move your view and interact with cockpit controls.

Looking Around

- **Right Mouse Button + Drag:** Pan view
- **Mouse Scroll Wheel:** Zoom in or out

Adjusting Head Position

- **Shift + A / D:** Move left or right
- **Shift + W / S:** Move forward or backward
- **Shift + Q / E:** Move down or up (useful for improving visibility over the dashboard)
- **Shift + Space:** Reset to the default cockpit view

Saving Custom Views

- Position your view (for radios, instruments, or panels)
- Press **Shift + F5, F6, F7, or F8** to save it
- Recall the view later using **Shift + F1–F4**

Using Switches and Knobs

- Hover until the **hand icon** appears, then **left-click** to activate switches
- Click the **yoke** to hide or show it for better visibility
- For knobs (radios, GPS, autopilot):

- Scroll the mouse wheel to adjust values (fastest method)
- Or click and drag left/right
- Use the **frequency swap button (<->)** to activate standby frequencies

BASIC FLIGHT CONTROLS EXPLAINED

These are the three primary control surfaces every pilot must understand:

Ailerons (Roll Control)

- Controlled by moving the yoke or joystick left/right
- Causes the aircraft to bank
- Keyboard default: **NUM 4 / NUM 6**

Elevator (Pitch Control)

- Push forward to lower the nose
- Pull back to raise the nose
- Controls climb and descent
- Keyboard default: **NUM 8 / NUM 2**

Rudder (Yaw Control)

- Controlled by rudder pedals or joystick twist
- Moves the nose left or right without banking
- Essential for coordinated turns and crosswind control
- Keyboard default: **NUM 0 / Enter**

Tip: If you don't have rudder pedals, enable **Auto-Rudder** in the Assistance settings to simplify control.

Trim

Trim relieves constant pressure on the controls and is critical for smooth flying.

- Use **pitch trim** frequently to maintain altitude and speed
- Map trim up/down to easily accessible buttons—this is one of the most-used controls in flight

TAKEOFF, CRUISE, AND USING THE PAUSE FEATURE

Assuming you've started on the runway or completed taxi:

Basic Takeoff (Single-Engine Trainer – Cessna 172)

1. Release the **parking brake** (Ctrl + Space or click the lever).
2. Smoothly apply **full throttle**.
3. Use **rudder input** to maintain the runway centerline.
4. At rotation speed (approximately **55 knots**), gently pull back on the yoke or stick to lift off.
5. Establish a positive climb and maintain runway heading.

For aircraft-specific procedures, consult the Pilot's Operating Handbook (POH) for the airplane you're flying.

Cruise Flight

- Level off at your desired altitude.
- Reduce engine power appropriately.
- Use **pitch trim** to maintain altitude hands-off and reduce workload.

USING THE PAUSE FEATURE

Pausing is an essential learning tool in MSFS 2024.

- **Active Pause (P):** Freezes the aircraft in place while systems and sound may continue. Useful for brief interruptions or studying instruments mid-flight.
- **Menu Pause (Esc):** Completely stops the simulation and audio while opening the menu. Best for longer breaks or adjusting settings safely.

USING MSFS 2024 FOR EFFECTIVE FLIGHT TRAINING

MSFS 2024 is an excellent supplement for real-world flight training when used with structure and intention.

Best Training Practices

- **Cockpit Familiarization:** Learn switch locations, avionics layouts (such as the G1000), and cockpit flows before entering a real aircraft.
- **Procedure Repetition:** Practice checklists, emergencies, and standard flows until they become automatic.
- **Instrument Scan Development:** Improve scan discipline without the pressure or cost of real flight time.
- **Maneuver Practice:** Rehearse procedures and visual references for maneuvers like steep turns and slow flight.
- **Replay Analysis:** Use the built-in replay tools to review control inputs and flight path.
- **Scenario-Based Training:**

  Use **Slew Mode** to reposition instantly for:

  - Engine failure simulations
  - Final approach landing practice
  - Emergency procedure drills
- **Navigation Skills:** Practice VOR tracking, GPS navigation, and flight planning.
- **Weather Training:** Safely experience strong winds, low visibility, and IFR conditions.
- **Time Efficiency:** Skip long cruise segments and focus on weak areas.

IMPORTANT TRAINING CONSIDERATIONS

- Home simulation **supplements** but does not replace real instruction.
- Physical sensations of flight cannot be replicated.
- Practice correct procedures to avoid developing bad habits.
- For realistic ATC interaction, consider online networks such as **VATSIM** or **PilotEdge**.

Mastering the simulator's interface, controls, and setup is essential to fully benefit from its training potential.

COMMON CHALLENGES & TROUBLESHOOTING

- **Aircraft Pulls Left on Takeoff:** Caused by torque and P-factor. Apply **right rudder** smoothly.
- **Engine Won't Start:** Ensure walkaround items are removed, battery and fuel are ON, or use **Ctrl + E**.
- **Low FPS or Stuttering:** Reduce Terrain/Object LOD and close background applications.
- **Controls Not Responding:** Verify correct control profile and assignments are active.

Next Steps: Beyond the Basics

You're ready to expand your skills:

- Practice traffic patterns and landings regularly
- Use built-in training lessons from the **Activities** menu
- Begin using real-world checklists
- Transition to more complex aircraft
- Experiment with night flying, weather challenges, and longer cross-country routes.

CHAPTER TWO

HOW TO START FLYING IN MICROSOFT FLIGHT SIMULATOR 2024 FOR PS5

GETTING STARTED: GAME MODES AND FREE FLIGHT OVERVIEW

This section is primarily written for **PlayStation 5 users**, but the information applies equally to **PC and Xbox players**. It provides a brief overview of the simulator's main modes and offers guidance on where new pilots should begin.

The core experience in **Microsoft Flight Simulator 2024** is built around several key modes: **Free Flight**, **Career**, **Challenge League**, **World Photographer**, and **Activities**. Each mode serves a different purpose, but most players—especially beginners—will spend the majority of their time in **Free Flight**.

The Marketplace

The **Marketplace** allows you to purchase additional aircraft, scenery, and upgrades beyond what is included in your edition of the simulator. At launch, Marketplace content on **PS5 is limited**, but beginning in **2026**, support is expected to expand to include third-party developers.

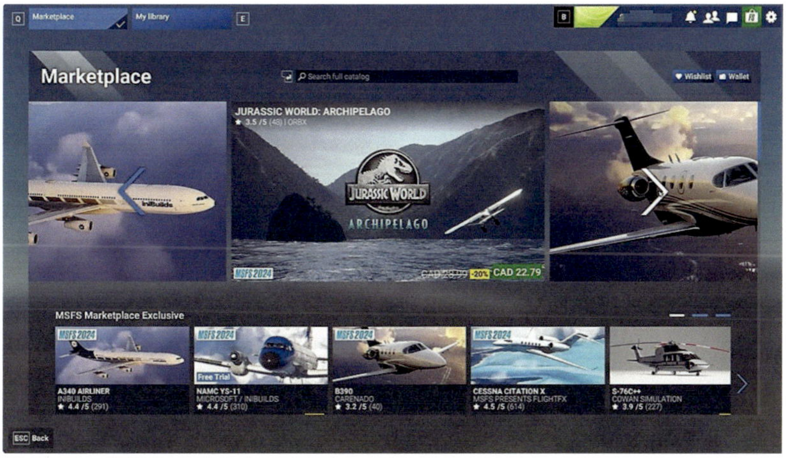

Currently, most Marketplace aircraft are created by **first-party developers**—studios commissioned by Microsoft to build specific aircraft. A notable example is the **Airbus A321 XLR**.

Free Flight Mode Explained

Free Flight is the largest and most flexible mode in the simulator. It allows you to fly **anywhere in the world**. You can zoom in on the global map, select a location using white map markers, or search for destinations by name.

For example, typing **New York** will display:

- Major airports
- Helipads

- Seaplane bases

You can also search for **points of interest**, such as the *Statue of Liberty*, and start a flight directly from that location or set it as a departure or arrival point.

Beginner Tip: If you are new to flight simulation and unfamiliar with airport codes or the phonetic alphabet, searching by **city or landmark name** is much easier than using ICAO airport codes.

Searching for cities like **Atlanta** will display multiple airports. Major airports may appear under formal names, such as *Hartsfield-Jackson Atlanta International Airport (KATL)*. If you know the airport code, you can enter it directly, or simply search by name if the in-game search feels limiting.

Aircraft Selection and Configuration

On the left side of the screen, you can:

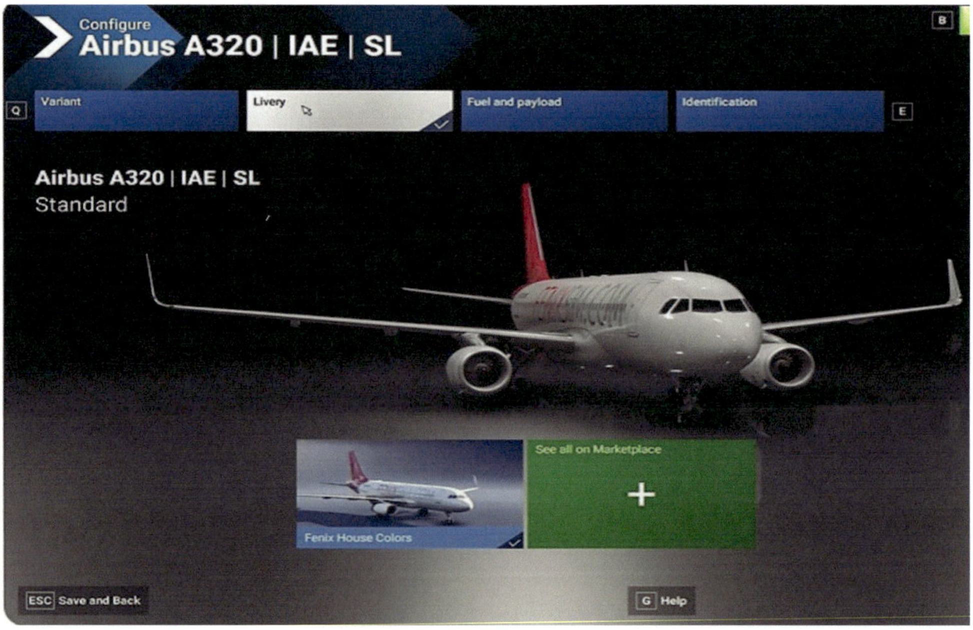

- Select your aircraft
- Change liveries (if available)
- Edit aircraft identification
- Adjust fuel and payload

At the top-right corner, you can configure **flight conditions**, including:

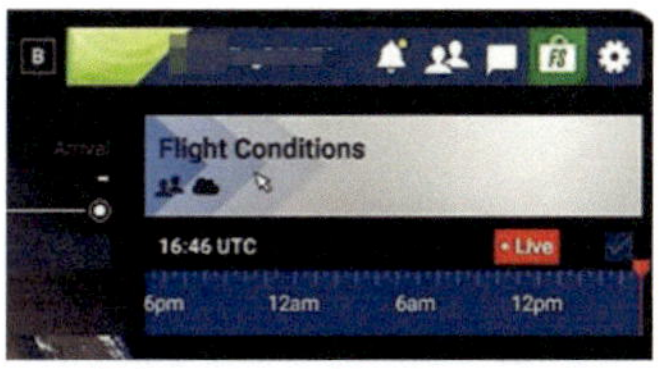

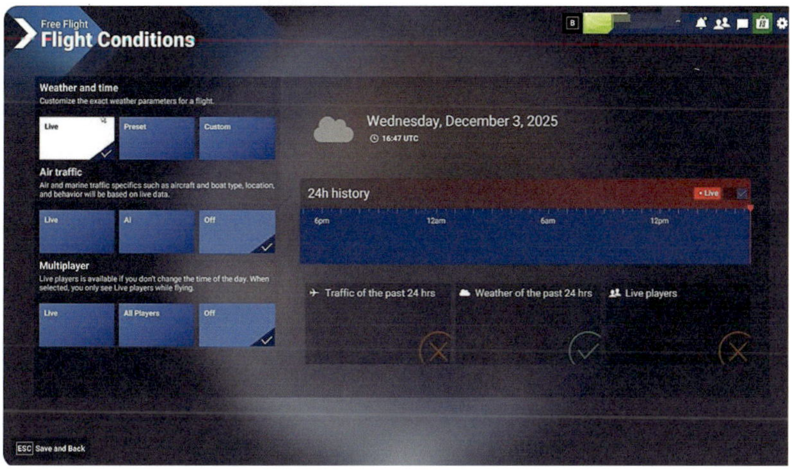

- Live or preset weather
- Time of day and season
- Air traffic (AI, live, or off)
- Multiplayer settings

Multiplayer Note:

On **PS5**, multiplayer is limited to **PS5 users only**. Xbox and PC players can see each other, but PS5 operates in a separate multiplayer environment and is not cross-platform compatible.

Creating a Simple Flight

To begin a flight:

1. Select a **departure airport** (an arrival is optional).
2. If desired, allow the simulator to automatically generate a flight plan.

For short flights or smaller airports, it's best to choose a **general aviation aircraft**, such as the **Cessna 172**. This aircraft is widely used for real-world **private pilot training (PPL)** and is ideal for beginners due to its simplicity and forgiving handling.

Once selected, the simulator will estimate the flight duration (for example, a short trip may take around **17 minutes**). When ready, click **Start Flight** to load into the world.

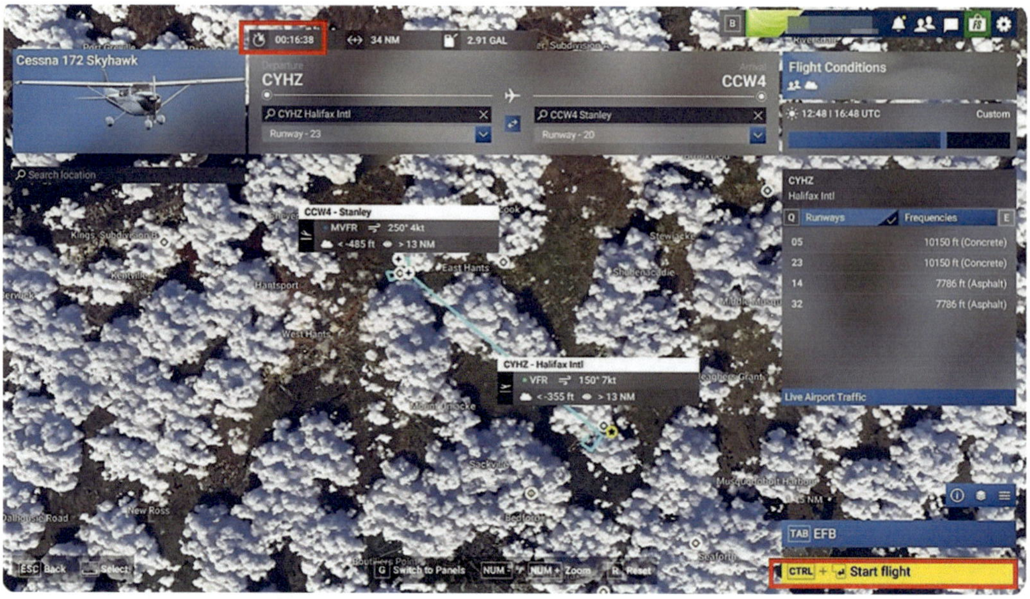

Runway vs. Gate Starts

By default, Free Flight places you **on the runway with engines running**. If you prefer a more realistic experience:

- Zoom into the airport
- Select a **ramp or gate**
- Start the aircraft **cold and dark**, meaning all systems are off and must be powered up manually

This option is especially useful for airliner operations or for learning proper startup procedures.

Career Mode Overview

Career Mode gives you access to the entire world, just like Free Flight, but adds a structured progression system that simulates a pilot's professional journey. You begin as a **brand-new pilot**, working toward your **Private Pilot License (PPL)** through guided training and certification paths.

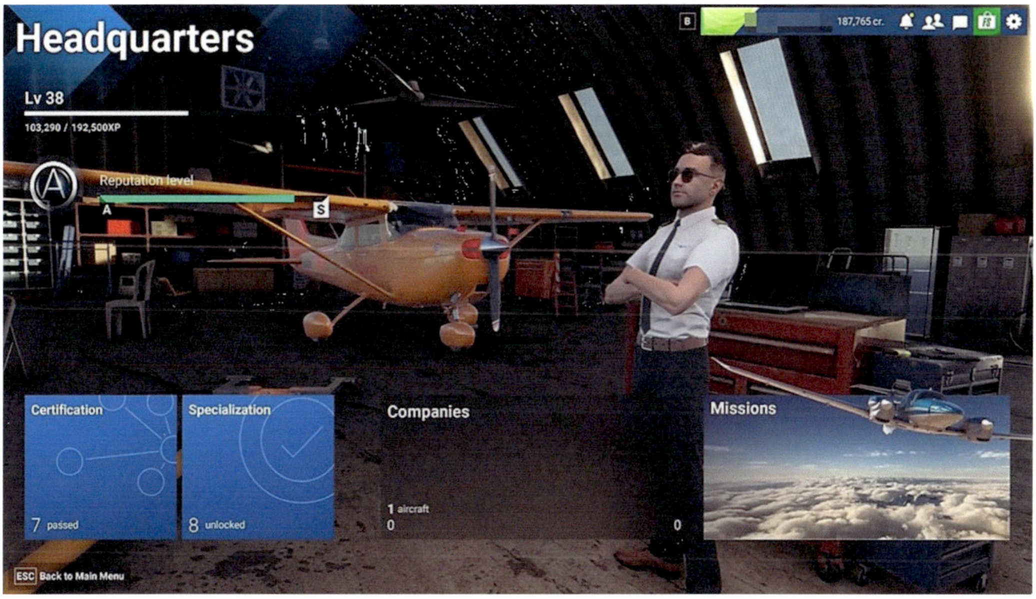

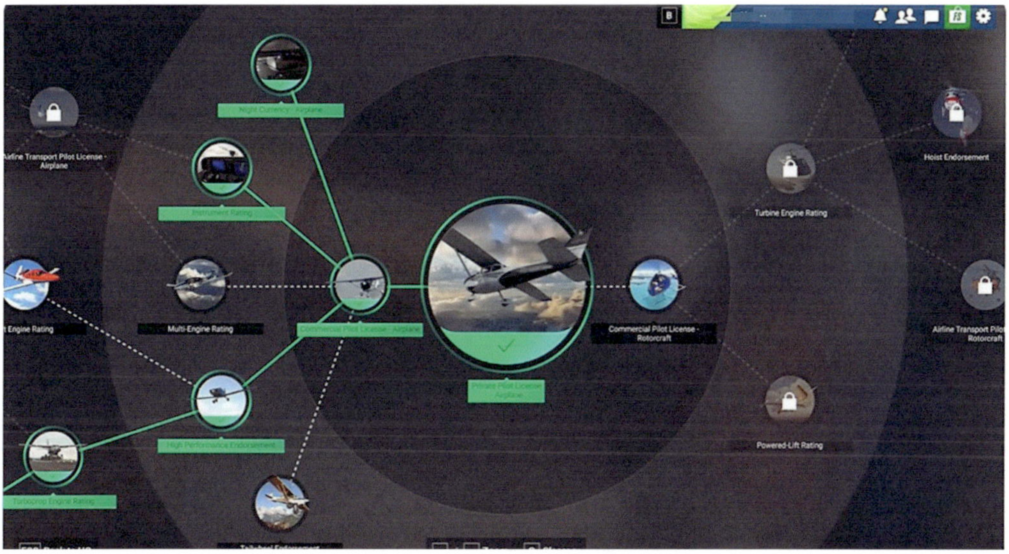

The training follows a **clear, step-by-step progression**, designed to teach core flying skills and gradually unlock new opportunities. Rather than focusing on full realism, the simulator simplifies certain procedures—such as aircraft startup—by using quick-start systems instead of detailed *cold-and-dark* operations. For most **PS5 users**, this streamlined approach is practical and accessible.

Licenses, Ratings, and Progression

After earning your **Private Pilot License**, you can expand into additional **ratings and endorsements**, eventually progressing toward advanced aircraft. A **heavy airliner rating** is planned but not yet available and will be introduced in a future update.

Career Mode also allows you to branch into **rotorcraft operations**, where you can train as a **helicopter pilot** and experience a different style of flight and mission structure.

Missions, Employment, and Income

Early in your career, you work for **other operators**, flying their aircraft and earning money through assigned missions. These missions vary in type and difficulty and are accessed through the **Missions** menu.

As you gain certifications and accumulate enough funds, you can transition into **freelance work** and eventually **own your own company**. At this stage:

- You must purchase your own aircraft
- Operating costs increase (maintenance, wear and tear, expenses)
- Earnings are higher, but profits depend on managing expenses

Your final income is determined by what remains after all operating costs are deducted.

Platform Differences

On **console (PS5 and Xbox)**, this is currently the **primary built-in career experience**. On **PC**, however, players have access to a wide range of **third-party career add-ons**, including free, subscription-based, and one-time purchase options that offer deeper or alternative career systems.

Home Screen Modes and Gamified Experiences

Returning to the **Home Screen**, the simulator presents several distinct ways to experience the world of flight.

- **Free Flight** is your primary mode for unrestricted exploration. If you simply want to fly anywhere in the world, this is where you begin.
- **Career Mode** offers a more structured, gamified experience with progression, certifications, missions, and income.

Challenge League

For players looking for **short, competitive experiences**, **Challenge League** provides a quick and engaging option. Each week features **three rotating challenges**, typically including:

- A rally-style race
- A low-altitude flight challenge
- A precision landing challenge

Your performance earns points, which allow you to advance through competitive leagues. These challenges reset weekly, keeping the experience fresh.

On **PS5**, competition is limited to other PS5 users. While participation is optional and competition is not required, many players find the challenges enjoyable simply as standalone activities rather than leaderboard contests.

Note: These weekly challenges are also accessible through the **Activities** section.

World Photographer Mode

World Photographer is designed for players who enjoy exploration and creativity, effectively turning the simulator into a **digital tourism experience**.

In this mode, you complete photography missions by capturing specific landmarks, locations, or wildlife. Each mission includes a **star-based rating system**, where:

- More stars indicate greater difficulty

- Bonus objectives increase your score

For example, a mission such as **"USA's Most Spectacular Bridges"** may require you to photograph a specific structure like the **Golden Gate Bridge**, with additional bonus conditions such as:

- Including San Francisco's financial district in the frame
- Capturing the image at night
- Including the moon in the photograph

The simulator places you near the target location, allowing you to focus on composition rather than navigation.

Using World Photographer in Free Flight

You can also complete photography challenges in **Free Flight** by:

1. Flying to the target location manually
2. Entering **Photo Mode**
3. Capturing the required image

When successful, you receive an on-screen notification confirming the stars earned. However, Free Flight does not display all mission criteria upfront, making it harder to complete bonus objectives.

Wildlife and Nature Photography

World Photographer also includes **nature-focused missions**, such as photographing national parks, wildlife safaris, and animals in their natural habitats. These missions provide:

- Population estimates
- Color-coded zones indicating higher or lower chances of sightings

Starting in a **red zone** increases your chances of spotting wildlife, while green zones offer fewer opportunities. Despite this, wildlife photography can be challenging, adding to the sense of exploration and discovery.

Overall, this mode is best suited for players who enjoy **slow-paced exploration, creativity, and visual storytelling**, rather than traditional flying objectives.

Activities and Flight Training

The final major section on the Home Screen is **Activities**. This is where you'll find **all challenges in one place**, including those featured in **Challenge League**. Instead of being limited to three weekly challenges, Activities gives you access to the **entire challenge library** at any time.

Available activities include:

- Rally races
- Low-altitude flight challenges
- Precision landing challenges

You can still compete on **global leaderboards** or compare scores with friends, but your progress here is not restricted by weekly rotations or league placement.

Future Content:

Planned additions such as **Red Bull Air Race** and **National Championship Air Races** have been announced but are not yet available.

Discovery Flights

Discovery Flights are introduced alongside **World or City Updates**. These curated flights guide you through notable landmarks and scenic routes, highlighting what to look for as you fly. They are ideal for sightseeing and exploring newly updated regions without complex planning.

Flight Training: Where Beginners Should Start

For first-time players, **Flight Training** is the recommended starting point. This mode teaches the **fundamentals of flying** in a structured, consequence-free environment.

Training begins with the **Cessna 172**, a simple and forgiving aircraft widely used for real-world pilot training. Lessons cover:

- Basic aircraft handling
- Takeoff and landing procedures
- Power management and trim
- Pitch, roll, turns, and altitude control

The training modules do not need to be completed in order, allowing you to focus on specific skills as needed.

VFR and IFR Navigation

Flight Training also introduces navigation concepts:

- **VFR (Visual Flight Rules):** Flying using visual landmarks and external references
- **IFR (Instrument Flight Rules):** Flying using cockpit instruments to follow approach paths and land in low-visibility conditions

Understanding both is essential for realistic flight operations and later progression into complex aircraft.

Recommended Learning Path

Although **Career Mode** includes pilot certification progression, it is strongly recommended to begin with **Flight Training** first. Training mode allows you to learn without penalties, while Career Mode tracks mistakes and applies consequences.

Starting with a **small aircraft like the Cessna 172** builds a solid foundation in flight fundamentals before transitioning to complex aircraft such as airliners. Jumping directly into large jets without understanding pitch, roll, and power management can make learning unnecessarily difficult.

Even experienced sim pilots continue learning over time, making structured training the most effective way to build long-term confidence and skill.

HOW TO CONNECT A PS5 CONTROLLER TO A PC (PERFECT FOR MICROSOFT FLIGHT SIMULATOR 2024)

If you want to use a **PlayStation 5 DualSense controller** with **Microsoft Flight Simulator 2024 on PC**, this guide walks you through the entire setup—from Bluetooth pairing to ensuring full compatibility in Flight Sim.

Pairing the PS5 Controller with Windows

Step 1: Pair the PS5 Controller with Windows

1. On **Windows 11**, open the **Start Menu** and search for **Bluetooth**.
2. Select **Bluetooth & devices**, then click **Add device**.
3. Choose **Bluetooth** from the list.

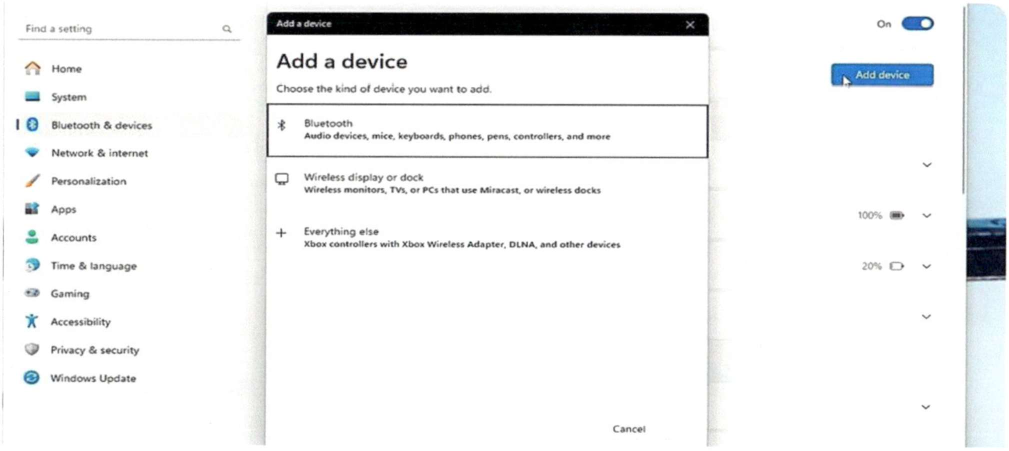

4. On your PS5 controller, **hold the PlayStation (PS) button and the Share button at the same time**.

5. When the light around the touchpad starts blinking, the controller is in pairing mode.
6. Select **Wireless Controller** when it appears on your PC.
7. Once Windows shows it as **Connected**, Bluetooth pairing is complete.

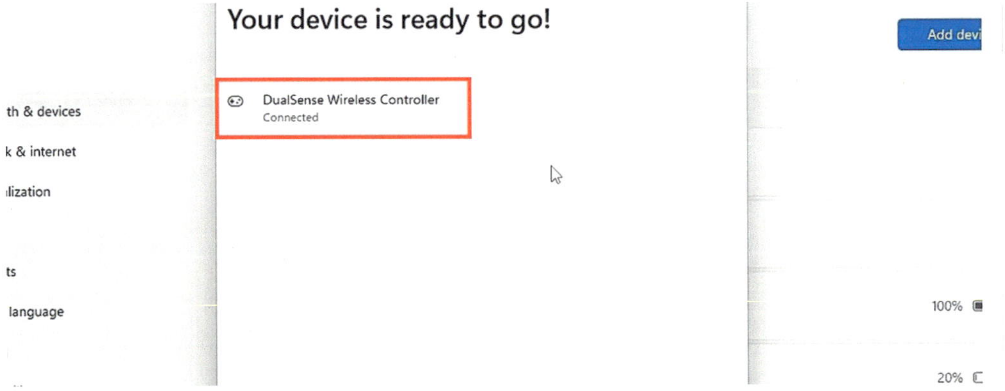

Step 2: Install DS4Windows for Full Compatibility

Windows can detect the controller, but **Flight Simulator requires additional software** to properly recognize and map it.

1. Go to **ds4windows.com** and download the **latest version**.

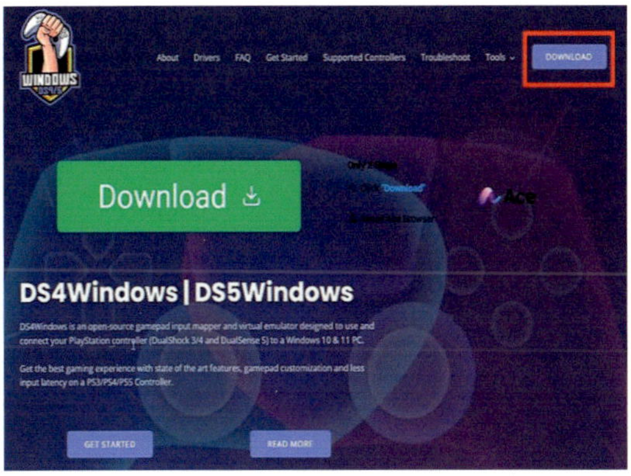

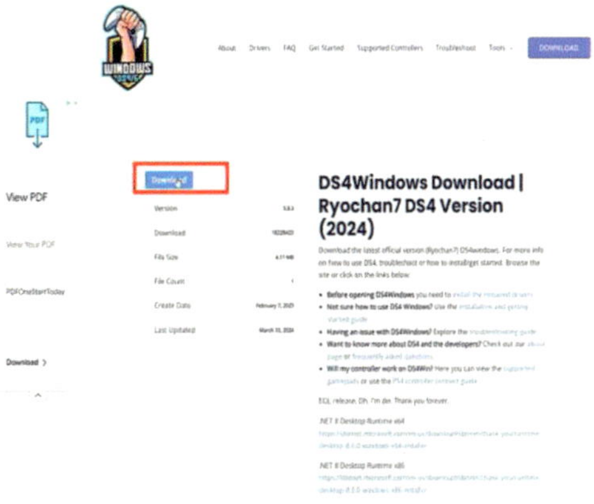

2. Open the downloaded ZIP file, right-click it, and select **Extract All**.

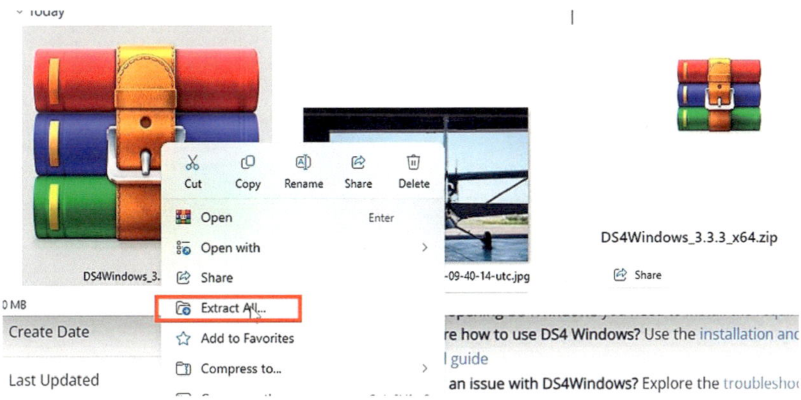

3. Open the extracted folder and **double-click the DS4Windows .exe file**.

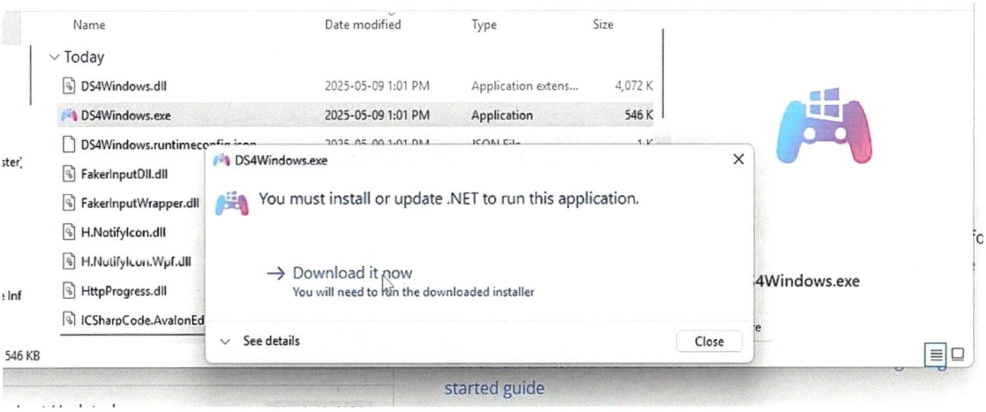

Step 3: Install Required System Components

1. When prompted, download and install the **Microsoft .NET Desktop Runtime**.

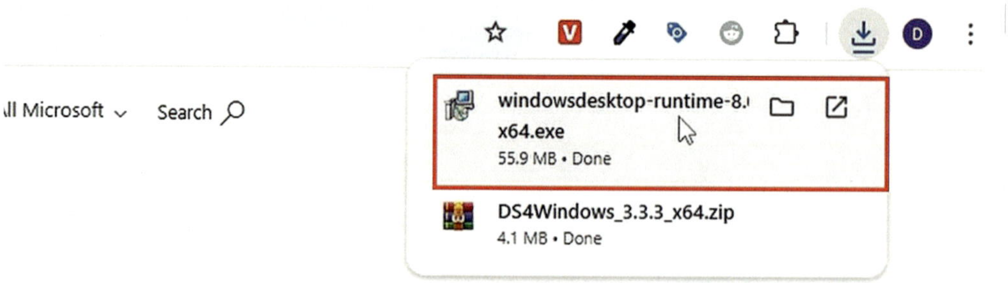

2. After installation completes, reopen **DS4Windows**.
3. When asked where to store settings, select **AppData** (recommended).

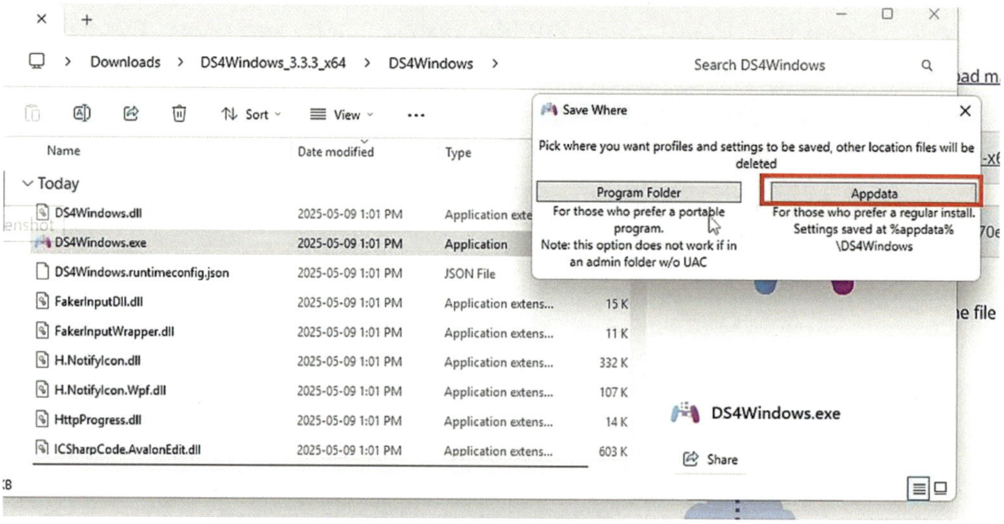

4. In the device setup screen:
   - Enable **DualSense (PS5) support**
   - Enable PS4 support only if needed

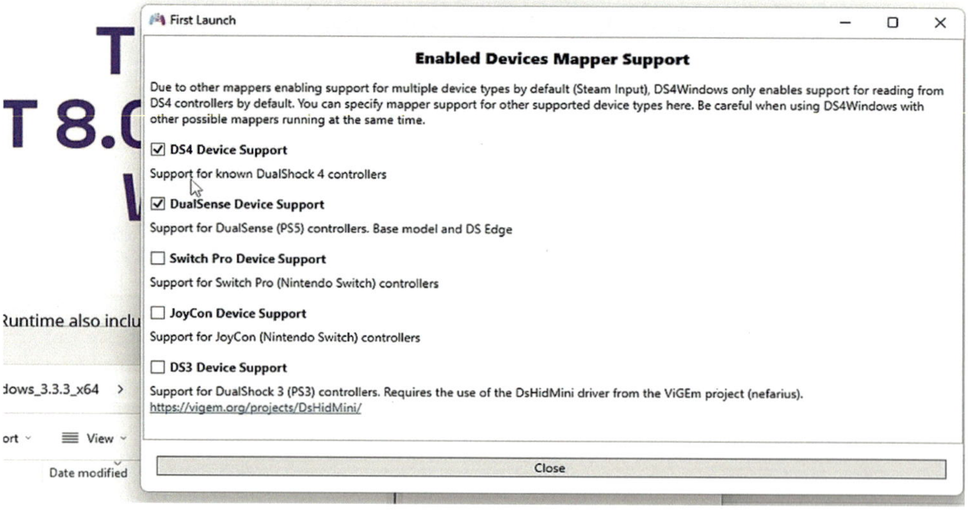

5. Click **Close**, then proceed to **install the driver** when prompted.

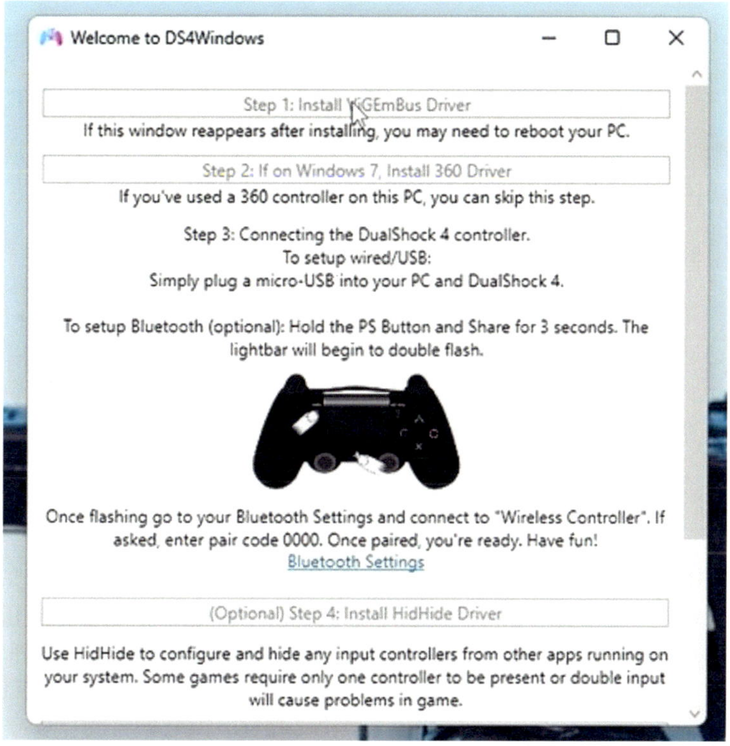

Once the driver installation finishes, the mandatory setup is complete.

Step 4: Connect the Controller in DS4Windows

1. Click **Start** inside DS4Windows.

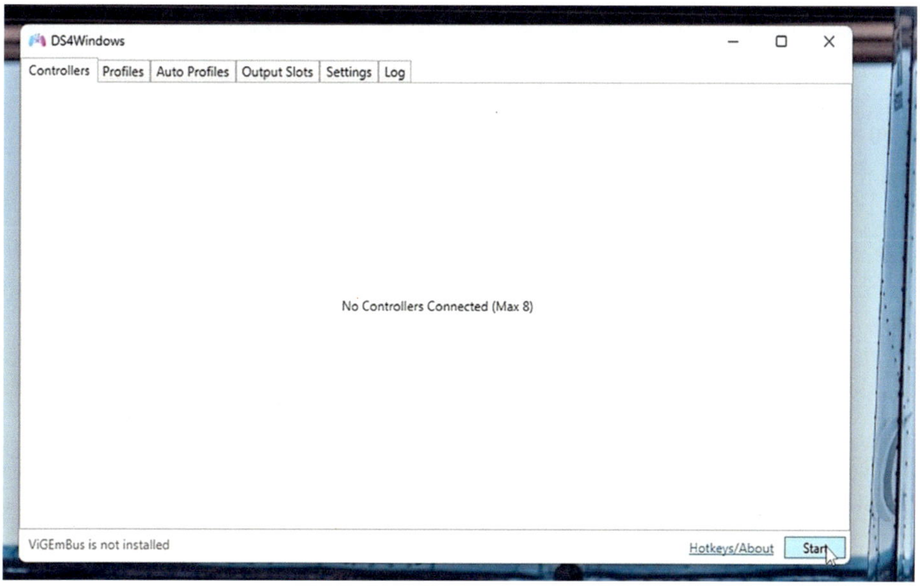

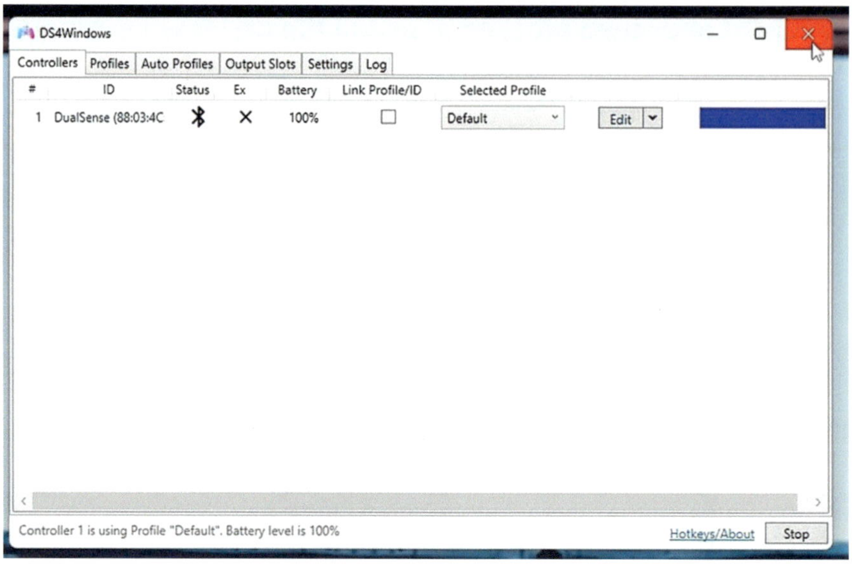

2. If your controller is already on, it will connect automatically.
3. If not, press the **PlayStation button** once to wake it up.
4. When the controller appears as connected in DS4Windows, it's ready for use.

Final Step: Launch Microsoft Flight Simulator 2024

With DS4Windows running in the background, launch **Microsoft Flight Simulator 2024**. The simulator will now properly detect the PS5 controller, allowing you to map controls or use the default layout for flying.

Making DS4Windows Easy to Use (and Avoiding Controller Conflicts)

To keep things simple long-term, it's best to move DS4Windows out of your Downloads folder.

Move DS4Windows to a Safe Location

1. Open your **Downloads** folder.
2. **Right-click the unzipped DS4Windows folder** (not the ZIP file).
3. Select **Cut**, then paste it somewhere permanent—such as **Documents** or **Program Files**.

This prevents the app from being accidentally deleted when cleaning out your Downloads folder later.

To launch it, just open the folder and double-click the **DS4Windows.exe** file.

Pin DS4Windows to the Taskbar

To make startup faster:

1. Open **DS4Windows**.

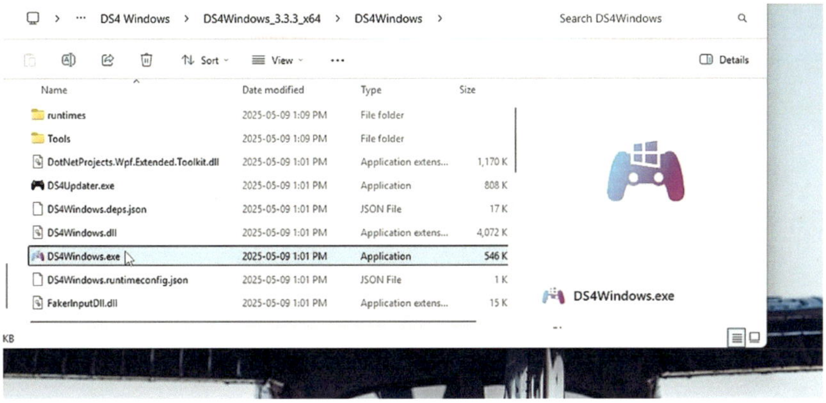

2. When its icon appears on the taskbar, **right-click it**.
3. Select **Pin to taskbar**.

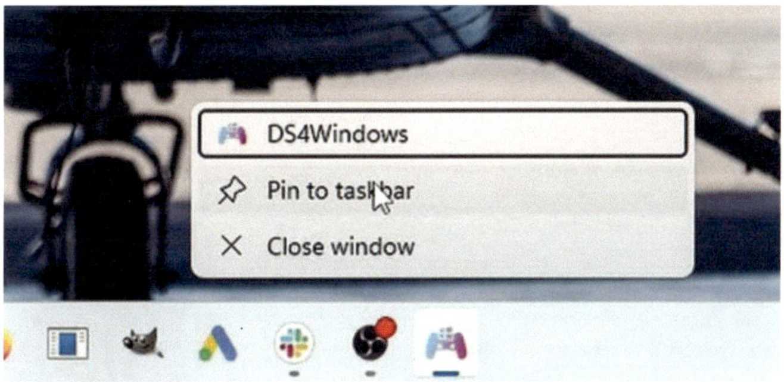

From now on, you can launch it with a single click.

Important: Always start DS4Windows before launching Microsoft Flight Simulator. It doesn't need to stay visible—just let it run in the background.

Preventing Duplicate Controller Inputs (HidHide Setup)

Without additional setup, Windows may detect your controller **twice**:

- A virtual Xbox controller (created by DS4Windows)
- The native Sony DualSense controller

This can cause conflicts in Flight Simulator.

Install and Configure HidHide

1. Download and install **HidHide** (recommended by DS4Windows).

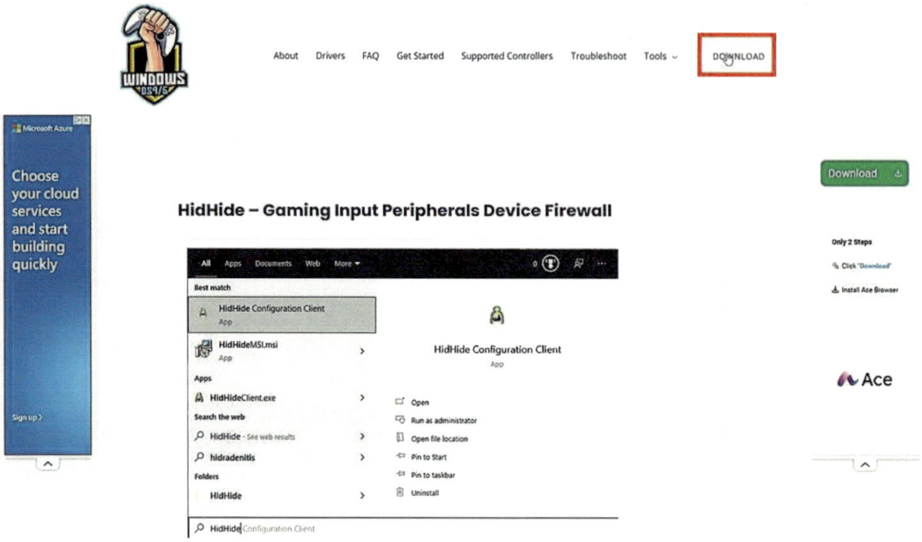

2. Open the **Start Menu**, search for **HidHide**, and launch **HidHide Configuration Client**.

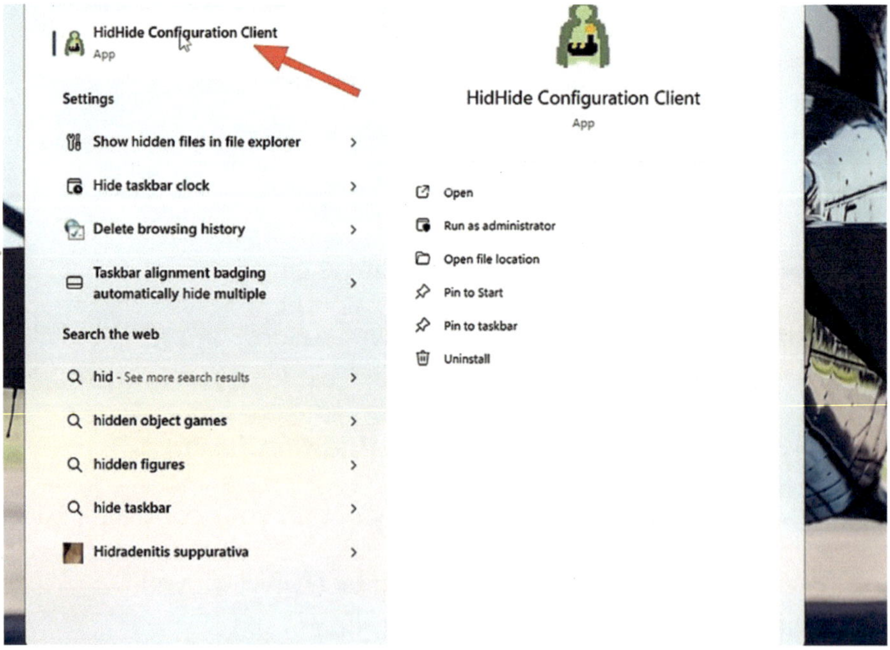

3. With DS4Windows running, you'll see **two controller entries**:
   - Xbox (virtual)
   - Sony (physical)

4. **Hide the Xbox controller entry**.

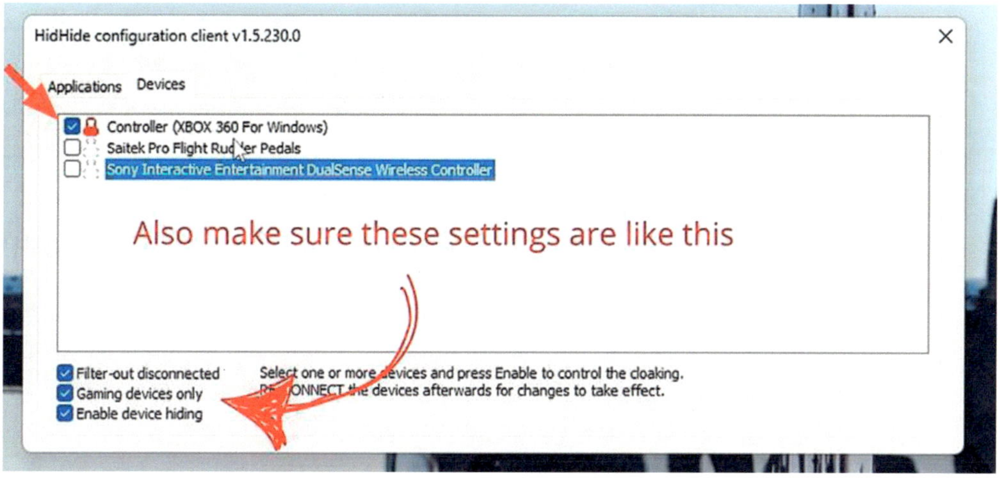

This ensures Flight Simulator only sees one controller input, preventing double bindings or erratic behavior.

HidHide is also useful if you use multiple controllers or other input devices.

Disable Steam Input (If Using Steam)

If Flight Simulator is launched through Steam, Steam Input can create another layer of duplication.

1. Open **Steam**.
2. Right-click **Microsoft Flight Simulator** → **Manage**.
3. Open **Controller Layout**.

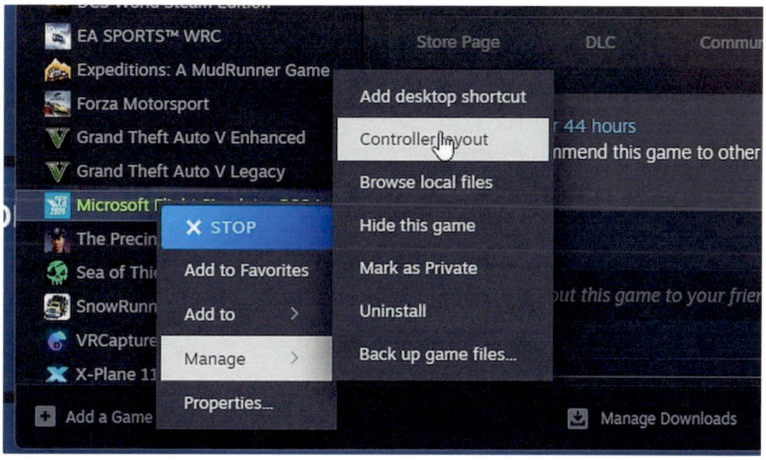

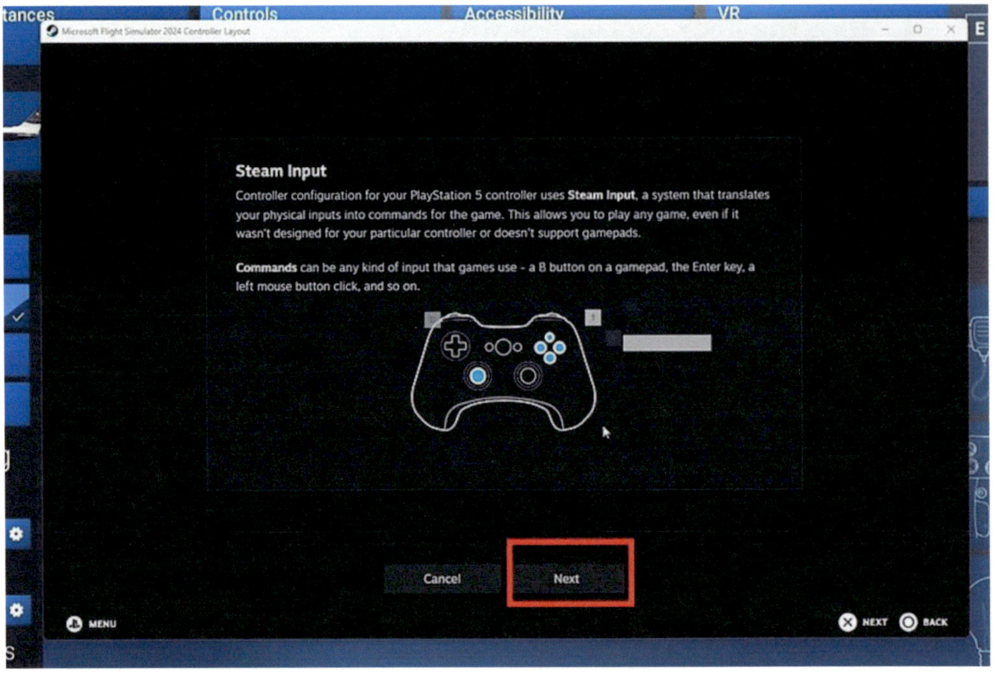

4. Close the layout window.
5. From the same menu, select **Disable Steam Input**.

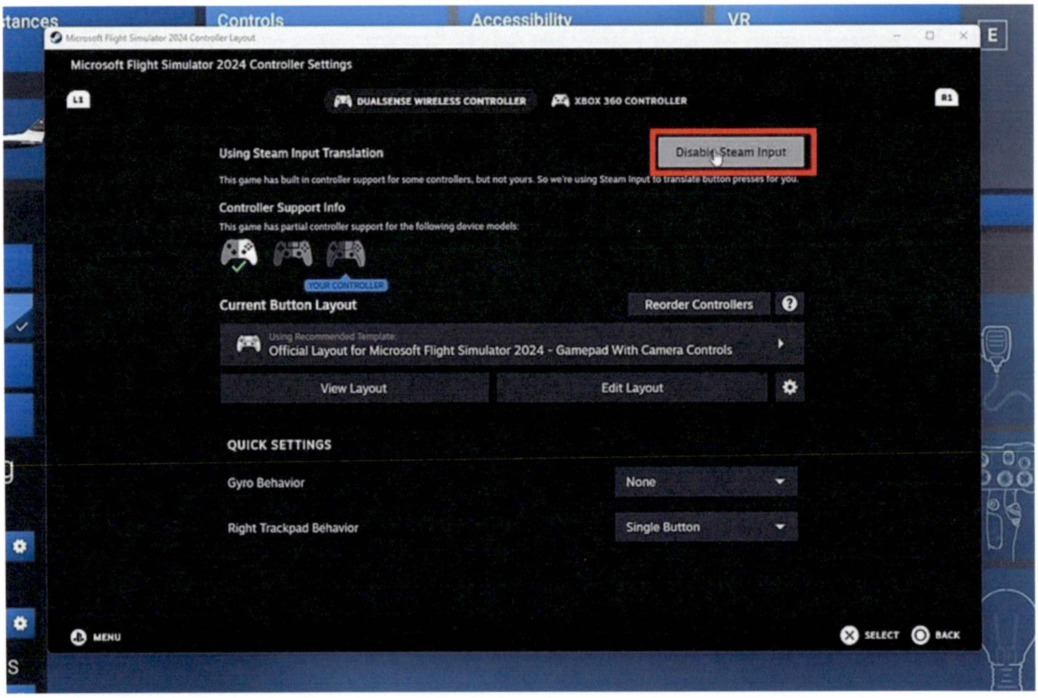

This ensures Steam doesn't interfere with DS4Windows.

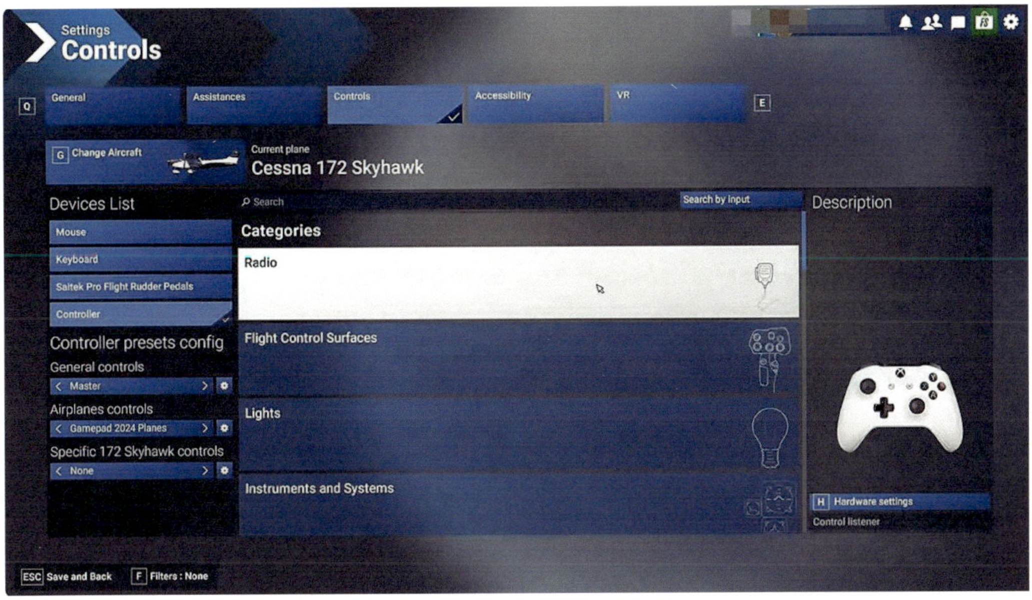

PS5 DUALSENSE CONTROLLER GUIDE – MICROSOFT FLIGHT SIMULATOR 2024

If you're wondering **what each button does on the PS5 DualSense controller** in *Microsoft Flight Simulator 2024*, this quick-reference cheat sheet breaks it all down in a clear and practical way.

D-Pad Controls

- **Up:** Raise flaps
- **Down:** Lower flaps
- **Right:** Toggle landing gear
- **Left:** Career quick reply

Main Buttons

- **Triangle:** Mission action toggle (smoke, spray, scoop, hook, etc.)
- **Circle:** Decrease throttle
- **X:** Increase throttle
- **Square:** Brakes

Analog Sticks

- **Left Stick:** Aircraft control (pitch, roll, yaw)
- **Left Stick Click:** Toggle visual assists
- **Right Stick:** Camera movement
- **Right Stick Click:** Reset camera

Triggers

- **Left & Right Triggers:** Rudder control
- **Triggers (EFB):** Zoom in / out

Touchpad

- Switch between **cockpit and external camera**
- Reset camera when in **Showcase view**

Bumpers & Modifier Combinations

R1 + L1

- Toggle **Photo Mode**

R1 + Controls

- **Left Stick Click:** Activate cursor mode
- **X:** Throttle to next detent
- **Circle:** Throttle to previous detent
- **Triangle:** Deploy spoilers
- **Square:** Toggle parking brake
- **D-Pad Up:** Disengage autopilot
- **D-Pad Down:** Shut down engine
- **D-Pad Right:** Toggle water rudder

L1 + Controls

- **Left Stick Click:** Toggle gyroscope mode
- **X:** Toggle smart camera
- **Circle:** Enter/exit aircraft (when stationary)
- **Triangle:** Pause simulation
- **Touchpad:** Open Electronic Flight Bag (EFB)
- **D-Pad Up:** Quick view (up)
- **D-Pad Down:** Close-up view
- **D-Pad Left:** Quick view (left)
- **D-Pad Right:** Quick view (right)
- **Any D-Pad Direction (External View):** Move camera
- **Left Stick:** Move camera position
- **Right Stick:** Look around
- **Left Trigger:** Lower camera
- **Right Trigger:** Raise camera

Showcase Camera Shortcuts

Camera Controls

- **Circle:** Toggle drone lock
- **X:** Toggle follow mode
- **Right Stick Click:** Reset camera
- **Right Trigger:** Raise camera
- **Left Trigger:** Lower camera

Exposure

- **L1 + Square:** Decrease exposure
- **R1 + Square:** Increase exposure

Zoom

- **Triangle + Right Trigger:** Zoom in
- **Triangle + Left Trigger:** Zoom out

Camera Speed

- **R1 + D-Pad Up:** Increase rotation speed
- **R1 + D-Pad Down:** Decrease rotation speed
- **R1 + X:** Increase drone speed
- **R1 + Circle:** Decrease drone speed

Camera Rotation

- **L1 + Right Stick Left/Right:** Roll camera

Custom Button Assignments (User-Defined)

- **Zoom Cockpit View:** Triangle + D-Pad Right
- **Unzoom Cockpit View:** Triangle + D-Pad Left
- **Zoom External View:** Triangle + D-Pad Right
- **Unzoom External View:** Triangle + D-Pad Left
- **Slew Mode:** Square + D-Pad Left
- **Toggle Drone Camera:** Square + D-Pad Right
- **Autopilot Master Toggle:** R1 + D-Pad Up
  (Replaces the default "Disengage Autopilot" — recommended for better control)

HERE'S HOW CAREER MODE WORKS ON PS5

Microsoft Flight Simulator 2024 has officially landed on PlayStation 5, marking the franchise's first appearance on Sony's platform. For many PS5 players, this will be their first encounter with the series—a simulator that blends open-world aviation with a structured, goal-driven career system.

Career Mode is designed to be the heart of MSFS 2024. It offers purpose, progression, and a sense of identity beyond free flight. Originally described by Microsoft as the backbone of the 2024 release, the mode delivers a broad range of aviation activities inspired by real-world flying careers. While some systems feel more refined than others—and a few ideas are simpler than early previews suggested—Career Mode remains the most accessible and engaging entry point for new pilots.

Below is a practical overview of what PS5 players can expect when stepping into Career Mode.

Creating Your Pilot Avatar

Career Mode begins with avatar creation, a feature exclusive to the 2024 edition. Players can customize their pilot's appearance with multiple facial features, hairstyles, outfits, accessories, and voice options. The simulator also supports voice input, allowing you to use your own voice when communicating with air traffic control.

Although largely cosmetic, your avatar serves as your persistent identity across certifications, missions, and company operations, reinforcing a sense of progression throughout your aviation career.

Choosing Your Starting Base

Your journey begins at a small aero club of your choosing. Large international airports are intentionally excluded, encouraging new pilots to train in quieter environments with shorter runways and simpler traffic patterns.

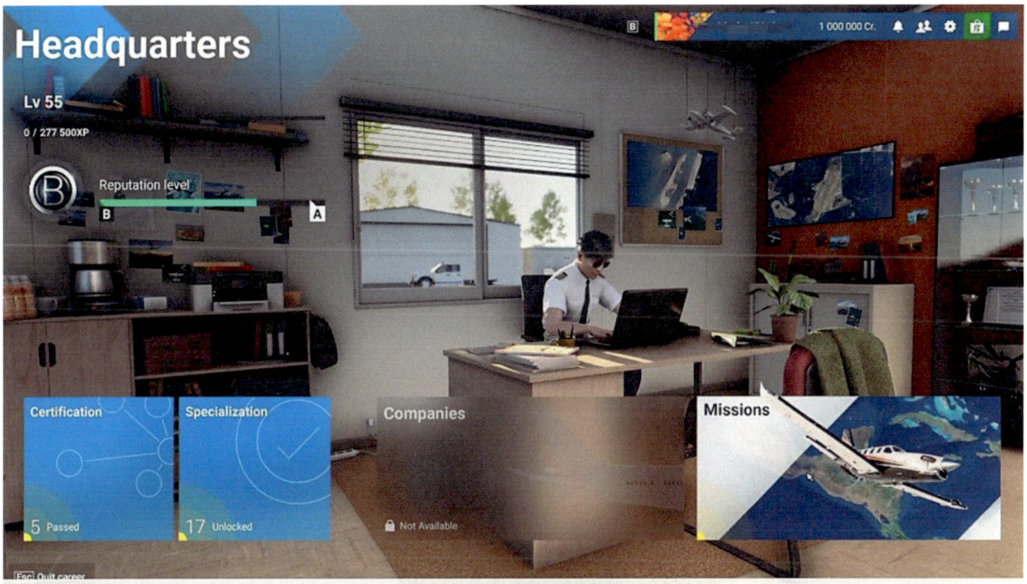

Using the world map, you're free to select an airport anywhere on the globe—whether it's a familiar local airfield or a remote strip surrounded by mountains or coastline. Once selected, a mentor character introduces you to the fundamentals of flight and outlines your certification path.

This onboarding experience closely follows the original design vision, easing new players into the simulator before advancing to more demanding missions.

Walkaround Mode and Pre-Flight Checks

Walkaround Mode remains a core component of Career Mode, though its scope is more focused than initially expected.

Before each flight, you'll inspect the aircraft's exterior. Interactive elements—such as pitot covers and wheel chocks—must be properly handled. Forgetting to remove pitot covers can result in incorrect airspeed readings, while leaving chocks in place will prevent the aircraft from moving during taxi.

These checks add meaningful depth to the experience, encouraging attention to detail and reinforcing real-world aviation habits. Neglecting them can lead to serious consequences once airborne.

First Flights and Flight Training

Your first flight introduces essential piloting skills under the guidance of your mentor, including:

- Pre-flight procedures
- Engine start-up
- Taxiing
- Takeoff
- Basic aircraft handling
- Simple altitude and heading adjustments

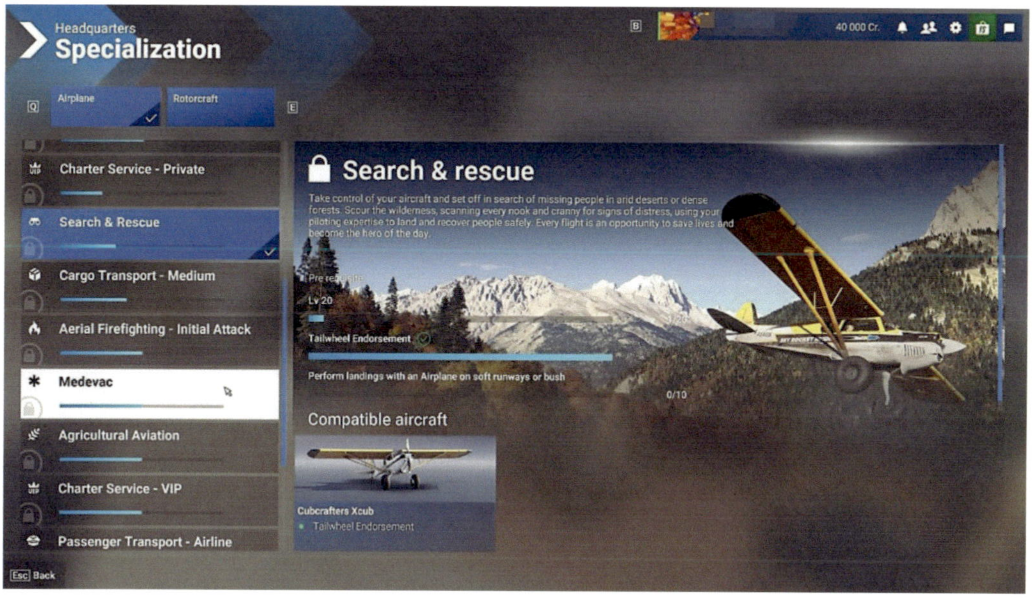

Career Mode includes a structured set of training modules that form the foundation of your progression. These lessons prepare you not only for certification exams but also for the challenges encountered during missions.

While some training modules are shorter or more streamlined than early previews suggested, the overall system provides a smooth learning curve from beginner to intermediate pilot.

Certifications and Career Specializations

Progression in Career Mode revolves around certifications. Completing training and passing evaluations unlocks new mission types and grants access to more advanced aircraft—both fixed-wing and rotary.

The certification system currently includes:

- Core pilot licenses
- Ratings for advanced aircraft categories
- Special authorizations tied to mission-specific roles

Rather than forcing a linear path, the system allows flexibility, enabling players to explore multiple aviation careers and switch specializations over time.

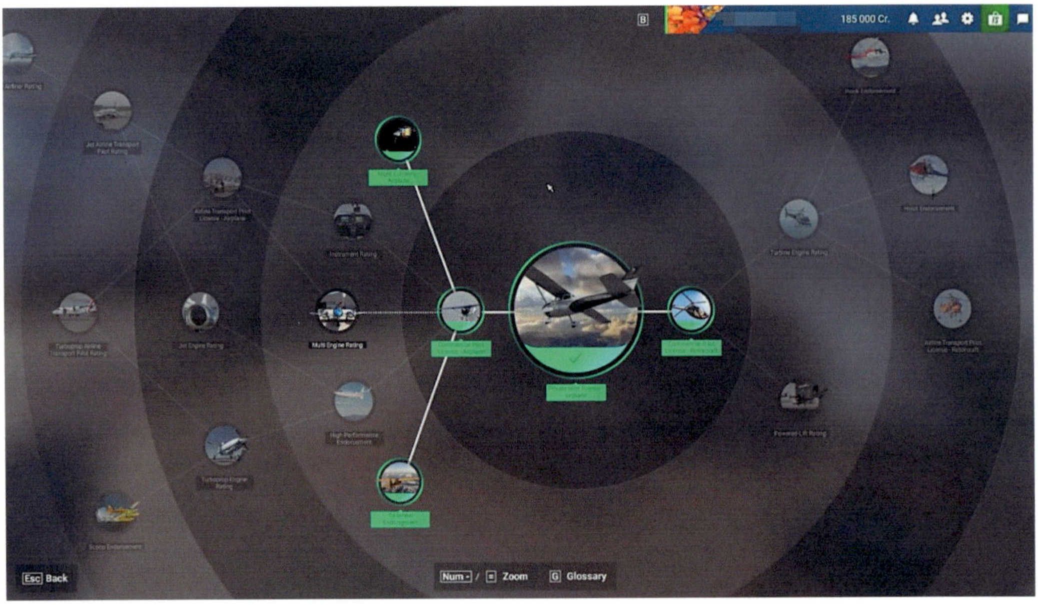

Aircraft Availability in Career Mode

Aircraft availability is one of the areas that differs most from early expectations.

While MSFS 2024 includes a large aircraft roster, not all aircraft are usable in Career Mode. The mode primarily supports aircraft included in the Standard Edition and selected models that align with existing mission types.

Premium, Deluxe, and third-party aircraft are not consistently supported in Career Mode at launch. Although support continues to expand, players should expect to fly a curated subset of the overall fleet when pursuing career missions.

The Dynamic Mission System

At the core of Career Mode is a dynamic mission system that reflects the evolving in-game world. Missions are influenced by factors such as weather, airport activity, emergencies, and time of day.

Mission opportunities appear across the global map, ranging from short local flights to multi-stage assignments. As the day progresses, new missions emerge while others expire, creating a sense of realism and ongoing activity.

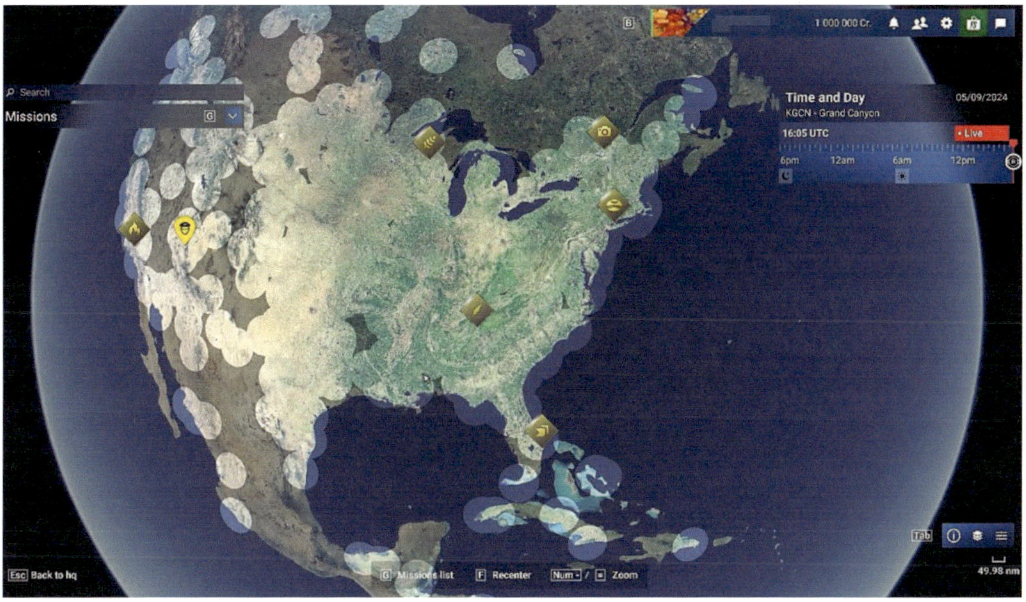

While the variety of mission categories is broad, availability is uneven. Some mission types appear less frequently than players might expect, with the system favoring consistency over sheer volume.

Mission Types

Career Mode features a diverse mix of civilian, commercial, and emergency aviation roles. Currently supported mission categories include:

- Air ambulance operations
- Search and rescue
- Cargo delivery
- Mountain rescue
- Passenger transport
- Executive and VIP transport
- Agricultural operations
- Aerial photography
- Aerial firefighting
- Helicopter cargo transport
- Survey and inspection missions

Mission availability varies by location, aircraft type, and environmental conditions, meaning some mission types appear more frequently than others. Overall mission quality can differ based on airport layout, weather, and terrain.

While ongoing updates continue to improve mission stability, PS5 players may occasionally encounter placement issues or scenarios that require restarting a mission.

Mission Evaluation

Each mission includes clearly defined success criteria and is scored across multiple performance factors:

General Flight Performance

Pilots are evaluated on overall handling, including smooth control inputs, proper taxiing, compliance with ATC instructions, and avoiding airframe overstress. Even non-mission flights contribute to performance tracking.

Mission-Specific Objectives

Every mission type has unique requirements. For example, aerial advertising missions require pilots to collect a banner at precise speeds and altitudes, then fly an accurate pass over the target area to release it correctly.

Meeting both general and mission-specific standards is key to achieving high ratings.

Reputation and Progression

Successful missions build reputation, which directly affects career advancement. A higher reputation unlocks:

- Better-paying contracts

- More complex and demanding missions
- Exclusive assignments unavailable to new pilots

Reputation acts as a progression gate, rewarding consistent, reliable performance. Mission earnings fund long-term goals, though the economic system is intentionally lighter than a full business simulator.

From Pilot to Operator

Career Mode allows players to transition from hired pilot to independent operator. As earnings grow, players can invest in their own aircraft fleet and expand operations globally.

Most aircraft purchases begin with used models, which may suffer from wear and require ongoing maintenance. Aircraft condition is influenced by how they are flown:

- Hard landings and poor handling increase wear on engines and landing gear
- Smooth, efficient flying reduces maintenance costs and extends aircraft lifespan

Over time, players can expand from small aircraft to larger and more complex operations, adding a strategic layer to progression.

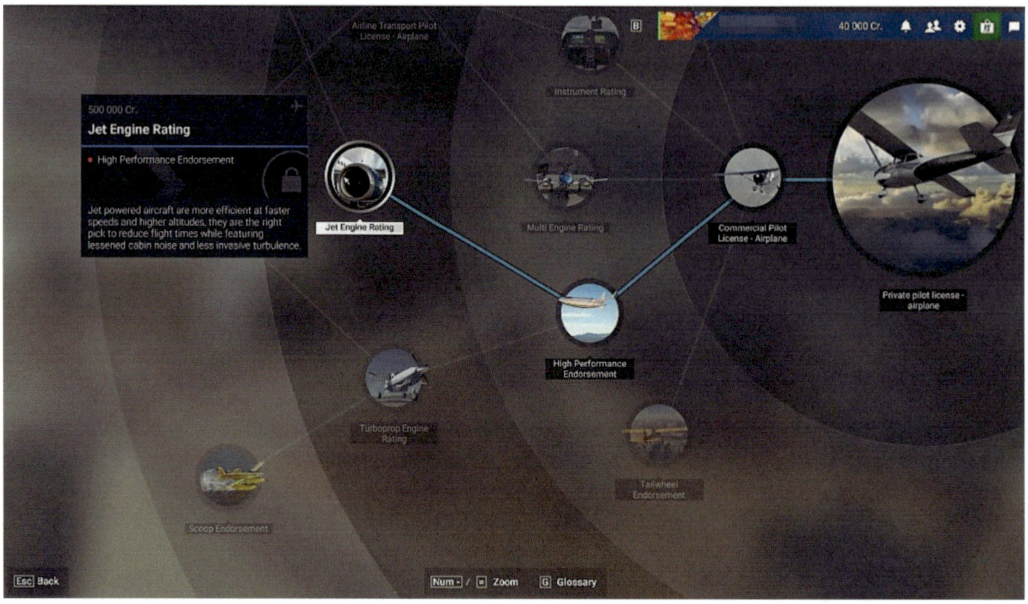

Realism and Accessibility

Career Mode balances realism with accessibility. While it is not a full pilot-training program, it introduces key aviation concepts such as:

- Weight and balance management
- Weather effects
- Basic checklist procedures
- Airspace structure
- ATC communication

This approach allows new PS5 players to learn real aviation principles without being overwhelmed by complex regulations, making Career Mode an approachable entry point into flight simulation.

The PS5 Experience

The PlayStation 5 version of *Microsoft Flight Simulator 2024* launches with the latest updates, including stability improvements, refined mission logic, and optimizations informed by PC and Xbox feedback.

Although Career Mode on PS5 shares known limitations—such as partial aircraft support and occasional mission inconsistencies—it benefits from solid performance and a fresh platform launch.

One year after its introduction, Career Mode remains ambitious. While not all early promises have fully materialized, it still delivers a structured, rewarding aviation experience. For PS5 players new to the franchise, it offers clear progression, meaningful objectives, and a wide range of flying activities that extend well beyond simple point-to-point flights.

MICROSOFT FLIGHT SIMULATOR 2024 (PS5) – THINGS TO KEEP IN MIND

Microsoft Flight Simulator 2024 is a technically impressive experience, featuring advanced weather, realistic aircraft behavior, and a fully simulated world. On PS5, this depth can feel overwhelming for newcomers and slightly disorienting for experienced PC pilots adjusting to console workflows.

The good news is that once you understand the controls and interface, the PS5 version offers the same expansive aviation sandbox that has defined the series for decades. Whether you're learning to keep a Cessna steady or seeking maximum realism in complex aircraft, the following tips will help you fly smarter and with more confidence on PS5.

- **Start with "All Assists" If You're New:** MSFS 2024 includes a comprehensive **"All Assists"** preset designed for beginners. Enabling it reduces workload and allows you to focus on core fundamentals such as pitch, roll, power, airspeed, and situational awareness. Think of it as training wheels—it keeps you airborne and learning until you're ready to gradually remove assistance and take full control.
- **Fix the Overly Sensitive Cursor:** This is one of the most important quality-of-life adjustments on PS5. The cockpit cursor effectively replaces a mouse, but its default sensitivity is too high.
- Go to **Settings → Accessibility → Effects & Animations → Cursor Settings**, then reduce cursor acceleration and maximum speed. This makes cockpit interaction, menu navigation, and switch manipulation far more precise and manageable.
- **Fine-Tune Assistance for Realism:** For experienced pilots or players coming from PC, assistance settings can be customized far beyond basic presets. You can disable features such as auto-mixture, control sensitivity aids, visual navigation helpers, and flight planning guidance. Rather than simple on/off switches, MSFS 2024's assistance options act as a realism gradient, letting you strike a balance between authenticity and usability on PS5.
- **Write Things Down During Tutorials:** The built-in tutorials are excellent but fast-paced, often delivering a lot of information at once. Don't hesitate to pause and jot down key control combinations, camera shortcuts, or

menu access commands. You don't need to memorize full procedures, but noting essential inputs—such as switching views or opening avionics—can prevent costly mistakes later, like accidentally shutting down an engine mid-flight.

- **Customize the In-Flight Toolbar:** The in-flight toolbar provides quick access to weather, camera controls, ATC, avionics shortcuts, and more. On PS5, customizing this toolbar via the **gear icon** is especially helpful, as controller navigation is less precise than a mouse. Removing unnecessary panels and keeping only what you use most streamlines gameplay and reduces interruptions during flight.
- **Fine-Tune Your DualSense Controller:** The DualSense is surprisingly effective for flight simulation, but default sensitivity settings won't suit everyone. MSFS 2024 lets you adjust thumbstick sensitivity, trigger response, dead zones, curves, acceleration, and touchpad zones. These tweaks mainly improve comfort and control. If you find yourself over-banking or constantly correcting, smoothing the sensitivity curves can make aircraft handling feel far more stable and predictable.
- **Dial In Gyro Controls:** Gyro controls can make lateral movements feel more natural, mimicking a yoke-like motion. While divisive, they're highly customizable—sensitivity, dead zones, neutral position, and range can all be adjusted. Spend a few minutes experimenting before dismissing gyro entirely; once tuned, many players find it significantly enhances immersion and precision.
- **Spend Early Hours in Cockpit View:** External cameras are great for sightseeing, but cockpit view is where real learning happens. Instruments like airspeed, altitude, RPM, and vertical speed teach you how the aircraft actually behaves. Relying too much on external views or HUD elements can lead to overcorrection. Flying from the cockpit builds the instincts needed for smooth control, accurate landings, and confident decision-making.
- **Alternate Between Missions and Career Certifications:** Career progression is tied to certifications, which require credits earned through Missions. This structure works in your favor. Certifications unlock new aircraft and roles, while Missions provide real-world scenarios to apply and refine those skills. Switching between the two keeps progression fresh and balanced, preventing burnout while reinforcing learning.
- **Use Free Flight for Focused Practice:** Free Flight isn't just for exploration—it's an ideal training environment. Use it to practice takeoffs, traffic patterns, landings, or test new aircraft. Starting options matter too;

choosing parked, runway-ready, or airborne lets you target exactly what you want to improve, making practice more efficient.

- **Complete Every Mission Stage for Maximum Credits:** You can skip walkarounds, taxiing, and cruise segments, but doing so reduces your payout. If you're saving for aircraft or certifications, complete every phase of the job. It takes longer, but rewards scale accordingly—and it reinforces proper procedures and good flying habits.
- **Use Custom Views for Better Cockpit Awareness:** Pressing **L1 + D-pad** directions lets you instantly access custom views for instruments, throttle controls, GPS displays, and external checks. These shortcuts reduce camera juggling and provide quick access to critical data—some of which isn't visible on the external HUD—improving situational awareness, especially during approach and landing.
- **Check the Marketplace for Free Content:** The Marketplace includes more than paid add-ons. Microsoft offers free world and city updates for PS5 that enhance terrain detail, landmarks, and points of interest, often unlocking new activities. These updates meaningfully expand the simulation at no cost—well worth downloading.
- **Learn Trim as Early as Possible:** Trim is essential for stable, hands-off flight. Properly adjusted, it balances the aircraft's natural pitch, eliminating the need for constant thumbstick pressure. Once mastered, cruising becomes smoother, less fatiguing, and far more enjoyable. Learning trim early is the single biggest quality-of-life upgrade you can make.
- **Choose High-Earning Specializations:** If your goal is fast credit generation, prioritize **VIP transport** and **cargo operations**. While activities like rescue missions or sightseeing may be more engaging, VIP and cargo jobs consistently offer the highest payouts.

CHAPTER THREE

MICROSOFT FLIGHT SIMULATOR 2024 – PS5 CONTROLLER BUTTONS GUIDE

Let's break down the key controls for Microsoft Flight Simulator 2024 on the PlayStation 5.

BASIC CONTROLLER OVERVIEW

- **Left Stick:** Controls movement and flight surfaces (pitch, roll, yaw).

- **Right Stick:** Controls the camera, regardless of mode—external, walkaround, or showcase camera.

- **Square:** Crouch. Useful in walkaround mode for planes with low wing heights or to access covers.
- **L1 + Circle:** Enter or exit the aircraft. Hold L1 and press Circle to get in or out.

Walkaround Mode

- **Square:** Crouch (for accessing low areas or panels).
- **Right Stick:** Move the camera freely.
- **L1 + Circle:** Enter or exit the aircraft.

These are the main buttons you need while exploring outside the plane.

In-Flight Controls & D-Pad Functions

- **Left D-Pad:** Quick ATC toggle (Career Mode only).

  - Use this to contact ATC for taxiing, IFR clearance, or tower changes without opening the communications tab.
- **Right D-Pad:** Gear toggle.
  - Raises or lowers retractable landing gear (not all planes have this).

- **Down D-Pad:** Lower flaps.
  - Each press reduces the flap by a notch. Multiple presses extend full flaps.

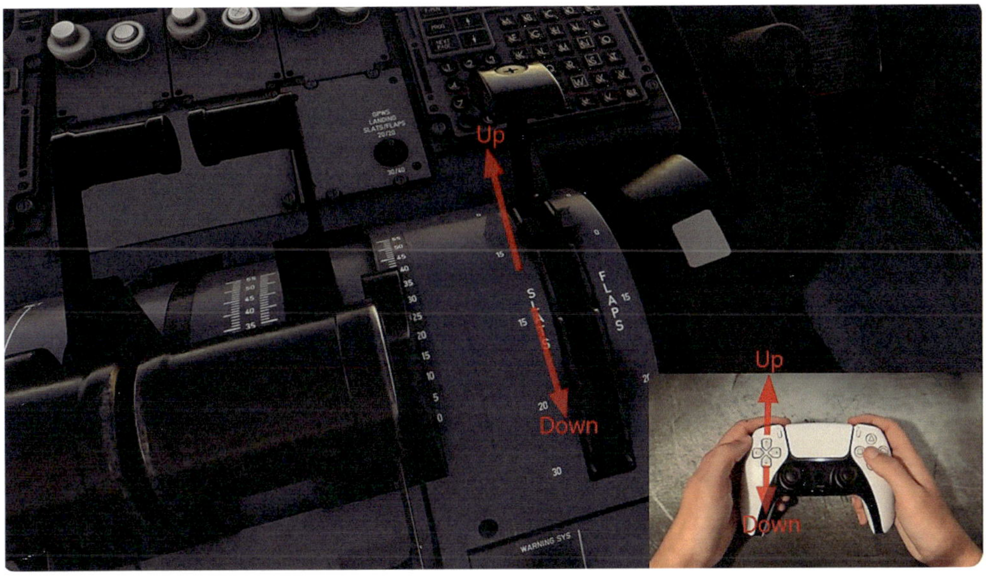

- **Up D-Pad:** Raise flaps.

Career Mode Exclusive

- **Triangle:** Special function primarily for Career Mode; not used in Free Flight.

MISSION & CAMERA FUNCTIONS

Triangle – Mission Toggles

In **Career Mode**, the **Triangle** button is primarily used for mission-specific actions:

- **Firefighting:** Toggle water scoops.
- **Aerial Advertising:** Lower the banner hook.
- **Aerobatics (Extra 300, etc.):** Toggle smoke.

In Free Flight, Triangle mainly controls smoke for aerobatic planes.

Throttle Control

- **X:** Increase throttle. Tap for small increments, hold for continuous acceleration.

- **Circle:** Decrease throttle. Tap to reduce incrementally, hold to slow down faster.

Brakes

- **Square:** Press and hold to apply brakes. Release to disengage.

Left Analog Stick – Aircraft & Visual Aids

- **Movement:** Controls aircraft pitch and roll.

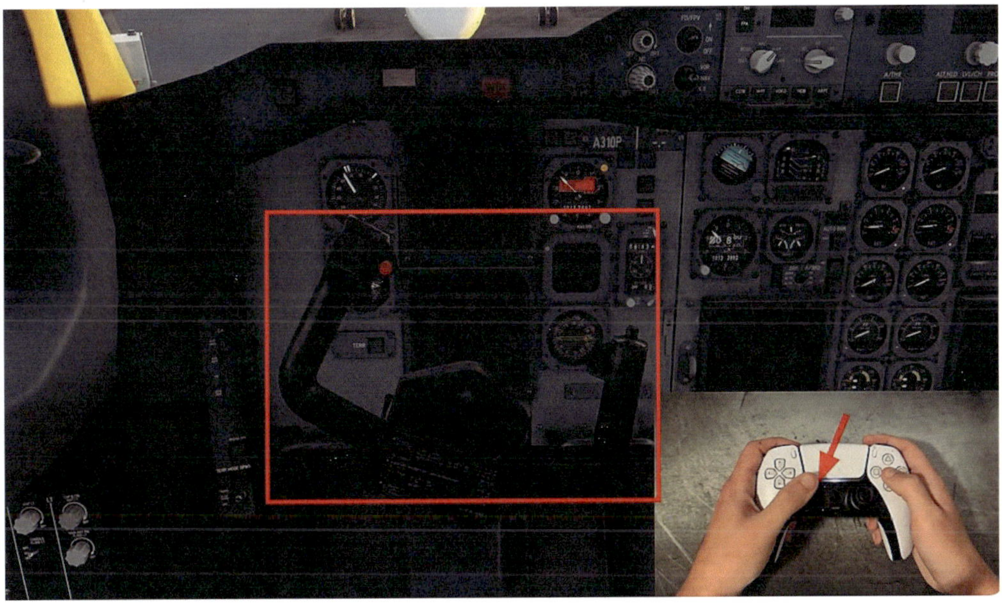

- **Click Left Stick:** Toggle visual aids on or off:

- Taxi ribbon
- Flight path
- Active waypoint markers

These visual aids are extremely helpful for beginners.

How to enable visual aids:

1. Pause the game → **Settings** → **Assistance**
2. Scroll to **Visual Assistance**
3. Enable: **Taxi Ribbon**, **Flight Path**, **Display Active Waypoint Marker**

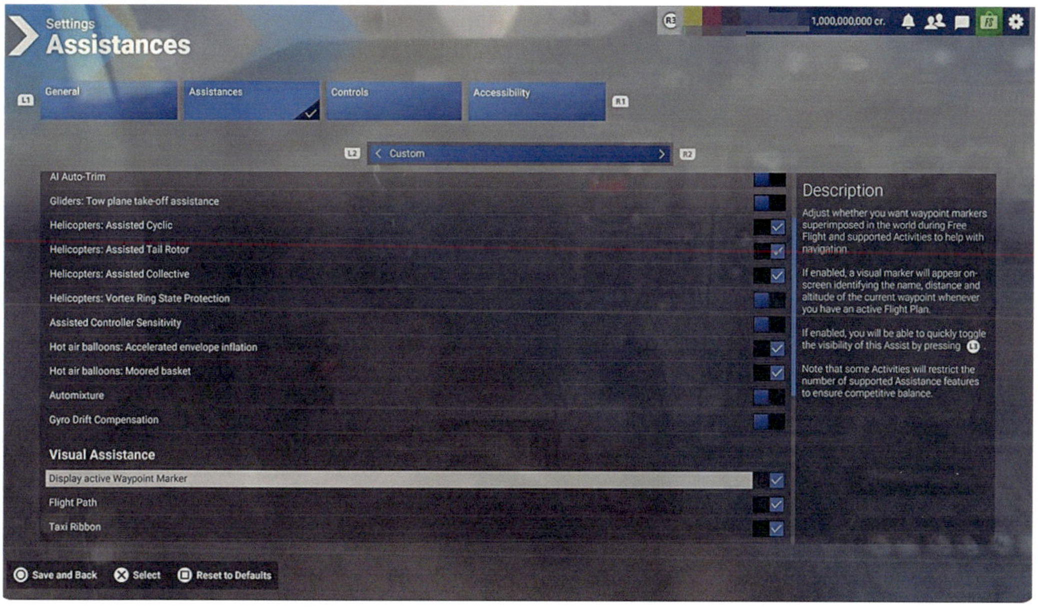

Right Analog Stick – Camera Control

- **Movement:** Adjust camera freely in cockpit or external view.

- **Click Right Stick:** Reset camera to default view (works for both cockpit and external views).

Triggers – Rudder & Zoom

- **Left Trigger:** Apply left rudder (useful when taxiing or correcting crosswinds).
- **Right Trigger:** Apply right rudder.
- **In EFB:**
  - Left Trigger: Zoom out
  - Right Trigger: Zoom in

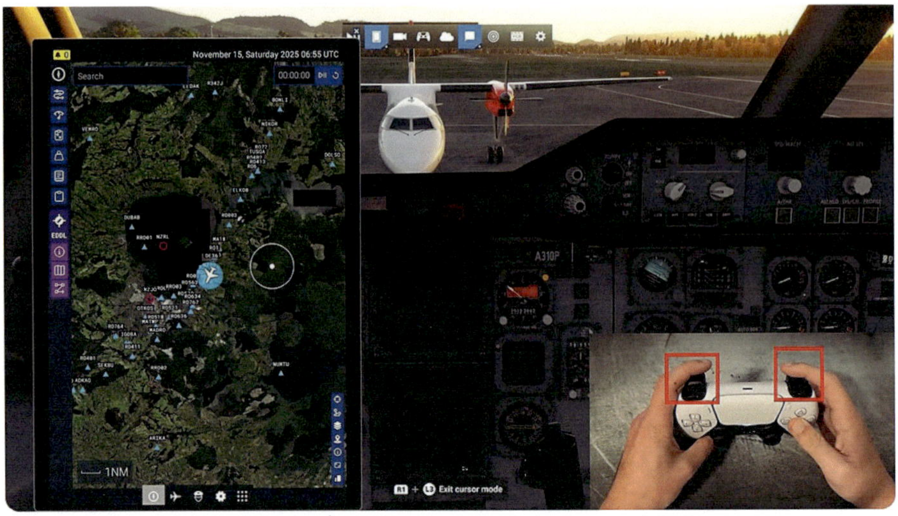

Touchpad – Camera Switching

- Press the **Touchpad** to switch between:
  - Cockpit view

  - External view
  - Drone/showcase cameras → returns to default cockpit or external camera

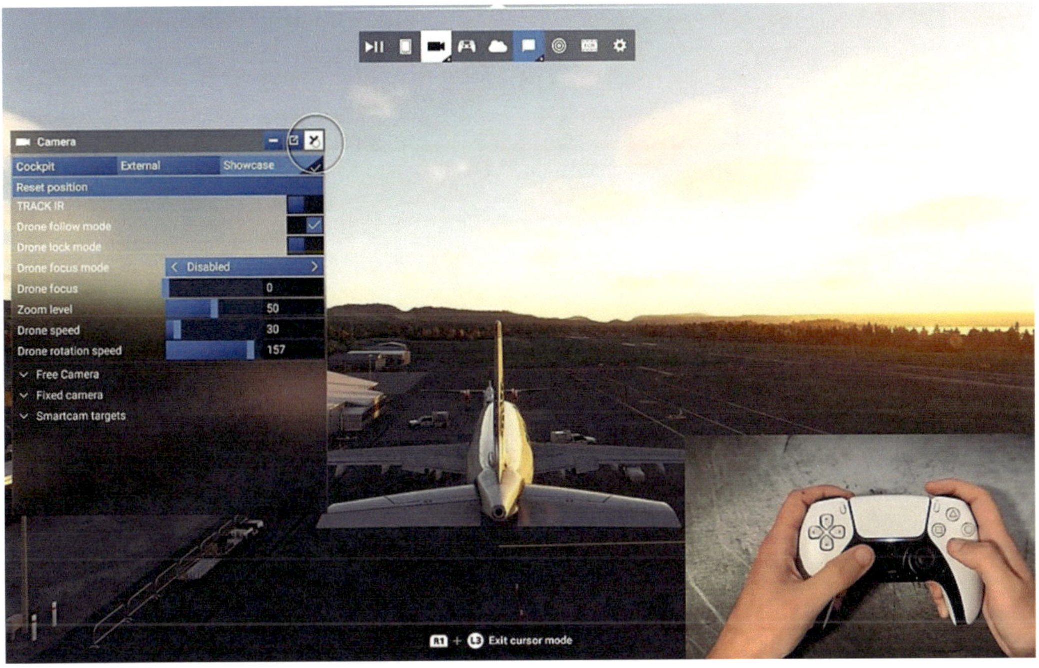

R1 & L1 FUNCTIONS

Photo Mode Toggle

- **R1 + L1 (press simultaneously):** Activates **Photo Mode**, essentially the **showcase camera** with a grid overlay and on-screen controls.

- **R2/L2:** Adjust focus
- **R1/L1:** Adjust exposure
- **Triangle + triggers:** Zoom in/out

Photo Mode is useful for capturing scenic views or mission snapshots.

R1 – Combination Button Functions

Holding **R1** while pressing another button activates secondary functions:

Cursor Mode

- **R1 + Left Stick Click:** Toggles **cursor mode**, allowing you to access the toolbar:

- Pause menu
- EFB (Electronic Flight Bag)
- Camera settings
- Controller settings
- Weather and ATC communications
- Career mission objectives and flight control replay

Reverse Thrust & Detent Control

- **R1 + Circle:** Moves throttle to the **reverse thrust detent**.

  - Useful after landing to engage reverse thrust.
  - Works even if your plane stops at a partial throttle detent.
- **R1 + X:** Returns throttle to **full forward power**, disengaging reverse thrust.

This combination allows precise control over throttle detents, especially during landing and ground operations.

Holding **R1** while pressing another button unlocks additional in-flight controls. Here's a breakdown:

R1 + Face Buttons

Speed Brakes

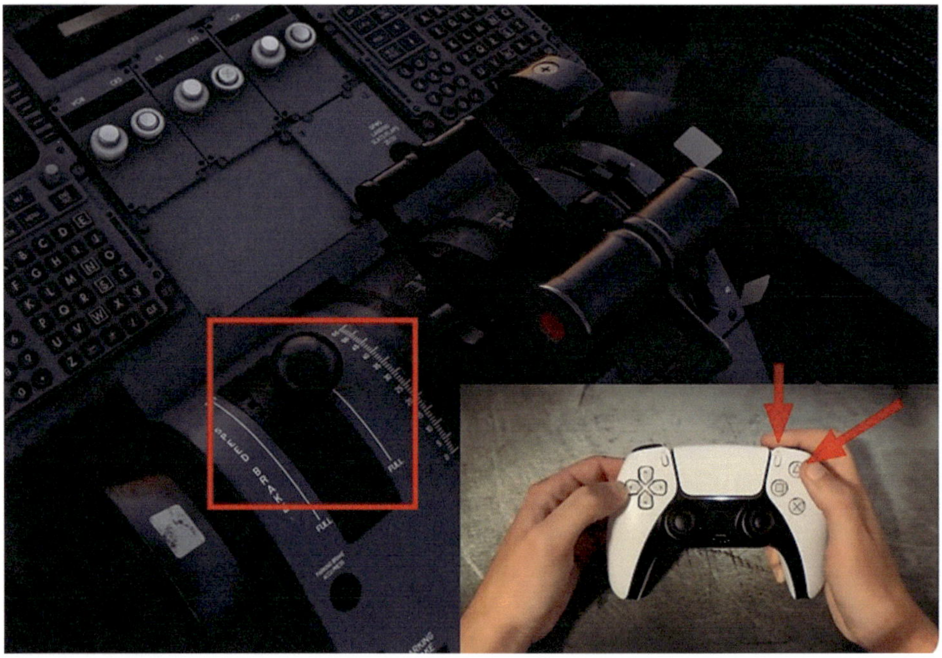

- **R1 + Triangle:** Toggles **speed brakes** on.
- Press again (**R1 + Triangle**) to retract them.

Most R1/L1 functions work as toggles, so the same button activates and deactivates the feature.

Parking Brake

- **R1 + Square:** Engages or disengages the **parking brake**.

Useful if your plane isn't moving even after applying throttle.

Quick Trim

- **R1 + Right Stick (forward/back):** Adjusts **pitch trim** quickly.

- Stick forward → Nose down
- Stick back → Nose up

Handy for leveling your aircraft without using cockpit trim controls.

Always complete walkaround checks before starting the plane.

R1 + D-Pad

Autopilot & Quick Start/Shutdown

- **R1 + Up: Disengage autopilot** quickly.
- **R1 + Down: Quick start** the aircraft without doing a full cold-and-dark startup.

- **R1 + Hold Down:** Quick shutdown of the aircraft.

Water Rudders

- **R1 + Right: Deploy water rudders** (for floatplanes and seaplanes).

- Press again (**R1 + Right**) to retract them.

L1 COMBINATION FUNCTIONS

Holding **L1** unlocks additional camera and flight control features, making exploration, movement, and certain flight tasks much easier.

L1 + Left Stick Click: Gyroscope Mode

- **Function:** Toggles **gyroscope (motion control) mode**.
- **Details:**
  - Enables motion-based flying using the DualSense controller.
  - Move the controller forward/back to pitch the aircraft, and tilt left/right for roll.
  - On the ground, tilting left/right controls the **rudder** for taxiing.
- **Tip:** You can disengage by pressing L1 + Left Stick Click again to return to analog stick flight.

Gyroscope mode gives a flight-stick-like experience and allows full control even when using **cursor mode**, meaning you can interact with ATC, the EFB, or other menus without worrying about losing control of the aircraft.

L1 + Circle: Enter/Exit Aircraft

- **Function:** Enter or exit the plane.

- **Details:** Only works when the aircraft is stationary.

Pressing this while flying is not possible.

L1 + D-Pad: Quick Views

- **Up/Down:** Cycle through **cockpit camera angles**, helping you inspect instruments or specific cockpit areas.
- **Left/Right:** Perform **quick side views**:
  - **L1 + Right D-Pad:** Quick view right
  - **L1 + Left D-Pad:** Quick view left

Great for situational awareness without manually moving the camera.

L1 + Left Stick: Walkaround Mode

- **Function:** Moves the camera around the aircraft cabin like an FPS game.
- **Details:**
  - **Left Stick:** Move forward, backward, left, right.
  - **Right Stick:** Look around.
  - **Left Trigger:** Lower the camera
  - **Right Trigger:** Raise the camera

Useful for planes with low or awkward default camera positions, inspecting the cockpit, or simply exploring.

Summary of L1 Combinations

Function	Combination	Notes
Gyroscope Mode	L1 + Left Stick Click	Motion-based flying; toggle on/off
Enter/Exit Aircraft	L1 + Circle	Only when plane is stationary
Quick Cockpit Views	L1 + D-Pad Up/Down	Cycle through preset views
Quick Side Views	L1 + D-Pad Left/Right	Inspect cockpit sides easily
Walkaround Mode	L1 + Left Stick	FPS-style movement; use triggers to adjust height, right stick to look

Holding **L1** essentially activates an **advanced camera/control mode**, allowing motion control, quick views, and full cabin exploration while still maintaining control of your aircraft.

CHAPTER FOUR

WORLD AND ENVIRONMENT

GLOBAL WORLD RENDERING

Global World Rendering in **Microsoft Flight Simulator 2024** uses an advanced "digital twin" system that processes massive amounts of cloud-based data to recreate the entire planet in unprecedented detail.

Key Rendering Technologies

- **Enhanced Photogrammetry & TIN Cities:** The world features over **500 TIN (triangular irregular network) cities** and more than 100,000 square kilometers of high-detail countryside photogrammetry.
- **Detailed Biomes:** The world is categorized into **27 highly detailed biomes**. These biomes dynamically generate hundreds of species of vegetation, including grass, rocks, and flowers, all of which adapt to seasonal changes.
- **Photometric Lighting System:** A completely new lighting system renders light more accurately than previous versions, improving how colors and shadows appear globally.
- **Dynamic Terrain & Surface Details:** For the first time, ground surfaces are not just flat textures; they feature modeled dips, craters, logs, and rocks that physically impact your aircraft upon landing.

Environmental & Life Systems

- **Global Wildlife:** The world is populated with land-based wildlife and free-ranging livestock in their natural habitats.
- **Live Maritime Traffic:** Waterways are filled with real-time worldwide maritime traffic, from large tankers to small trawlers.
- **Atmospheric Effects:** New rendering capabilities include enhanced cloud types, auroras, tornadoes, and real-time weather phenomena.

Performance & Technical Requirements

- **Cloud Streaming:** To maintain high fidelity, the simulator streams up-to-date satellite imagery and meteorological data. A minimum connection of **10 Mbps** is required, with **50–100 Mbps** recommended for photorealistic detail in dense areas.

- **Optimization:** Recent updates, such as Sim Update 3 and 4 (released throughout 2025), have focused on optimizing grass rendering, scenery object culling, and reducing texture "pop-in" via new level-of-detail (LOD) curves.
- **Hardware:** Recommended specs include at least an **Intel Core i7-10700K** and a **GeForce RTX 2080** to handle the heavy rendering load of the global map.

WEATHER SYSTEMS & EFFECTS

In 2026, **Microsoft Flight Simulator 2024** features an evolved weather system that integrates real-time global modeling with enhanced local atmospheric physics.

Key Weather Systems

- **Live Weather Integration:** Continues a partnership with Meteoblue to ingest hourly automated forecast grids (wind, temperature, humidity, and precipitation) which are interpolated into a continuous 3D representation.
- **Atmospheric Simulation:** Uses a 3D grid or voxel system with **64 altitude layers** to render detailed cloud formations and localized weather phenomena like 3D fog and haze.
- **Persistent Weather Fronts:** Live weather fronts now persist in the simulation rather than suddenly appearing or disappearing based on local METAR updates.

Environmental & Visual Effects

- **Enhanced Cloud Varieties:** New representations for high-altitude thin **cirrus clouds** and more realistic towering cumulus and cumulonimbus (CB) structures.
- **Precipitation Dynamics:** Enhanced rain effects include **simulated rain on aircraft windows** and streaks visible during forward momentum.
- **Photometric Lighting:** A revamped lighting system more accurately renders atmospheric scattering, improving the visual quality of sunsets, sun rays through mist, and moonlight.
- **Dynamic Terrestrial Interaction:** Wind now physically affects ground vegetation (trees, bushes, grass) and creates more natural water surface responses.

Flight Dynamics & Interaction

- **Advanced Turbulence:** Includes enhanced modeling for **cloud turbulence**, wake turbulence, and mountain waves that interact more convincingly with aircraft flight dynamics.
- **Thunderstorm Prediction:** Improvements in Sim Update 3 (2025) reduced unrealistic lightning rates and improved the accuracy of thunderstorm cell prediction.
- **Hazardous Weather:** While visual fidelity is high, some pilots noted in early 2026 that the physical consequences of flying through severe convective clouds (like hail or extreme icing) still require further tuning for full realism.

Third-Party Enhancements

Several tools offer deeper customization as of early 2026:

- **REX Atmos Core:** Injects real-time changes to atmospheric parameters like haze, sky coloring, and cloud shading without altering core files.
- Active Sky FS: Provides an alternative weather engine with historical weather playback, custom clear air turbulence, and advanced data synthesis from METARs and GRIB files.

SEASONS, BIOMES & ENVIRONMENTAL EFFECTS

In Microsoft Flight Simulator 2024, the environment is driven by an evolved engine that introduces fully integrated seasons, a diverse biome system, and enhanced physical interactions with the world.

Integrated Four Seasons

Unlike previous versions, seasonal changes are built directly into the simulator.

- **Dynamic Vegetation:** Trees change color over time (e.g., green in summer, yellow in September, and orange/yellow in October).
- **Leaf Transition:** By November, many deciduous trees lose their leaves, while evergreens remain green.
- **Snow Effects:** Snow appears on the ground in winter months and features realistic melting effects.
- **Control:** Users can manually adjust date settings to observe these transitions, such as moving from lush spring (April/May) to winter hibernation (December).

Biomes and Vegetation

The world is categorized into **27 highly detailed biomes** containing hundreds of species of vegetation.

- **Enhanced Detail:** The simulator generates nearly **3 trillion trees**.
- **Regional Accuracy:** Specific biomes feature regionally appropriate flora, such as palm and date trees in desert cities or banana and coconut trees in rainforests.
- **Ground Realism:** For the first time, players can exit the aircraft to explore biomes on foot, encountering 3D-modeled grass, rocks, stones, and flowers.
- **Customization:** The SDK allows for the creation of unique biomes and vegetation using XML files.

Environmental and Atmospheric Effects

The simulation includes several new dynamic environmental phenomena that impact both visuals and flight mechanics:

- **Atmospheric Simulation:** A new photometric lighting system renders colors accurately based on cloud makeup. It also introduces new cloud types, such as high-altitude **cirrus clouds**, and **3D fog and haze** calculated via a revamped scattering system.
- **Dynamic Hazards:** The environment now features active **wildfires** with animated flames and smoke, as well as **tornadoes** and **active volcanoes** with lava explosions and ash clouds.
- **Physical Interactions:** Wind realistically affects trees, bushes, and water. Ground surfaces (gravel, rocks) now interact physically with aircraft wheels during takeoff and landing.
- **Living World:** The world is populated with animal species (wildlife and livestock) placed in their appropriate habitats, alongside live maritime and flight tracking.

AIRPORTS, NAVIGATION & AIRSPACE

In Microsoft Flight Simulator 2024 (MSFS 2024), airports, navigation, and airspace have been significantly overhauled for 2026 with new streaming technologies, expanded airport categories, and updated data cycles.

Airports and Facilities

- **Upgraded Airport Count:** The sim features up to **160 "upgraded" handcrafted airports** depending on the edition:
  - **Standard:** 150 airports.
  - **Deluxe:** 155 airports.
  - **Premium Deluxe/Aviator:** 160 airports.
- **New Airport Types:** For the first time, MSFS 2024 natively includes specialized facilities such as **glider airports, heliports, and oil rigs**.
- **Enhanced Realism:** Airports now feature regionally accurate representations of humanity, including **passengers moving through terminals** and detailed airport ground service vehicles.
- **Cloud Streaming:** High-quality airport assets and mesh are streamed on demand based on your distance to the airport, reducing local storage requirements.

Navigation and Avionics

- **Data Updates:** The simulator automatically installs real-world **AIRAC cycles** (e.g., cycle 2510 as of late 2025/early 2026) to ensure navigation data remains current.
- **In-Game Flight Planner:** A new native flight planner supports **IFR and VFR map layers**, IFR charts, vertical profile planning, and **ETOPS planning**.
- **Electronic Flight Bag (EFB):** All stock aircraft are equipped with a powerful EFB that provides real-time access to weather, NOTAMs, and airport information.
- **Navigraph Integration:** Users can access **Jeppesen IFR charts** for over 7,200 airports and track live traffic from VATSIM or IVAO directly through the in-game toolbar or EFB.

Airspace and ATC

- **ATC Improvements:** Recent updates have overhauled ATC to use **real-world phraseology and flows**. This includes better STAR (Standard Terminal Arrival Route) support and improved descent point estimations.
- **Prohibited Airspace:** The Career mode enforces penalties for violating **prohibited airspace** and taking off without permission.
- **Airspace Boundaries:** Navigation databases now include updated **FIR/UIR boundaries** for more accurate global airspace management.

CHAPTER FIVE

UNDERSTANDING FLIGHT MODEL AND PHYSICS

Flight physics and modeling are based on the continuous interaction of forces and the aircraft's orientation in three-dimensional space. In 2026, understanding these principles remains central to both pilot training and high-fidelity flight simulation.

The Four Fundamental Forces of Flight

An aircraft in flight is constantly governed by four vector forces that must be balanced for stable flight.

- **Lift:** The upward force generated primarily by the wings. It is created through a combination of **Bernoulli's Principle** (lower air pressure on the curved top of the wing) and **Newton's Third Law** (downward deflection of air pushing the wing upward).
- **Weight:** The downward force of gravity acting through the aircraft's center of gravity.
- **Thrust:** The forward force produced by engines (propellers or jets) that overcomes air resistance.
- **Drag:** The resistive force opposing forward motion, caused by air friction and pressure differences.

Flight Dynamics and Control Axes

To maneuver, pilots and automated systems control the aircraft along three rotational axes:

1. **Pitch (Lateral Axis):** The nose-up or nose-down movement, controlled by the **elevators** on the tail.

2. **Roll (Longitudinal Axis):** The tilting of the wings, controlled by **ailerons** on the wing's trailing edges.

3. **Yaw (Vertical Axis):** The left or right rotation of the nose, controlled by the **rudder**.

Advanced Aerodynamic Concepts

- **Angle of Attack (AoA):** The angle between the wing's chord line and the oncoming air. Increasing AoA produces more lift, but exceeding a critical angle leads to a **stall**, where airflow separates from the wing and lift drops sharply.
- **Stability:** Aircraft are designed with inherent stability, such as **dihedral** (upward-angled wings) to provide natural roll stabilization.
- **Air Density and Altitude:** As altitude increases, air becomes thinner, which reduces both the lift generated by the wings and the thrust produced by the engines.

Performance Rules for Pilots

- **70/50 Rule:** A check for takeoff safety where a pilot should have 70% of their takeoff airspeed by the time they reach 50% of the calculated takeoff distance.
- **3-to-1 Rule:** A descent guide stating that for every 1,000 feet of altitude to lose, the aircraft should fly 3 nautical miles forward (simulating a standard 3-degree glide slope)

WHAT IS A FLIGHT MODEL

In aviation and simulation, a **flight model** (or flight dynamics model) refers to the mathematical or physical representation of an aircraft's behavior in the air. Depending on the context, it can mean a digital simulation, a physical research tool, or a hobbyist's craft.

1. Digital Flight Dynamics Model (FDM)

In flight simulators, an FDM is a set of mathematical equations and data used to calculate the physical forces acting on a simulated aircraft.

- **How it Works:** It processes inputs (like control surface movements) and environmental variables (like air density) to output the aircraft's position, orientation, and velocity.
- **Common Approaches:**
  - **Lookup Tables:** Uses pre-recorded data from real flight tests to determine performance at specific speeds or altitudes (common in older sims like FSX).

- **Blade Element Theory:** Breaks the aircraft into hundreds of small sections (elements) and calculates the air forces on each piece individually in real-time (used in X-Plane).
- **Computational Fluid Dynamics (CFD):** High-fidelity simulations that calculate 3D airflow around the entire aircraft body (used in modern MSFS updates).

2. Physical Flight Models

These are tangible aircraft used for testing or hobbyist purposes.

- **Research Models:** Scaled-down versions of aircraft (often used in wind tunnels) to test aerodynamic properties before building a full-size version.
- **Hobbyist Flying Models:** Small-scale aircraft designed for recreation. These include:
  - **Free Flight (FF):** Launched into the air without active external control.
  - **Radio Control (RC):** Managed remotely by a pilot using a transmitter.
  - **Control Line (CL):** Tethered by wires that allow the pilot to control pitch while the plane flies in a circle.

3. Commercial Aircraft Model

In the travel industry, this simply refers to the specific type or series of a commercial plane (e.g., Boeing 787-9 or Airbus A350). Passengers can often find this information in flight booking details or via flight tracking services.

THE ROLE OF PHYSICS ENGINES IN FLIGHT SIMULATOR REALISM

Modern flight simulators have come a long way, delivering experiences that feel strikingly close to real-world flying. At the heart of this realism lies one critical component: the **physics engine**. This system governs how aircraft behave in virtual airspace, ensuring that every takeoff, maneuver, and landing follows the same physical rules as real aviation.

If you've ever wondered why some simulators feel authentic while others feel more arcade-like, the answer often comes down to how advanced their physics engines are. These engines are responsible for translating aerodynamics, weather, and pilot input into believable aircraft behavior.

What Is a Physics Engine?

A physics engine is software designed to simulate real-world physical forces in a digital environment. In flight simulators, it calculates how aircraft respond to **lift, drag, thrust, gravity**, and environmental factors.

Rather than simply moving an aircraft through space, the physics engine models how forces interact continuously. Control inputs, aircraft design, air density, and weather are all processed in real time, creating flight behavior that feels natural and responsive. Without this layer, a simulator would feel more like a game than a meaningful simulation or training tool.

Why Physics Engines Matter in Flight Simulation

Flight is governed by complex physical laws, and the accuracy of a simulator depends on how well those laws are reproduced. A strong physics engine delivers:

- **Realistic Flight Dynamics**

  Control inputs produce believable results. Pitching up affects lift and airspeed, banking increases load factor, and improper handling leads to stalls or instability.

- **Environmental Interaction**

  Wind, turbulence, temperature, and air density all influence performance, just as they do in real flight.

- **Training Value**

  Accurate physics allow pilots to practice real-world scenarios such as stalls, crosswind landings, and emergency handling.

- **Immersion**

  When aircraft respond naturally to both pilot input and environmental changes, the experience feels authentic and engaging.

How Physics Engines Work

A physics engine acts as the simulator's decision-maker, constantly calculating how the aircraft should behave:

1. **Input Collection** – Reads pilot controls, aircraft configuration, and environmental data.

2. **Force Calculation** – Determines lift, drag, thrust, and gravity using aerodynamic models.
3. **Real-Time Updates** – Continuously adjusts the aircraft's position, speed, and orientation.
4. **Feedback** – Displays motion visually and through controller or yoke response.

This cycle runs many times per second, creating smooth and responsive flight behavior.

Physics Engines in Popular Flight Simulators

Microsoft Flight Simulator (MSFS)

MSFS combines detailed physics modeling with real-world data. Its engine simulates airflow over individual aircraft components and integrates live weather systems. This results in flight behavior that feels smooth, immersive, and visually convincing.

X-Plane

X-Plane uses **blade element theory**, dividing aircraft surfaces into small sections and calculating how each interacts with the air. This approach emphasizes aerodynamic accuracy and is widely respected in professional and training environments.

Both simulators prioritize realism, but each approaches physics calculation differently.

Where Physics Engines Truly Shine

- **Stalls and Spins:** Realistic modeling of angle of attack, airflow separation, and recovery behavior.
- **Crosswind Landings:** Accurate interaction between wind, aircraft alignment, and control surfaces.
- **Turbulence:** Unpredictable vertical and lateral forces that challenge aircraft control and pilot skill.

These scenarios highlight the difference between simplified motion and true flight simulation.

The Future of Physics Engines

Advances in computing continue to push realism further. Future developments may include:

- **AI-enhanced physics** that adapt dynamically to pilot behavior
- **More detailed atmospheric modeling**, including wake turbulence and microbursts
- **Improved VR integration**, making motion and spatial awareness even more convincing

Why Physics Engines Matter

The physics engine is the backbone of any serious flight simulator. It transforms raw inputs into believable flight behavior, capturing the complexity of aerodynamics and environmental interaction. Whether you're training, exploring, or flying for enjoyment, it's the physics engine that makes virtual flight feel real.

THE PHYSICS OF AVIATION EXPLAINED

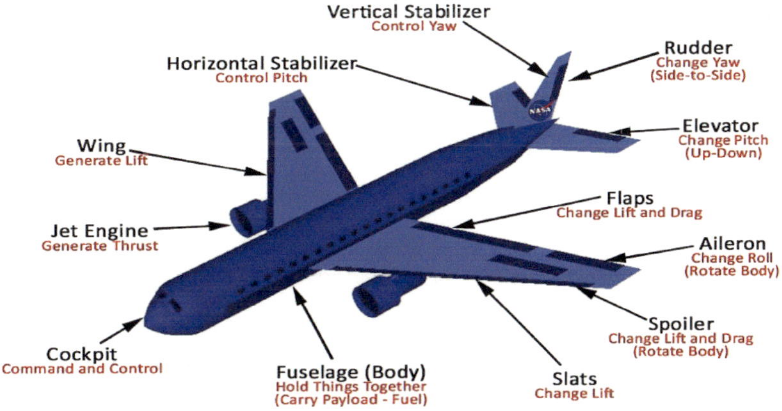

The Four Forces of Flight

Every aircraft in flight is governed by four fundamental forces that determine whether it climbs, cruises, or descends:

1. **Lift** – The upward force that counteracts gravity and keeps the aircraft airborne.
2. **Weight** – The downward force caused by Earth's gravitational pull.
3. **Thrust** – The forward force produced by engines or propellers.
4. **Drag** – The resistance created by air friction and pressure differences.

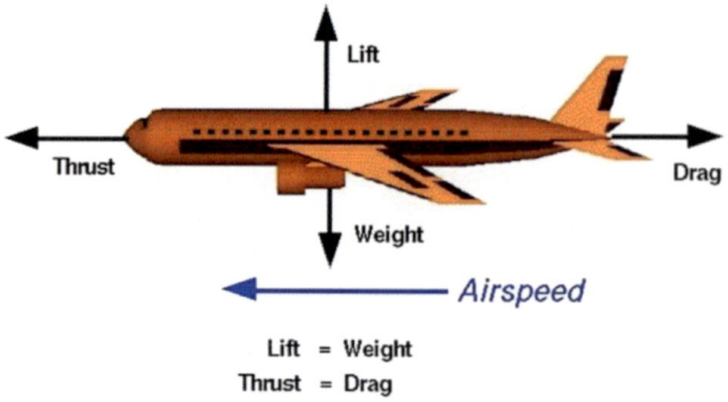

The aircraft flies straight and level at a steady airspeed.

For steady flight, thrust must overcome drag, while lift must equal weight. These forces are constantly changing with speed, altitude, aircraft configuration, and atmospheric conditions.

How Lift Is Generated: Bernoulli and Newton Working Together

Lift is often considered the most intriguing aspect of flight. How does an aircraft weighing several tons rise into the air? The answer lies in wing design and airflow behavior.

Airfoil Shape and Flow Turning

Aircraft wings, known as **airfoils**, are curved on the top and flatter underneath. As air approaches the wing, it splits at the leading edge. Due to the wing's shape and the **Coandă effect**—the tendency of airflow to follow a curved surface—air moving over the top of the wing accelerates.

Bernoulli's Principle

Faster-moving air creates lower pressure. Because air above the wing travels faster than air below it, a pressure difference forms. Higher pressure beneath the wing pushes upward, generating lift.

Newton's Third Law

Lift can also be explained through action and reaction. As the wing deflects air downward, the air pushes back with an equal and opposite force, lifting the aircraft upward. This explanation is rooted in the conservation of momentum.

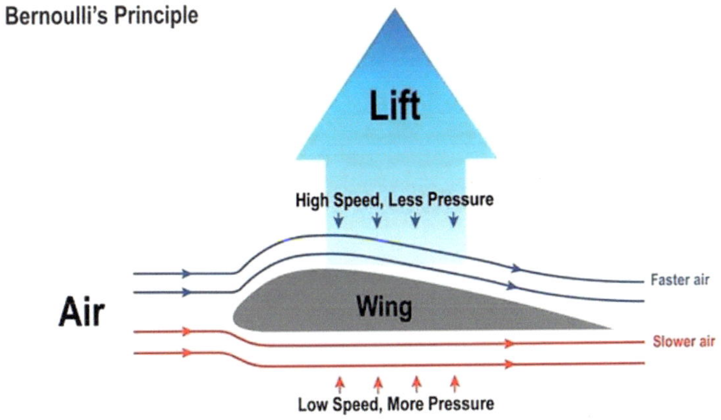

In practice, both principles work together. Engineers describe lift using **circulation** and **vorticity**—advanced fluid-dynamics concepts that explain how air "swirls" around the wing and why trailing vortices form behind it.

Wingtip vortices form when high-pressure air from beneath the wings spills around the wingtips into the low-pressure region above. This pressure imbalance creates rotating streams of air that trail behind the aircraft, increasing drag and posing a hazard to following aircraft.

Angle of Attack and Stall

Lift depends not only on wing shape but also on the **angle of attack**, which is the angle between the wing's chord line and the oncoming airflow. Increasing this angle increases lift—up to a limit.

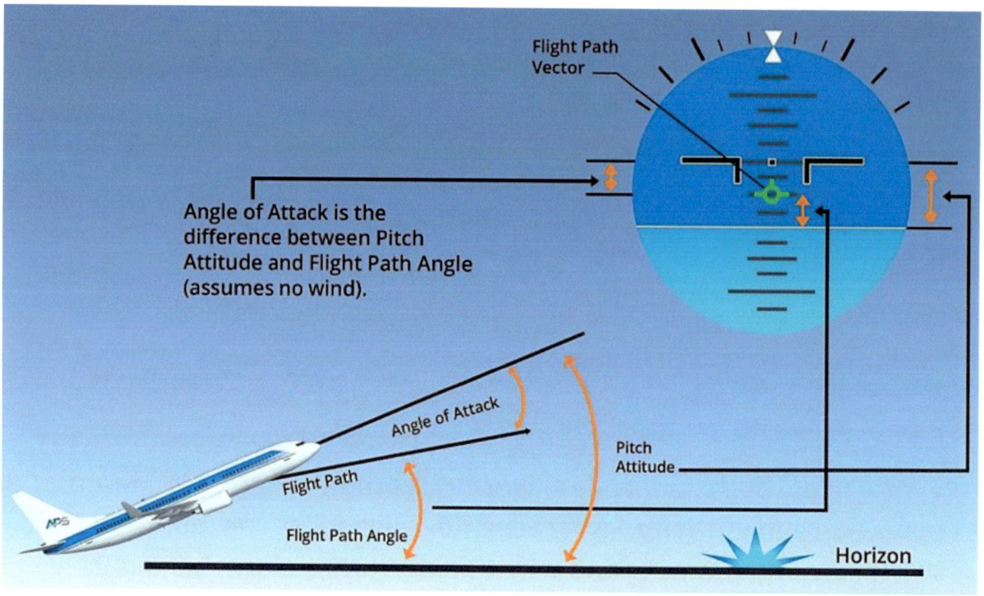

Beyond a critical angle (typically around **15 degrees**), airflow separates from the wing surface, causing turbulence and a sudden loss of lift. This condition is known as a **stall**.

Pilots carefully manage angle of attack during takeoff, cruise, and landing to maintain safe and efficient flight.

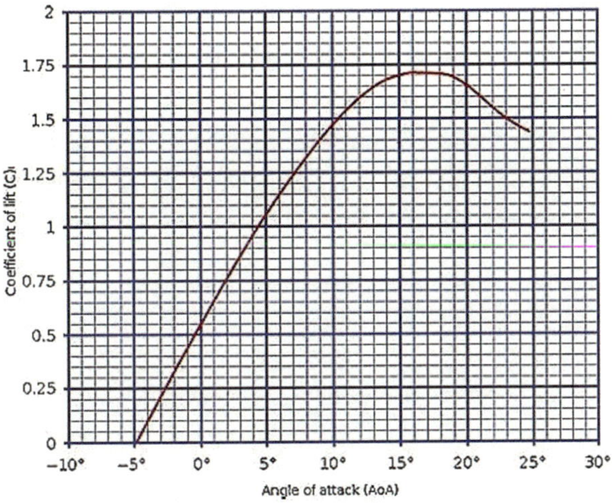

Drag: The Invisible Opponent

Drag constantly resists forward motion and appears in several forms:

- **Parasitic Drag** – Caused by air friction over the aircraft's surfaces and external components.
- **Induced Drag** – A result of lift production, created by wingtip vortices.
- **Wave Drag** – Occurs at transonic and supersonic speeds due to shock waves.

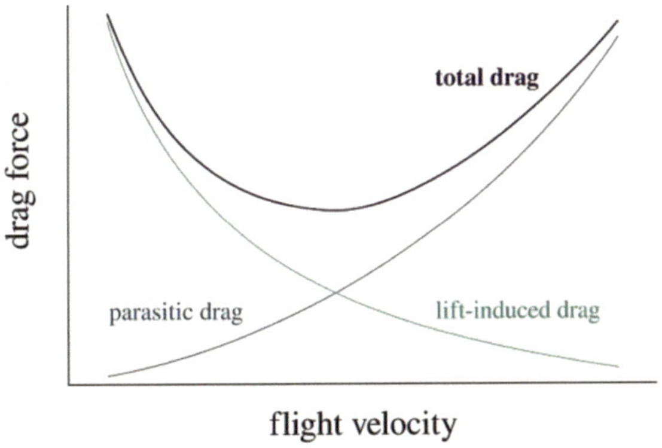

To reduce drag, modern aircraft feature smooth surfaces, streamlined fuselages, and **winglets**, which weaken wingtip vortices and improve fuel efficiency.

Thrust: The Power Behind Flight

Thrust moves an aircraft forward, allowing the wings to generate lift. Different propulsion systems achieve this in different ways:

- **Propeller Engines** – Spinning blades push air backward, producing forward thrust. Common in small and early aircraft.

- **Jet Engines** – Compress air, mix it with fuel, ignite it, and expel hot gases backward, propelling the aircraft forward.
- **Turbofan Engines** – A type of jet engine with a large front fan, used in most commercial airliners for better efficiency and reduced noise.
- **Rocket Engines** – Used in spaceflight, producing thrust without relying on atmospheric air.

Engineers design engines to maximize the **thrust-to-weight ratio** while minimizing fuel consumption and emissions.

The Physics of Stability and Control

Flying straight and level is only part of the challenge—safe maneuvering depends on precise control and stability. Aircraft motion is defined around **three rotational axes**:

1. **Pitch (lateral axis)** – Nose-up or nose-down movement, controlled by the **elevator**.
2. **Roll (longitudinal axis)** – Banking left or right, controlled by **ailerons**.
3. **Yaw (vertical axis)** – Side-to-side movement of the nose, controlled by the **rudder**.

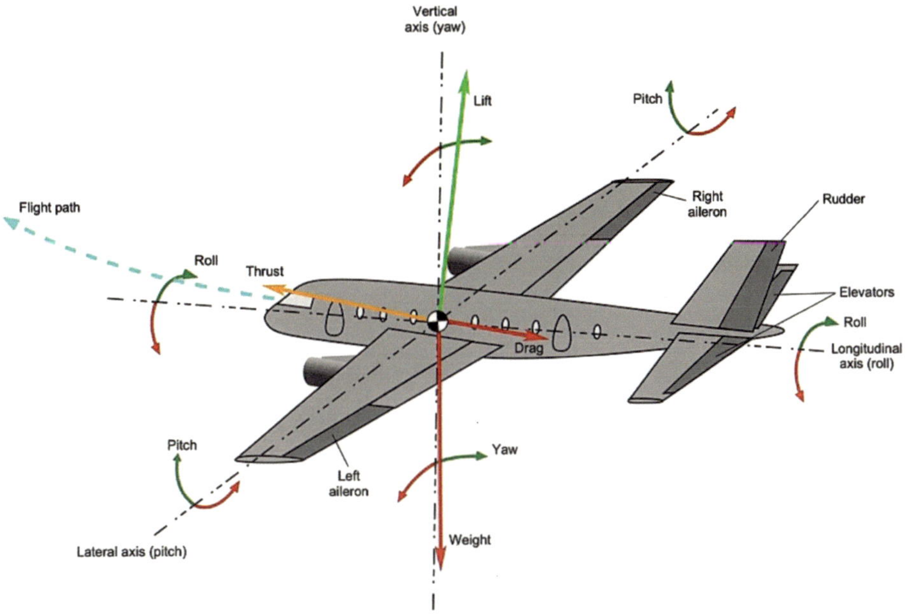

A well-designed aircraft is naturally stable, meaning it tends to return to steady flight after a disturbance. Engineers achieve this by placing the **center of lift slightly behind the center of gravity**, creating a self-correcting balance.

Atmospheric and Altitude Effects

Aircraft operate within Earth's atmosphere, where conditions change significantly with altitude:

- **Air Density** – Decreases with altitude, reducing lift and engine efficiency.
- **Speed of Sound** – Drops as temperature decreases, affecting high-speed flight near Mach 1.
- **Weather** – Turbulence, wind shear, and storms demand constant pilot awareness and control.

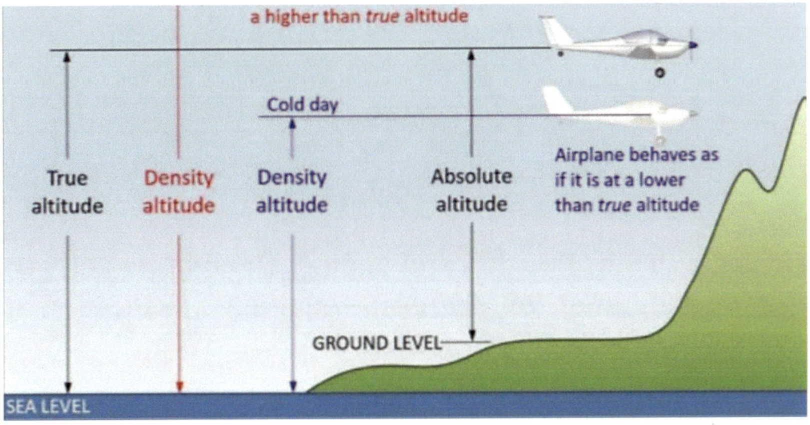

These factors explain why commercial airliners typically cruise between **30,000 and 40,000 feet**, where thinner air improves fuel efficiency without excessively compromising lift.

Supersonic and Hypersonic Flight

As aircraft approach **Mach 1**, air begins to compress into shock waves, dramatically increasing drag and instability. To manage this, engineers employ:

- **Swept Wings** – Reducing wave drag at high speeds.
- **Delta Wings** – Providing stability and control at supersonic velocities.
- **Area Rule Design** – Narrowing sections of the fuselage to weaken shock waves.

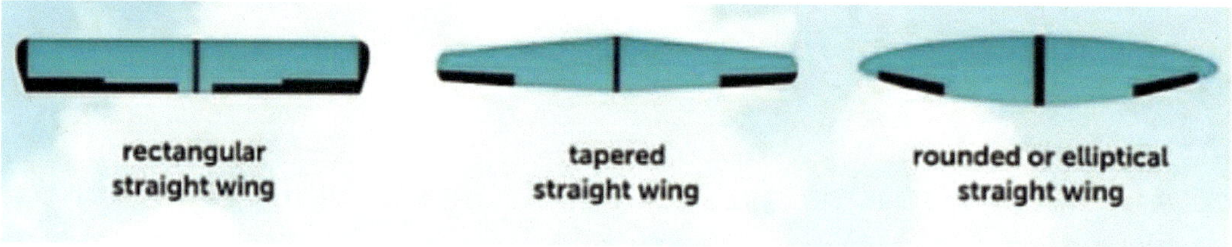

Straight Wing

Swept Wing

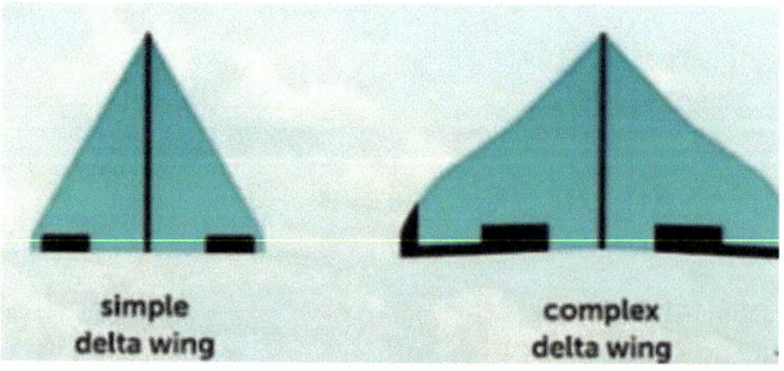

Delta Wing

At **hypersonic speeds (Mach 5 and above)**, air compression generates extreme heat—often thousands of degrees—requiring advanced materials, thermal shielding, and active cooling systems.

Fuel Efficiency and Modern Innovations

Physics directly shapes the economics of aviation. Fuel consumption rises with drag and weight, so modern aircraft focus heavily on efficiency:

- **Composite Materials** – Lightweight carbon-fiber structures reduce mass.
- **High-Bypass Turbofan Engines** – Optimized for quiet, efficient subsonic flight.
- **Winglets and Laminar Flow Control** – Minimizing aerodynamic drag.
- **Electric and Hybrid Propulsion** – Emerging technologies aimed at reducing emissions.

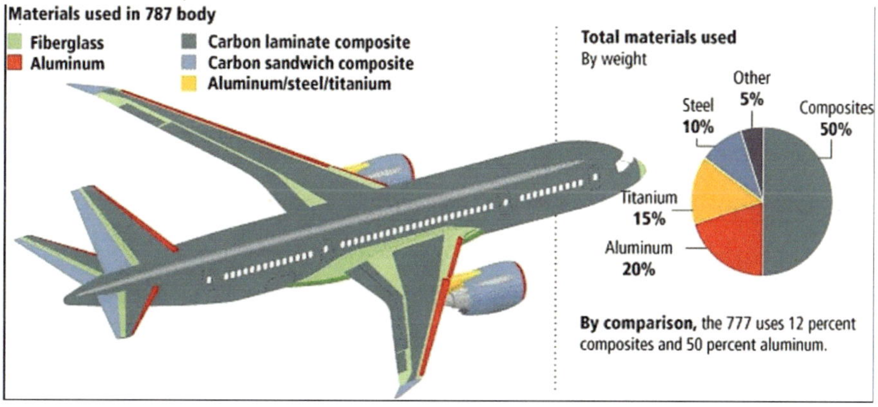

Today, aviation physics is increasingly intertwined with environmental science as the industry works toward lower carbon footprints.

Relativity and GPS Navigation

Even **Einstein's theory of relativity** plays a role in aviation. GPS satellites experience time differently due to their speed (special relativity) and weaker gravity at altitude (general relativity). Without constant correction, GPS positioning would drift by several kilometers per day—making precise navigation impossible.

Human Factors: The Physics of the Pilot

Aviation medicine studies how flight physics affects the human body. Rapid acceleration, tight turns, and sudden altitude changes expose pilots to **g-forces**. At high g-loads, blood can be pulled away from the brain, causing **blackouts** or loss of consciousness.

Pilots undergo specialized training and, in high-performance aircraft, wear **g-suits** to maintain blood flow and remain conscious—especially critical in military aviation.

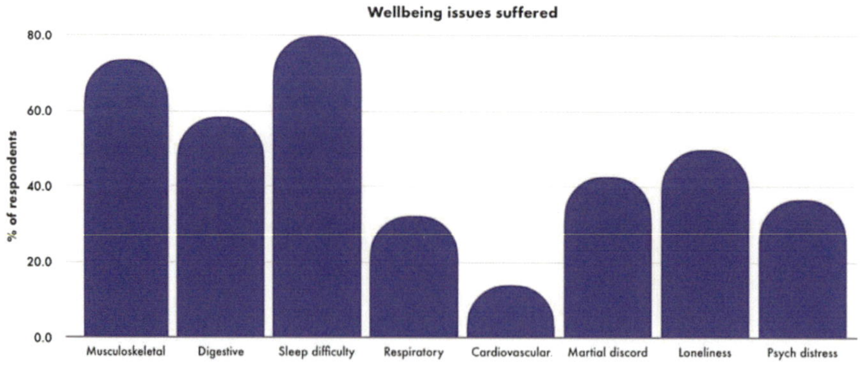

The Future of Aviation

Advances in physics continue to reshape what is possible in flight:

- **Supersonic Passenger Aircraft** – Faster travel with improved efficiency and lower noise.

- **Electric Vertical Takeoff and Landing (eVTOL)** – Urban air mobility and air taxis.
- **Hypersonic Travel** – Intercontinental flights in under two hours.
- **Spaceplanes** – Vehicles capable of operating in both atmosphere and space.

As technology evolves, physics remains the foundation driving safer, faster, and more sustainable aviation.

ATMOSPHERIC EFFECTS ON AERODYNAMICS

Atmospheric conditions significantly influence aerodynamics by altering **air density**, which is the primary driver for lift and drag. These effects are often summarized by **Density Altitude**, a measure of how aircraft performance is degraded by high temperatures, low pressure, and high humidity.

1. Primary Atmospheric Drivers

- **Altitude and Pressure**: As altitude increases, atmospheric pressure drops, leading to less dense air. This directly reduces the number of air molecules available to generate **lift** and **thrust**, increasing the required takeoff distance and decreasing the rate of climb.
- **Temperature**: High temperatures cause air molecules to spread apart, decreasing density. This "thin" air provides less force on airfoils and reduces engine power because less oxygen is available for combustion.
- **Humidity**: Water vapor is lighter than dry air (nitrogen and oxygen). Therefore, as humidity increases, air density decreases. While its effect on aerodynamics is generally smaller than temperature, high humidity can still cause a significant performance penalty.

2. Effects on Aerodynamic Forces

- **Lift Reduction**: Since lift is proportional to air density, thinner air requires higher airspeeds or a higher **Angle of Attack** to maintain level flight.
- **Drag Variations**: While thinner air reduces total drag force, it can increase the **drag coefficient** due to lower Reynolds numbers and higher required angles of attack, which increase **induced drag**.
- **Propeller and Engine Efficiency**: Propellers are less efficient in thin air, producing less thrust. Jet and piston engines also produce less power because the mass of air entering the engine is reduced.

3. Weather-Specific Phenomena

- **Precipitation (Rain/Ice)**: Rain increases wing surface roughness and adds weight, leading to increased drag and reduced stall angles. Ice formation on wings can drastically alter their shape, destroying lift.
- **Atmospheric Turbulence**: Sudden gusts and wind shear cause rapid changes in lift and can disrupt the stable airflow over wings, leading to increased unsteadiness and potential loss of control.
- **Wind Shear & Vorticity**: Vertical or horizontal changes in wind speed (vorticity) can cause immediate lift gains or losses. Positive shear (speed increasing with height) may increase lift, while negative shear can lead to dangerous lift loss during takeoff or landing.

4. Aerodynamic Contrails

In humid conditions at high altitudes, the pressure and temperature drops over wings can trigger **aerodynamic contrails**. These form when local adiabatic cooling exceeds the ambient dew point, causing immediate condensation or freezing even without engine exhaust.

CHAPTER SIX

WEATHER AND ENVIRONMENTAL SIMULATION

Weather and environmental simulation involves using computational models or physical chambers to replicate natural processes for research, engineering, and policy-making. In 2026, these tools are increasingly integrated with AI to improve speed and resolution.

Key Types of Simulations

- **Weather Models:** Focus on short-term atmospheric predictions (days to weeks) by solving complex hydrodynamic differential equations.
- **Climate Models:** Simulate long-term global patterns (decades to centuries), including interactions between oceans, land surfaces, and ice.
- **Ecological Simulations:** Model species interactions, biodiversity, and ecosystem health under varying stressors like pollution or deforestation.
- **Urban Environmental Simulations:** Analyze heat islands, air quality, and energy consumption in cities using tools like the **Weather Research and Forecasting (WRF)** model.
- **Physical Testing Chambers:** Replicate extreme conditions (e.g., -40°F to 4000°F, 2.4M volt lightning, or saltwater fog) to test the durability of products like satellites and vehicles.

Core Applications

- **Infrastructure Design:** Engineers use Building Energy Models (BEM) to predict how structures will perform under future climate scenarios, helping to prevent summer overheating.
- **Disaster Preparedness:** Modeling hurricanes, wildfires, and floods allows authorities to plan emergency responses and design resilient infrastructure.
- **Product Reliability:** The Automotive and Aerospace industries use environmental chambers to simulate "dynamic environments" where rain transitions to sleet and snow while driving.
- **Policy Support:** Integrated Assessment Models evaluate the trade-offs between economic development and carbon emission strategies.

Major Simulation Platforms & Entities

- NVIDIA Earth-2: A 2026-era platform using AI-accelerated digital twins to visualize global climate change at high speeds.
- **NOAA Environmental Modeling Center (EMC):** Develops over 20 numerical weather prediction systems, including the Global Forecast System (GFS).
- **ECMWF:** Provides the Integrated Forecasting System (IFS), a global leader in high-resolution weather data.
- **JULES (Joint UK Land Environment Simulator):** Used by scientists and the IPCC to study land-surface processes and climate impacts.

ENVIRONMENTAL EFFECTS ON FLIGHT

Flight has significant environmental effects on climate, air quality, ecosystems, and human health. While aviation accounts for approximately **2.4% to 3% of global CO_2 emissions**, its total contribution to global warming is roughly **double to triple** that amount due to non-CO_2 effects at high altitudes.

1. Climate Change Impacts

The aviation industry is responsible for about **4% of observed human-induced global warming**.

- **Non-CO_2 Effects:** Emissions of nitrogen oxides (NOx), water vapor, and soot at high altitudes create persistent contrails and aviation-induced cloudiness (AIC). These clouds trap heat, and in 2018, they were responsible for two-thirds of aviation's total climate impact.
- **Altitude Sensitivity:** Radiative forcing (warming effect) is more intense at high altitudes. For example, supersonic aircraft flying at 17–20 km have a radiative forcing five times greater than subsonic aircraft.
- **Passenger Density:** Emissions per passenger are **four times higher** in first-class compared to economy due to the larger space and weight allocated per seat.

2. Air Quality and Health

- **Toxic Pollutants:** Engines emit nitrogen oxides (NOx), sulfur dioxide (SO_2), and ultrafine particles (UFPs). These contribute to ground-level ozone and particulate matter (PM2.5) pollution, linked to asthma, heart attacks, and roughly **74,300 premature deaths annually**.

- **Lead Contamination:** Piston engines in small private planes still use leaded fuel (Avgas), releasing thousands of tons of toxic lead into the atmosphere.

3. Noise Pollution

- **Human Health:** Aircraft noise near airports disrupts sleep and is linked to increased cardiovascular risk, high blood pressure, and impaired school performance in children.
- **Wildlife Impact:** Noise and light pollution from airports can distress wildlife, altering breeding patterns and communication.

4. Ecosystems and Resource Use

- **Water Pollution:** De-icing fluids (ethylene or propylene glycol) used in cold weather can run off into nearby water bodies, consuming dissolved oxygen and killing aquatic life.
- **Land and Habitat Loss:** Airport expansions often require clearing forests or wetlands, leading to significant biodiversity loss.
- **Waste Generation:** In 2019 alone, the aviation industry generated over **6 million tons of cabin waste**, including plastic packaging and disposable items.

5. Mitigation Strategies

The industry is targeting **net-zero emissions by 2050** through several pathways:

- **Sustainable Aviation Fuel (SAF):** Biofuels can reduce carbon emissions by up to 80% compared to fossil kerosene.
- **Technological Innovation:** Development of hydrogen-powered and electric aircraft is underway, with potential entry into service in the **2030s** for short-range flights.
- **Operational Changes:** Rerouting just **2% of flights** to avoid areas prone to contrail formation can reduce contrail-related warming by up to 60%.
- **Regulatory Measures:** The ICAO's CORSIA program is a global market-based measure to offset carbon emissions from international flights.

TERRAIN AND ENVIRONMENTAL INTERACTIONS ON FLIGHTS

Flight interactions with terrain and the environment in 2026 involve a complex balance between operational safety and the mitigation of long-term ecological impacts. While mountainous terrain poses immediate risks like

Controlled Flight Into Terrain (CFIT), environmental factors such as high-altitude emissions drive broader climate change concerns.

Terrain Interactions and Safety

Terrain awareness is a critical safety component, particularly in mountainous regions where topographical features directly influence aircraft performance and pilot decision-making.

- **Controlled Flight Into Terrain (CFIT):** CFIT remains a leading cause of aviation fatalities, often occurring when a functional aircraft is unintentionally flown into the ground. Factors include loss of situational awareness and misinterpretation of visual cues, such as "whiteout" effects in snow-covered areas.
- **Aerodynamic Challenges:** Mountains generate localized weather phenomena like **updrafts, downdrafts, and mountain waves**.
  - **Altimeter Errors:** Strong winds over ridges can cause local atmospheric pressure changes, leading to altimeter inaccuracies.
  - **Wind Effects:** Winds as low as 25 knots can create downdrafts that exceed the climb capability of light aircraft.
- **Operational Techniques:** Pilots are trained to approach ridges at a **45-degree angle** to allow for an easier escape turn if downdrafts are encountered.

Environmental Impacts of Flight

The environmental footprint of aviation is dominated by the operational phase, with high-altitude interactions causing significant warming effects.

- **Atmospheric Chemistry:** Aircraft engines emit CO_2, nitrogen oxides (NO_x), and soot. When released in the upper troposphere, these pollutants contribute to **radiative forcing**.
- **Non-CO2 Warming:** Aviation-induced cloudiness (AIC), including persistent contrails, may contribute more to global warming than CO_2 emissions alone—potentially up to three times as much.
- **Ground-Level Issues:** Near airports, environmental interactions include noise pollution, wildlife hazards (e.g., bird strikes), and air quality degradation from particulate matter and ozone.

Technological Interventions (2026)

Advanced systems are continuously updated to manage these interactions more effectively:

- **TAWS and GPWS:** Terrain Awareness and Warning Systems (TAWS) and Ground Proximity Warning Systems (GPWS) use digital terrain databases and GPS to provide visual and auditory alerts to pilots.
- **Precision Altimetry:** The FAA and other bodies are refining standards for **radio altimeters** to mitigate interference from new cellular signals (e.g., 5G), ensuring accurate height-above-terrain readings during critical flight phases.
- **Sustainable Aviation Fuels (SAF):** By 2026, the industry is increasingly adopting SAF to reduce soot and aromatics, which helps minimize the formation of persistent contrails.

CHAPTER SEVEN

AIRCRAFT OVERVIEW AND SELECTION IN MICROSOFT FLIGHT SIMULATOR 2024

Microsoft Flight Simulator 2024 features a **vast and diverse fleet** of up to 125 aircraft, categorized into different versions of the game, including general aviation, airliners, helicopters, and specialized aircraft like gliders and hot air balloons. Aircraft selection is done through the World Map's flight planning screen, where users can configure their aircraft's appearance, weight, balance, and other flight parameters.

COMPLETE LIST OF AIRCRAFT IN MICROSOFT FLIGHT SIMULATOR 2024

Microsoft Flight Simulator 2024, developed by Asobo Studio in partnership with Microsoft, introduces a **substantial collection of over 95 aircraft and rotorcraft**. Beyond just quantity, these aircraft feature **refined aerodynamics, upgraded cockpit instrumentation, and expanded mission-based experiences**, catering to both casual flyers and advanced enthusiasts seeking deeper realism.

Expanded Aircraft Roster Across Editions

Asobo Studio structured the simulator editions to meet different needs, offering a mix of **fixed-wing planes, helicopters, gyrocopters, and eVTOLs**:

- **Standard Edition:** 70 aircraft
- **Deluxe Edition:** 75 aircraft
- **Premium Deluxe Edition:** 90 aircraft
- **Aviator Edition:** 125 aircraft

The Aviator Edition includes 30 additional payware expansions, featuring Microsoft's popular **"Local Legends"** and **"Famous Flyers"** series.

These totals combine **brand-new aircraft built for MSFS 2024** with **updated and reworked models** from previous releases.

Key Features Across All Aircraft

All aircraft, regardless of edition, come with **enhanced flight models** that leverage **advanced computational fluid dynamics (CFD)**. Key improvements include:

- **Engine Behavior:** More realistic performance and responsiveness.
- **Aerodynamics:** Refined surfaces for improved lift, drag, and handling.
- **Ground Handling:** Authentic taxiing, braking, and takeoff/landing behavior.
- **Avionics:** Upgraded glass cockpit systems, more accurate autopilot, and realistic **FMC** functionality.
- **Rotorcraft Controls:** Enhanced collective and cyclic responsiveness, noticeable in hover and transition to forward flight.

These improvements make every aircraft feel more authentic, whether you're flying a single-engine trainer or a complex commercial jet.

Microsoft Flight Simulator 2024: Complete Aircraft Overview

Microsoft Flight Simulator 2024 delivers a **massive lineup of 95+ aircraft and rotorcraft**, with each edition offering progressively more planes, enhanced flight models, and specialized features. From classic trainers to cutting-edge jets and VTOLs, MSFS 2024 caters to every type of virtual pilot.

Standard Edition – 70 Notable Aircraft

The **Standard Edition** includes 70 aircraft spanning **classic, modern, and experimental designs**. Highlights include:

- **Iconic Aircraft:** Hughes H-4 Hercules ("Spruce Goose"), Curtiss JN-4 Jenny, Ryan NYP "Spirit of St. Louis"
- **General Aviation & Trainers:** Cessna Citation CJ4, Beechcraft Bonanza G36, CubCrafters NX Cub
- **Military & Specialty:** Fairchild Republic A-10 Thunderbolt II, North American P-51 Mustang, Erickson S-64F Aircrane
- **Commercial Airliners:** Airbus A320neo, Airbus A330-743L Beluga XL
- **Other Notables:** Draco X, Bell 407

This edition caters to **casual flyers, sightseeing enthusiasts, and vintage aircraft aficionados**.

Deluxe Edition – 75 Aircraft

Building on the Standard Edition, the **Deluxe Edition adds five extra aircraft**, focusing on **general aviation, amphibious operations, and agricultural flights**. Notable additions include:

- Cessna 188 AGTruck (agriculture)
- Beechcraft Baron G58 (twin-engine GA)
- Amphibian Aerospace Albatross G111/HU16
- Cessna 408 SkyCourier
- Dornier Seastar

These aircraft feature **unique flight decks and system depth**, ideal for **bush-flying, floatplane operations, or specialized missions**.

Premium Deluxe Edition – 90 Aircraft

The **Premium Deluxe Edition** includes all Standard and Deluxe aircraft plus **specialized jets, turboprops, and heavy-lift helicopters**. Highlights:

- Boeing 787-10 Dreamliner (advanced autopilot & FMS)

- Boeing C-17 Globemaster III (cargo/military)
- Boeing CH-47D Chinook (rotorcraft)
- Pilatus PC-24
- Cirrus SR22
- Pipistrel Taurus M

This edition emphasizes **complex airliner operations, advanced rotorcraft handling, and versatile mission profiles**.

Aviator Edition – 125 Aircraft + Payware

The **Aviator Edition** is for **dedicated simmers**, combining all previous editions plus **30 payware expansions** from Microsoft, including the **"Local Legends"** and **"Famous Flyers"** collections. This edition introduces **historic, rare, and experimental aircraft**:

- Dornier Do 31 (Experimental VTOL)
- Boeing 707-320C (Classic jetliner)
- Short SC.7 Skyvan (Compact utility aircraft)
- Antonov An-2 (Soviet-era biplane)
- Granville Gee Bee R2 / Z (Challenging racing aircraft)

Payware aircraft feature historically accurate cockpits, **engine simulations replicating original torque and RPM behaviors**, and realistic **amphibious and glider physics**.

Refined Flight Models and Systems

Across all editions, aircraft benefit from:

- **Advanced aerodynamics & engine logic**: Improved stall handling, turbocharger modeling, and prop RPM management
- **Detailed avionics & FMS**: Realistic glass cockpit systems, autopilot behavior, and management of complex jet systems
- **Rotorcraft optimization**: Authentic collective and cyclic responses, transitional lift, and tail rotor authority

From **IFR airliners to bush flying in GA planes**, MSFS 2024 balances **authenticity and accessibility**, offering:

- Multiple camera views and interactive checklists
- Realistic flight conditions and accurate avionics

- Diverse flight profiles: sightseeing, military cargo, rotorcraft missions, and long-haul jets

This edition structure ensures every pilot, from **casual enthusiasts to technical virtuosos**, can find an aircraft and mission suited to their skill level and interests.

HOW TO INSTALL FREE ADD-ONS IN MICROSOFT FLIGHT SIMULATOR 2024

In this section, you'll learn how to download a free add-on from **flightsim.to** and install it correctly in **Microsoft Flight Simulator 2024** using the **Community folder**.

Step 1: Locate the Community Folder

The easiest way to find your Community folder is directly through the simulator:

1. Launch **Microsoft Flight Simulator 2024**.
2. Click on **Marketplace**.

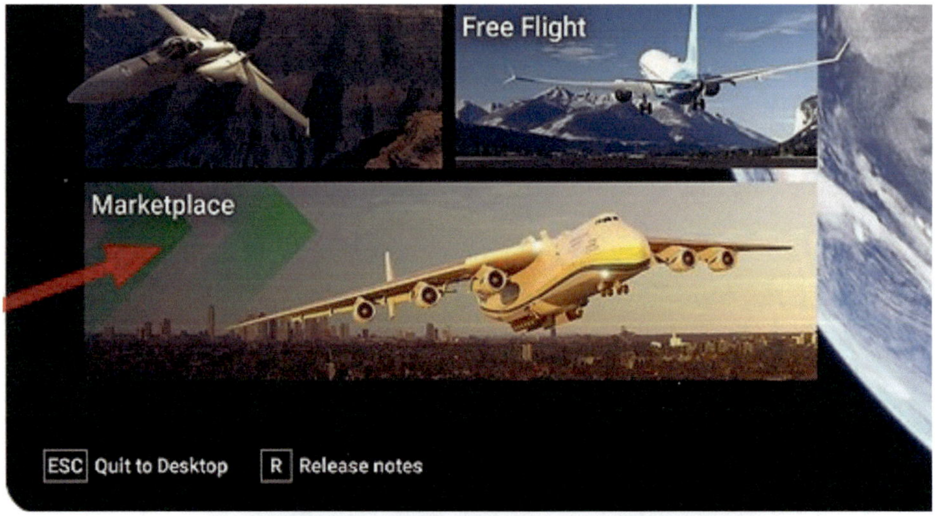

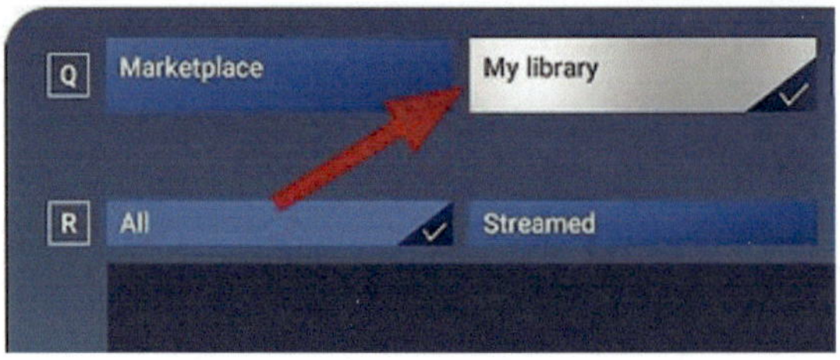

3. Select **My Library** and wait for it to load.
4. Click the **cogwheel (settings icon)** on the right.
5. Here, you'll see the **Community folder location**.

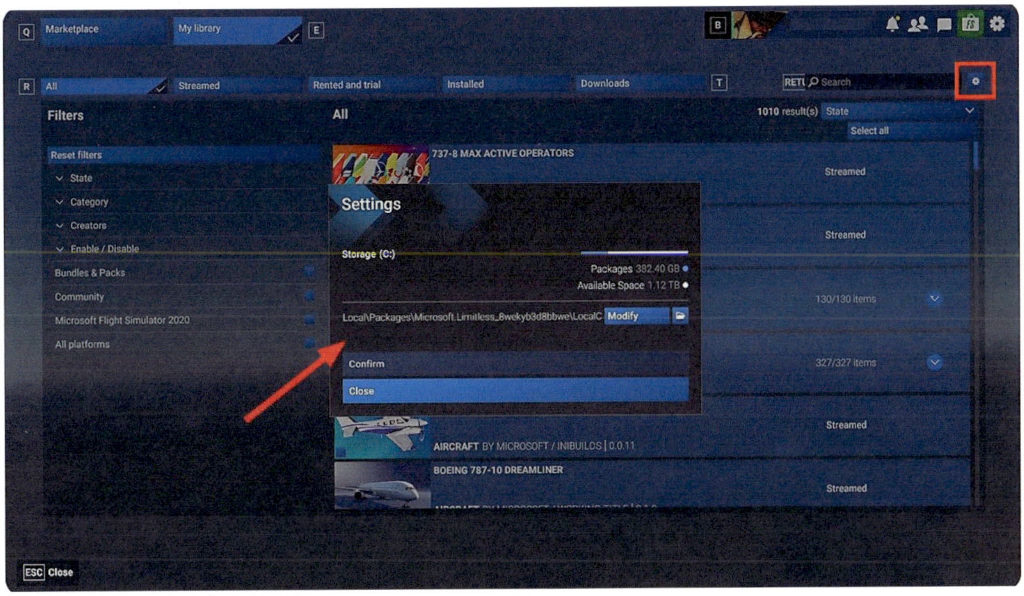

6. Click it to open the folder in File Explorer.
7. Inside, you'll find the **Community** folder—this is where all third-party add-ons are installed.

Step 2: Download an Add-on from flightsim.to

1. Open a web browser and go to **flightsim.to**.
2. Use the search bar to find an add-on. In this example, we search for **Ålesund Airport (Norway)**.

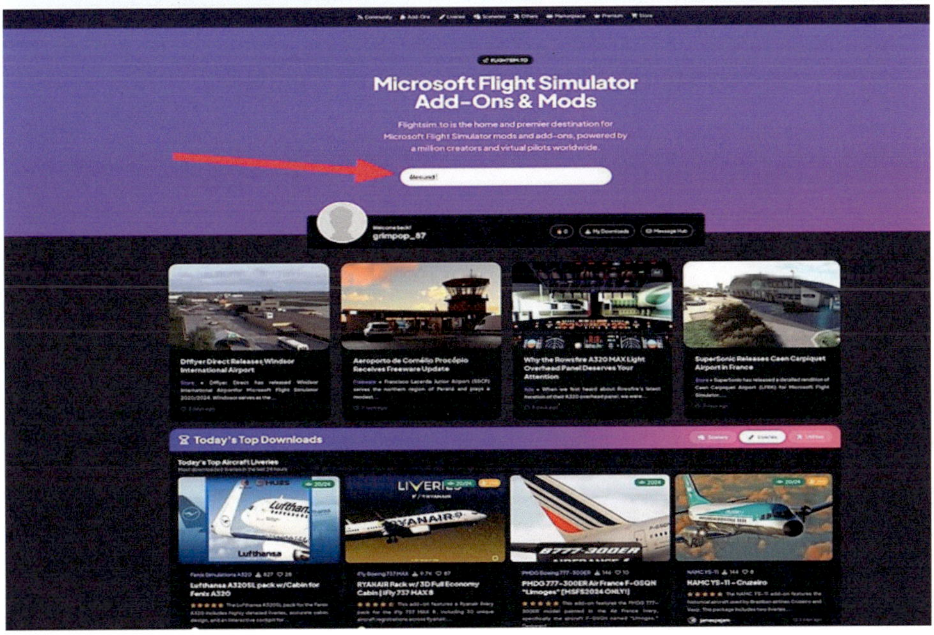

3. Select the add-on you want to install.
4. **Important:** Make sure the add-on is compatible with **Microsoft Flight Simulator 2024**.
   - Look for a checkmark confirming MSFS 2024 support.
   - Some add-ons are only compatible with MSFS 2020, which will be marked accordingly.
5. Click **Download**.
6. Skip the donation if you wish, then complete the "not a robot" check.
7. Wait for the download to finish.

Step 3: Extract the Add-on Files

1. Once downloaded, click **Show in folder**.
2. The file will usually be in **ZIP format**.
3. Right-click the ZIP file and select **Extract All**.
4. Click **Extract**.
5. After extraction, you'll see a folder—this is the add-on you need.

Step 4: Install the Add-on

1. Open the previously located **Community** folder.
2. Drag the extracted add-on folder directly into the **Community** folder.

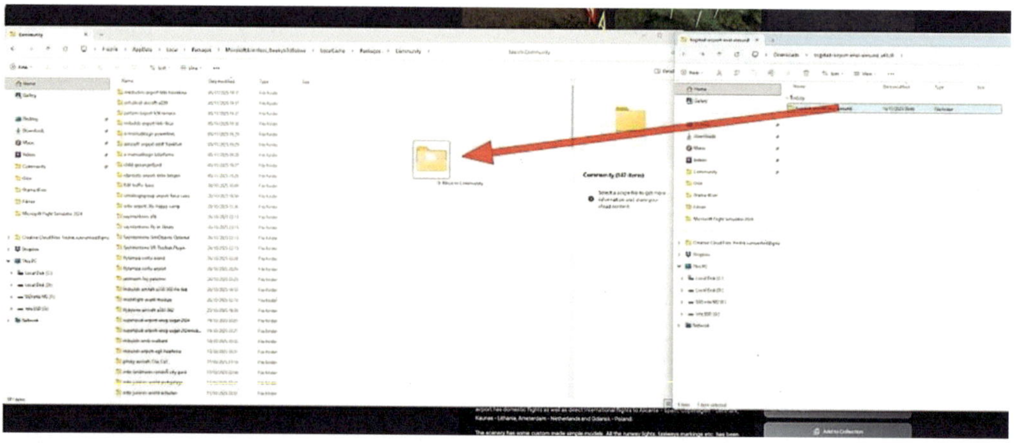

3. Wait for the copy process to finish (time varies based on file size).

Step 5: Restart the Simulator

To apply the changes:

- **Restart Microsoft Flight Simulator 2024**.
- Once loaded, the new scenery or add-on should be active in the sim.

CHAPTER EIGHT

MILITARY AND SPECIALIZED AIRCRAFT

Microsoft Flight Simulator 2024 (MSFS 2024) expands its military and specialized fleet with key additions like the **Fairchild Republic A-10C Thunderbolt II**, the heavy-lift **Boeing C-17 Globemaster III**, and the versatile **Airbus A400M Atlas**, alongside specialized roles like firefighting with the **CL-415** and unique designs like hybrid rotorcraft, all available across different editions (Standard, Deluxe, Premium Deluxe, Aviator) for diverse mission profiles.

OVERVIEW OF MILITARY AND SPECIALIZED AIRCRAFT

In **Microsoft Flight Simulator 2024**, the roster of military and specialized aircraft has been significantly expanded to support a new mission-based Career Mode. These aircraft are categorized by their specific operational roles, ranging from tactical transport and combat training to specialized industrial and rescue operations.

Military Aircraft

The 2024 edition includes tactical airlifters and fighters, with some premium models developed in partnership with specialized third-party creators.

- **Tactical Airlifters:**
  - **Airbus A400M Atlas:** A multi-role tactical airlifter included in the **Standard Edition**.
  - **Boeing C-17 Globemaster III:** A strategic heavy-lift transport, exclusive to the **Premium Deluxe Edition**.
- **Combat and Trainers:**
  - **Fairchild Republic A-10 Thunderbolt II:** The iconic "Warthog" ground-attack aircraft (**Standard Edition**).
  - **Boeing F/A-18E Super Hornet:** Returning multi-role fighter (**Standard Edition**).
  - **Aero Vodochody L-39 Albatross:** A high-performance jet trainer (**Standard Edition**).
  - **North American T-6 Texan:** A classic advanced trainer for military pilots (**Standard Edition**).
- **Historical Military:**
  - **North American P-51 Mustang:** World War II fighter (**Standard Edition**).

- **Grumman G-21A Goose:** Amphibious military transport.
- **Saab 17 B:** Historical Swedish dive bomber, included in the **Aviator Edition**.

Specialized & Industrial Aircraft

These aircraft are designed for unique missions introduced in MSFS 2024, such as firefighting, search and rescue, and heavy construction.

- **Aerial Firefighting:**
  - **De Havilland Canada CL-415:** A purpose-built amphibious "Super Scooper" for wildfire suppression.
  - **Boeing 747-400 Global Supertanker:** The world's largest aerial firefighter (**Premium Deluxe Edition**).
- **Heavy Lift & Logistics:**
  - **Erickson S-64F Aircrane:** A heavy-lift helicopter used for timber harvesting and infrastructure construction.
  - **Boeing CH-47D Chinook:** Tandem-rotor heavy-lift helicopter (**Premium Deluxe Edition**).
  - **Airbus A330-743L Beluga XL:** Specialized cargo aircraft for transporting large aircraft components.
  - **Boeing 747-400 LCF Dreamlifter:** Large cargo freighter for specialized logistics (**Premium Deluxe Edition**).
- **Search, Rescue & Utility:**
  - **Air Tractor AT-802:** Used for agricultural crop dusting and fire suppression.
  - **Cessna 188 AGTruck:** Specialized agricultural aircraft (**Deluxe Edition**).
  - **AeroElvira Optica:** A unique "observation" aircraft with a helicopter-like glass cockpit for flightseeing and surveillance.
  - **Amphibian Aerospace Albatross G111/HU16:** A rugged search and rescue amphibian (**Deluxe Edition**).

HOW TO INSTALL AND CONFIGURE MILITARY AND SPECIALIZED AIRCRAFT

In Microsoft Flight Simulator 2024, military and specialized aircraft are managed through a combination of the in-game Marketplace and the local Community folder. Configuration is handled via the reimagined Control Settings, which now supports aircraft-specific profiles.

1. Installing Military & Specialized Aircraft

Aircraft can be acquired through two primary methods:

- **In-Game Marketplace:**
  - Navigate to **Marketplace** > **My Library**.
  - Check the **Streamed** tab for content owned from MSFS 2020. You may need to click **Enable** or **Download** to make these active in 2024.
  - New purchases directly from the 2024 Marketplace will automatically appear in your library for installation.
- **Community Folder (Third-Party Mods):**
  - Download military aircraft mods from sites like Flightsim.to.
  - Extract the downloaded folder directly into your **Community** folder.
  - **To find your Community folder:** Go to **Marketplace** > **My Library**, click the **Gear (Settings)** icon next to the search bar, and select **Open**.
  - **Common Paths:**
    - **Steam:** %appdata%\Microsoft Flight Simulator 2024\Packages\Community.
    - **MS Store:** %localappdata%\Packages\Microsoft.Limitless_8wekyb3d8bbwe\LocalCache\Packages\Community.

2. Configuring Aircraft Systems and Controls

MSFS 2024 uses a "three-profile" system (General, Airplane, and Specific) to manage controls.

- **Specific Aircraft Profiles:**
  - Select the military aircraft you wish to configure from the top-left of the **Controls** menu.
  - The simulator will automatically remember and load the specific profile assigned to that aircraft next time you fly it.
- **Specialized Functions:**
  - Use the **Filter** set to "All" or use the **Search** bar to find specialized military commands such as "Afterburner," "Winch," or specific weapon system toggles (if supported by the mod).
  - **Sensitivity:** Click **Hardware Settings** within the Controls menu to fine-tune axis response for high-performance jets.
- **Manuals:** Many complex military aircraft require specific procedures. Access official PDF manuals via the Microsoft Flight Simulator Manuals page.

3. Specialized Installation Tools

For complex military conversions (e.g., adding carrier traffic or specific tankers), specialized tools like **MilitaryMod 2024** may be required. These often involve running a .vbs script within the Community folder to correctly map models and traffic assets

FLYING MILITARY AND SPECIALIZED AIRCRAFT

In **Microsoft Flight Simulator 2024**, military and specialized aircraft are integrated through a new mission-driven **Career Mode** and expanded aircraft editions. The sim features more than 95 new or upgraded aircraft models, with specific editions offering deeper access to military and heavy-utility machines.

Military Aircraft

The 2024 version includes several first-party military planes and helicopters:

- **Fighters & Attack Jets**:
  - **Fairchild Republic A-10 Thunderbolt II**: Included in the **Standard Edition**.
  - **Boeing F/A-18E Super Hornet**: Available in the **Standard Edition**.
  - **Northrop T-38A Talon**: Provided as a launch bonus for PlayStation 5 pre-orders.
- **Military Transports**:
  - **Airbus A400M Atlas**: A tactical airlifter included in the **Standard Edition**.
  - **Boeing C-17A Globemaster III**: A heavy-lift transport available in the **Premium Deluxe Edition**.
- **Military Helicopters**:
  - **Boeing CH-47D Chinook**: A tandem-rotor heavy-lift helicopter in the **Premium Deluxe Edition**.
  - **Bell UH-1H Huey**: Released in partnership with Taog's Hangar as part of a free expansion.
- **Trainers & Historic Military**:
  - **Aero Vodochody L-39**: A jet trainer in the **Standard Edition**.
  - **North American P-51 Mustang** and **T-6 Texan**: Historic military trainers available in the **Standard Edition**.
  - **Beechcraft T-34B Mentor**: A classic Navy trainer added to the "military hangar" by Carenado.

Specialized & Utility Aircraft

The simulator introduces specialized aircraft for specific career roles beyond traditional flying:

- **Aerial Firefighting**: The **De Havilland Canada CL-415** is used for water-dropping missions.
- **Agricultural (Crop Dusting)**: The **Cessna 188 AGTruck** and **Air Tractor AT-802** are available for agricultural specialized missions.
- **Search & Rescue / Medevac**: Specialized helicopters like the **Airbus H125** and **H225** are used for hoist operations and emergency transport.
- **Heavy Utility & Experimental**:
  - **Erickson S-64F Aircrane**: A heavy-lift helicopter for specialized cargo roles.
  - **Airship Industries Skyship 600**: A modern blimp for aerial observation.
  - **Dornier Do 31**: An experimental VTOL transport included in the **Aviator Edition**.

Specialized Flight Features

Military and specialized aircraft benefit from the 2024 engine's updated physics:

- **Advanced Simulation**: Features over 10,000 rigid-body surfaces for detailed aerodynamic modeling and a new soft-body physics system for elements like cloth or ropes.
- **Career Specialization**: Aircraft are categorized by "targeted specializations," allowing them to be used in specific career paths like Search & Rescue or Remote Cargo Ops.
- **Mission Integration**: Flying these aircraft often involves interactive tasks such as pre-flight walkarounds, water scooping for firefighting, or cargo loading for heavy transports.

CHAPTER NINE

CUSTOM AND THIRD-PARTY AIRCRAFT

In Microsoft Flight Simulator 2024 (MSFS 2024), third-party aircraft are classified into two main categories: **Native** (built for the 2024 SDK) and **Compatible** (ported from MSFS 2020).

CUSTOM AND THIRD-PARTY AIRCRAFT IN MICROSOFT FLIGHT SIMULATOR 2024

Recent and Upcoming Releases (2026)

- **TFDi Design MD-11:** Released January 12, 2026, featuring a 2024-native variant with advanced LOD optimization, 3D default passengers, and career mode functionality.
- **iniBuilds A340:** Set to arrive on January 15, 2026, via the iniManager.
- **Carenado T-34B Mentor:** Added to the military hangar as a native 2024 release on January 12, 2026.
- **FlightSim Studio Boeing 727-100:** Released January 7, 2026, as a dual-compatible package for both MSFS 2020 and 2024.
- **Aeroplane Heaven Boeing P-26A 'Peashooter':** Released January 7, 2026.

Native vs. Compatible Aircraft

Native aircraft are optimized to support 2024-exclusive features like interactive walkarounds, missions, and the improved Electronic Flight Bag (EFB).

- **Native 2024 Examples:** AzurPoly C160 Transall, Black Box Islander BN2, and PMDG 777 series.
- **Legacy (2020) Compatibility:** Virtually all MSFS 2020 Marketplace purchases carry over to MSFS 2024. While they function in "Free Flight," they may not natively support Career Mode or new environmental interactions.

Career Mode Support

Only aircraft verified through the official **Marketplace** are typically validated for use in Career Mode missions.

- **Passenger Transport:** LVFR Airbus A330-900 NEO, A340-300.
- **Cargo/Heavy:** AzurPoly C160 Transall, Captain Sim Boeing 767 Freighter.

- **Specialized:** Black Box Simulations Islander BN2 (Skydive Aviation), Miltech Simulations Osprey MV-22.

Installation and Management

- **Community Folder:** Third-party aircraft downloaded from external sites (e.g., Flightsim.to) must still be placed in the Community folder.
- **Addon Linker:** Tools like the MSFS Addons Linker remain highly recommended for managing large collections across both the 2020 and 2024 versions.
- **Platform Lock:** Purchases only transfer if you remain on the same platform (e.g., Steam to Steam or Microsoft Store to Microsoft Store)

WHAT ARE CUSTOM AND THIRD-PARTY AIRCRAFT

Microsoft Flight Simulator 2024, custom and third-party aircraft refer to content developed by external teams rather than Microsoft's internal studios. These are divided into two main categories: **First-Party Partnered** (included in the base game or editions) and **Third-Party Add-ons** (purchased or downloaded separately).

1. Partnered "First-Party" Developers

Microsoft collaborated with 14 external teams to build the official aircraft roster for the various 2024 editions. While developed by third parties, these are considered "first-party" because they are included in the simulator's Standard, Deluxe, Premium Deluxe, or Aviator editions.

- **Key Partners & Their Contributions:**
  - **iniBuilds:** Airbus A321LR, A330 series, A400M Atlas, and A320neo v2.
  - **Got Friends:** Draco X, AeroElvira Optica, and Stemme S12G.
  - **FlightFX:** Cirrus Vision Jet, Archer Midnight, and Joby S4.
  - **Carenado:** Pilatus PC-12 NGX, Cessna 400 Corvalis TT, and Robinson R66.
  - **Blackbird Simulations:** De Havilland DHC-2 Beaver and Erickson S-64F Aircrane.

2. Independent Third-Party Add-ons

These are aircraft bought separately through the in-game **Marketplace** or from external developer stores like iniBuilds, Orbx, or Just Flight.

- **High-Fidelity Airliners:**

- **PMDG:** Boeing 777-300ER, 777-200ER, and 777F.
- **Fenix Simulations:** Airbus A320, A319, and A321 expansions.
- **TFDi Design:** MD-11 (launched January 12, 2026).

- **General Aviation & Military:**
  - **A2A Simulations:** Accu-Sim Comanche 250 and Aerostar 600.
  - **Black Square:** Piston and Turbine Duke, Velocity XL, and Beechcraft Starship.
  - **DC Designs:** F-14 Tomcat, F-4 Phantom, and Concorde.
  - **Miltech Simulations:** MV-22 Osprey and CH-47D Chinook.

3. Custom & Community Content (Freeware)

Custom aircraft also include community-made projects often hosted on sites like Flightsim.to.

- **Headwind Simulations:** Airbus A330-900neo (A339X).
- **FlyByWire Simulations:** A32NX (Airbus A320neo enhancement).

Compatibility & Career Mode

- **Career Mode Integration:** Currently, only aircraft available on the official Marketplace can be validated for Career Mode. Examples of compatible third-party planes include the **LVFR Airbus A330-900 NEO**, **Carenado B55**, and **Miltech Simulations MV-22**.
- **Installation:** For PC, third-party content downloaded outside the Marketplace is installed by dragging the unzipped folder into the simulator's **Community folder**.

TYPES OF CUSTOM AND THIRD-PARTY AIRCRAFT

In **Microsoft Flight Simulator 2024**, custom and third-party aircraft fall into several distinct categories based on their origin, level of complexity, and compatibility with the new simulator's features.

1. First-Party Partner Aircraft

These are aircraft developed by third-party studios specifically for Microsoft to be included as "default" aircraft in various game editions.

- **Airliners:** Includes the **Airbus A330 series** and **A400M Atlas** (by iniBuilds), and the **Boeing 737 MAX 8** (by Asobo).

- **Utility & Career-Specific:** Specialized aircraft like the **De Havilland CL-415** (Firefighting), **Erickson S-64F Aircrane** (BlackBird Simulations), and **Air Tractor AT-802**.
- **Helicopters:** New additions such as the **Robinson R66** (Carenado) and **Bell 407** (Nemeth Designs).
- **Historical & Experimental:** Featured in the **Aviator Edition**, including the **Antonov An-2**, **Dornier Do 31**, and **Boeing 707-320C**.

2. Native MSFS 2024 Third-Party Add-ons

These are premium "payware" aircraft built using the updated 2024 SDK to take full advantage of new physics, walkaround inspections, and career mode compatibility.

- **High-Fidelity Airliners:** Major developers include **PMDG** (777-300ER, 777F), **Fenix Simulations** (A320 family), and **iniBuilds** (A300-600R, A350).
- **General Aviation:** Advanced models like the **A2A Accu-Sim Aerostar 600** and **Black Square Starship**.
- **Military & Jets:** Aircraft such as the **AzurPoly C160 Transall** and **Just Flight Avro Vulcan**.

3. "Legacy" Compatible Aircraft (MSFS 2020 Ports)

Most aircraft purchased in the MSFS 2020 marketplace are "credited" to users in MSFS 2024. While many work via backward compatibility, their performance varies.

- **Functional Ports:** Examples like the **Ant's Tiger Moth** and **CowanSim 206L3** have been reported as working well in the new sim.
- **Broken or Limited:** Some complex 2020 aircraft, such as the **Black Box Islander BN2**, initially faced issues like lack of takeoff power or UI freezing when imported without specific 2024 updates.

4. Freeware and Community Content

Custom aircraft available through community platforms like Flightsim.to.

- **Native Freeware:** Examples include the **Fouga Castel C-25S Training Glider** by BlueMesh.
- **Liveries and Mods:** Thousands of community-made **liveries** for default planes and enhancements for existing systems.

WHERE TO FIND CUSTOM AIRCRAFTS

Custom aircraft for **Microsoft Flight Simulator 2024** can be found through both official in-game channels and third-party community websites:

Official In-Game Marketplace

The primary way to find custom aircraft, especially for console players (Xbox/PS5), is the **Marketplace**.

- **Where to look:** Launch the simulator and navigate to the **Marketplace** tab from the main menu.
- **Categories:** You can filter by "Aircraft," where developers like Carenado, Just Flight, and PMDG release premium custom models.
- **Updates:** Official updates and new releases typically go live every Thursday.

Third-Party Community Websites (PC Only)

PC users can download thousands of free and paid custom aircraft from external repositories.

- Flightsim.to: The largest community hub for MSFS 2024. It features dedicated categories for new aircraft releases, helicopters, and gliders.
- Fly Away Simulation: An all-in-one library that includes specific sections for MSFS 2024 free mods and aircraft.
- MSFS Addons: A reliable source for news and an updated list of every aircraft available for the 2024 simulator.

HOW TO CHOOSE QUALITY THIRD-PARTY AIRCRAFT

In 2026, choosing quality third-party aircraft for Microsoft Flight Simulator 2024 (MSFS 2024) requires distinguishing between native 2024 builds and older 2020 ports. Follow these guidelines to ensure you receive high-fidelity content:

1. Verify Platform Compatibility

While many MSFS 2020 aircraft are "forward compatible," they often lack native 2024 features like advanced physics or walk-around inspections.

- **Native 2024 Version:** Look for aircraft built specifically for the 2024 SDK. These include native features such as detailed walk-arounds and enhanced flight models.

- **Legacy Compatibility:** Some 2020 aircraft require specific installers (e.g., **Fenix** or **FlyByWire**) to function correctly in the 2024 community folder.
- **Upgrade Paths:** Confirm if a developer offers free 2024 updates for existing 2020 purchases, as some may charge for the transition.

2. Prioritize Top-Tier Developers

Consistent quality is often tied to the developer's reputation for support and "study-level" depth.

- **Tier-S (Highest Quality): Fenix Simulations** (A320 family), **PMDG** (777, 737), **A2A Simulations** (Piper Comanche), and **FlyByWire** (A380X) are widely regarded for industry-leading systems and visuals.
- **Tier-A (Reliable Excellence): Just Flight** (Hawk T1, Piper Arrow), **SimWorks Studios** (PC-12), **Got Friends**, and **IndiaFoxTecho**.
- **Specialized Jets: Flysimware's** Learjet 35A is noted for high-quality visuals and accurate bizjet systems.

3. Check for Performance Impact

MSFS 2024 is highly demanding on system resources. Before purchasing, research the following:

- **Frame Rate (FPS):** Some high-fidelity aircraft, such as the **iniBuilds A321**, have been reported to cause "choppy" performance compared to better-optimized models like the **PMDG 777**.
- **Bug Reports:** Check community forums for issues specific to 2024, such as missing wingflex, broken landing gear animations, or loading errors.

4. Consult Modern Community Resources

- **Latest Reviews:** Use platforms like FSElite or MSFS Addons for 2026-specific news and release updates.
- **Developer Forums:** Check the Official MSFS Forums for unofficial compatibility lists and "Tier Lists" maintained by the community.
- **YouTube Performance Tests:** Search for "live" feedback to see the aircraft's flight dynamics and cockpit clarity in real-time.

CHAPTER TEN

COCKPIT INSTRUMENTS AND AVIONICS

In Microsoft Flight Simulator 2024, cockpit instruments and avionics have been significantly upgraded through the **MSFS Avionics Framework**, developed primarily by Working Title. These systems are now more deeply integrated into the flight engine, featuring improved physics and system logic for electrical, hydraulic, and fuel systems.

Standard Avionics Packages

MSFS 2024 includes highly detailed simulations of real-world avionics units used by developers for various aircraft:

- **Garmin G1000 NXi:** A widespread glass cockpit for general aviation (e.g., Cessna 172), featuring a Primary Flight Display (PFD) and Multi-Function Display (MFD).
- **Garmin G3000 / G5000:** Advanced touch-screen systems used in light jets like the TBM 930 and Cessna Citation Longitude, featuring full VNAV support and integrated charts.
- **Garmin GNS 430/530:** Traditional GPS navigators often found in older general aviation aircraft.
- **Honeywell Primus Epic 2:** A sophisticated glass cockpit for high-end business aircraft like the Pilatus PC-12 and PC-24.
- **Collins ProLine 21 (WT21):** Standard avionics for business jets like the Beechcraft King Air and Citation CJ4.
- **Universal UNS-1:** A flight management computer (FMC) modeled for retrofitting older aircraft, such as the Saab 340.

Core Cockpit Instruments

The simulator reproduces the "Six Pack" of primary flight instruments for analog aircraft, which are often mirrored digitally in glass cockpits:

1. **Airspeed Indicator:** Measures speed relative to the air.
2. **Attitude Indicator (Artificial Horizon):** Shows the aircraft's orientation relative to the horizon.
3. **Altimeter:** Displays altitude above sea level.
4. **Turn Coordinator:** Indicates turn rate and quality.
5. **Heading Indicator / Compass:** Displays the aircraft's direction.

6. **Vertical Speed Indicator (VSI):** Shows the rate of climb or descent.

New Features in 2024

- **Integrated Electronic Flight Bag (EFB):** A tablet available in many cockpits to manage flight plans, charts, and aircraft weight/balance.
- **Real-World Charts:** For the first time, Jeppesen-powered charts can be displayed directly on glass cockpit screens via plugins like Navigraph.
- **Improved System Logic:** Advanced simulations for FADEC (Full Authority Digital Engine Control), autothrottle, and complex failure messaging (CAS).
- **Native Multi-monitor Support:** Enhanced ability to "pop out" instrument panels to separate screens or tablets.

INSTRUMENTS

Aircraft instruments in Microsoft Flight Simulator 2024 can be defined in several ways and combined into panels within the virtual cockpit. This section explains how instrument panels are set up and outlines the different methods available for creating and integrating gauges.

At the core of the system, **panel.cfg** acts as the "glue" that connects instruments to the aircraft within the simulator. Meanwhile, **panel.xml** is used to add automated behavior to gauges, such as alerts, messages, and electrical logic.

Instrument Types

Microsoft Flight Simulator 2024 groups aircraft instrumentation into three main categories, each increasing in complexity as you move from visual representation to full system logic.

External Cockpit

The external cockpit is what users see when viewing or flying the aircraft in third-person mode.

Instruments displayed externally—and some shared with glass cockpits—are defined in **cockpit.cfg**. This file controls how external instruments appear and behave when the aircraft is viewed from outside.

Steam Gauges

Many aircraft still use traditional analog, or "steam," gauges within the virtual cockpit.

These gauges are built directly into the aircraft's cockpit 3D model and are controlled using **Model Behaviors templates**, which define how each instrument responds to simulator data and pilot input.

Glass Cockpit Gauges

Modern aircraft often rely on digital, or "glass cockpit," displays. These gauges can be created using one of three methods:

- **WASM (WebAssembly):** Written in C++ using an external development environment such as Visual Studio. Several official aircraft samples demonstrate this approach.
- **JavaScript / HTML / CSS:** This method uses an HTML page for layout, JavaScript for logic, and CSS for styling. It offers flexibility and is widely supported within the simulator's UI system.

- **MSFS Avionics Framework:** A purpose-built, component-based API designed specifically for avionics development, using a React-like architecture. Many default and third-party aircraft rely on this framework.

The MSFS Avionics Framework

The MSFS Avionics Framework allows developers to build fully custom glass cockpits or to use prebuilt avionics packages included with Microsoft Flight Simulator 2024. These packages are complete systems that can be integrated directly into aircraft projects.

Most avionics packages support **plug-ins**, which allow developers to add aircraft-specific functionality while still using the base instrument set. Plug-ins are often required to display unique engine instruments or manage systems such as FADEC or custom autothrottle logic.

To support both legacy and modern aircraft, Microsoft Flight Simulator 2024 includes two versions of each avionics package:

- A **backward-compatible version** for aircraft migrated from MSFS 2020
- An **enhanced MSFS 2024 version** that takes advantage of new features and capabilities

For the best performance and user experience, developers are strongly encouraged to use the updated **V2 avionics packages** when creating aircraft for Microsoft Flight Simulator 2024.

NAVIGATING MODERN AVIONICS: A PILOT'S GUIDE TO GLASS COCKPITS

Glass cockpits have largely replaced traditional analog instrument panels in modern general aviation aircraft. These digital avionics systems—most commonly the Garmin G1000—provide enhanced situational awareness, integrated flight information, and powerful automation tools that fundamentally change how pilots manage and fly an aircraft.

For student and private pilots trained on round-dial instruments, transitioning to glass requires a new scanning technique, an understanding of system logic, and disciplined use of automation. This guide outlines the essential concepts and best practices for operating glass cockpits safely and effectively.

What Is a Glass Cockpit?

A glass cockpit replaces mechanical gauges with electronic flight displays. Most systems feature two primary screens:

- **Primary Flight Display (PFD):** Combines attitude, airspeed, altitude, heading, and vertical speed into a single, easy-to-read display.
- **Multi-Function Display (MFD):** Shows engine data, navigation charts, traffic, weather, terrain, and system status.

Modern glass cockpits integrate GPS navigation, autopilot control, terrain awareness, and traffic alerts into one cohesive digital suite. The Garmin G1000 is the most widely used system in training and personal aircraft.

Advantages of Glass Cockpits

- **Enhanced Situational Awareness:** Moving maps, traffic overlays, and synthetic vision provide a comprehensive view of the flight environment.
- **Efficient Navigation:** GPS-based routing and terrain displays simplify flight planning and reduce navigational errors.
- **System Integration:** Engine, electrical, and navigation data are centralized, minimizing the need to scan multiple instruments.
- **Workload Management:** Autopilot integration helps manage pilot workload, especially during IFR operations and high-task phases of flight.

Common Transition Challenges

Information Overload: The sheer amount of available data can overwhelm pilots new to glass cockpits, particularly when multiple alerts or display layers are active.

Mode Confusion: Pilots may lose track of autopilot or GPS modes, leading to unintended aircraft behavior if system status is not continuously monitored.

Overreliance on Automation: Excessive dependence on automation can erode situational awareness and delay recognition of system failures or incorrect inputs.

Skill Degradation: Glass cockpit flying should not replace fundamental skills such as hand flying, VOR navigation, or operating with backup instruments.

Effective Training Strategies

Master the System: Study the specific avionics installed in your aircraft. For Garmin G1000 users, Garmin simulators and structured tutorials are excellent tools. Practice building flight plans, switching navigation modes, and managing alerts.

Train with Realistic Scenarios: Use the avionics to handle real-world situations, such as weather diversions, holding patterns, or system malfunctions. Scenario-based practice builds practical, transferable skills.

Maintain a Disciplined Scan: Avoid excessive "heads-down" time. Keep a consistent scan of critical flight data and regularly look outside to maintain situational awareness.

Learn the Autopilot Thoroughly: Autopilot misuse is a common source of error. Understand and practice using NAV, HDG, VS, ALT, and FLC modes—and always be ready to disconnect and hand-fly.

Preserve Manual Flying Skills: Continue practicing basic maneuvers, slow flight, steep turns, and non-GPS approaches. If the glass goes dark, confident manual flying is essential.

HOW TO USE AVIONICS EFFECTIVELY

In Microsoft Flight Simulator 2024 (MSFS 2024), effective use of avionics relies on the new **Electronic Flight Bag (EFB)**, enhanced system depth for units like the G3000, and integrated flight planning.

1. Master the New Electronic Flight Bag (EFB)

Every aircraft in MSFS 2024 now includes a native EFB tablet, which is the central hub for mission and flight management.

- **Synchronize Flight Plans:** Plan your route directly in the EFB's new flight planner. Use the "SEND" menu to select **"SEND TO AVIONICS"** to instantly load the route into your aircraft's FMS/GPS.
- **Manage Performance:** Use the EFB to calculate fuel, payload, and takeoff/landing speeds (V-speeds), which are then reflected in your primary flight displays (PFD).
- **Monitor Systems:** The EFB provides real-time data on aircraft wear and tear, including tire and brake status, which is especially critical in Career Mode.

2. Utilize Advanced Glass Cockpit Features

Updated avionics suites like the **Garmin G3000** and **Universal UNS-1 FMS** offer significantly more functionality than in previous versions.

- **Customizable Displays:** The G3000 now features larger screens and three smaller, customizable touchscreens for managing navigation, radio, and system pages.
- **Instrument Scan Development:** Use the PFD's high-fidelity tapes to monitor optimal speed (green zone) and avoid stalls (white/red zones).
- **Vertical Profile Planning:** Leverage the new flight planner's ability to visualize vertical profiles to manage descents more effectively during IFR (Instrument Flight Rules) operations.

3. Effective Controls & Interaction

Interaction with avionics has been streamlined for better precision.

- **Precision Knob Turning:** For radios or GPS units with inner and outer rings, hover over the specific part and use the **Mouse Scroll Wheel** for the easiest adjustments.
- **Frequency Swapping:** Look for the swap button (often <->) on the avionics panel to make a standby frequency active after tuning.
- **Cursor Management:** Press the middle mouse button to unlock the cursor for clicking buttons, and right-click + drag to pan the view without losing focus on your instruments.

4. Training and Documentation

- **Interactive Flight School:** Use the built-in Training Missions to learn specific aircraft systems and navigation under a virtual instructor.
- **Official Manuals:** For complex aircraft like the Boeing 787-10 or Cessna Citation Longitude, download the official MSFS Aircraft Manuals to understand deep system logic.
- **Evaluated Checklists:** Enable "Evaluated" checklist mode to have the AI copilot highlight the specific buttons and knobs you need to interact with.

CHAPTER ELEVEN

USING GPS AND AUTOPILOT SYSTEM

Using GPS and autopilot in MSFS 2024 involves loading a flight plan, setting the navigation source to GPS, engaging autopilot modes (like Heading, Altitude, NAV/GPS), and letting the system guide the aircraft along the magenta route on your display, switching from HDG to GPS capture as you get closer to the planned track for seamless automated flight.

AUTOPILOT IN AVIATION: UNDERSTANDING MODERN FLIGHT AUTOMATION

In modern aviation, autopilot systems are among the most transformative innovations, improving flight safety, efficiency, and reducing pilot workload. Often misunderstood as "planes flying themselves," autopilots are actually sophisticated tools that work **in partnership with pilots**, automating routine tasks while allowing pilots to focus on decision-making, monitoring, and handling critical phases of flight. This guide explores how autopilot works, its capabilities, the underlying technology, and pilot training — including an in-depth look at **Autoland**, one of its most advanced functions.

What Is Autopilot?

Autopilot is a flight control system that manages an aircraft's trajectory without constant manual input. It can maintain **altitude, heading, and speed**, follow navigation routes, and even assist with landings under specific conditions. Despite its automation, pilots remain essential, particularly during takeoff, landing, and unexpected situations.

Key Components of an Autopilot System

Modern autopilots rely on several integrated components:

- **Flight Control Computer (FCC):** The "brain" of the system, processing sensor inputs and issuing real-time commands.
- **Sensors & Instruments:** Measure flight parameters such as altitude, airspeed, pitch, roll, and yaw. Typical sensors include **gyroscopes, GPS, altimeters, and inertial measurement units (IMUs)**.
- **Actuators:** Mechanical systems that move control surfaces — rudder, elevators, ailerons — according to FCC commands.

- **Flight Management System (FMS):** Coordinates autopilot with a pre-programmed flight plan, including waypoints, routes, and altitude profiles.

Major Autopilot Functions

Autopilot assists pilots with numerous tasks, enhancing flight precision and reducing workload:

1. **Altitude Hold:** Maintains a steady vertical level.
2. **Heading & Navigation Hold:** Keeps the aircraft aligned with a specific heading or follows a GPS/VOR-based route.
3. **Vertical Navigation (VNAV):** Automates climbs and descents according to FMS profiles.
4. **Lateral Navigation (LNAV):** Ensures the aircraft follows the programmed route accurately.
5. **Autothrottle:** Adjusts engine thrust to maintain target airspeed.
6. **Autoland:** Fully automated landings, particularly in low-visibility conditions.

Autoland: Precision in Low Visibility

Autoland is the pinnacle of autopilot capability, allowing aircraft to land automatically with minimal pilot intervention.

Requirements for Autoland:

- Runway equipped with **ILS Category III** systems.
- Functional **autopilot** and **autothrottle** systems.
- Dual or triple autopilot setup for redundancy.
- Operational **radio altimeter**.

Safety Features:

- Triple redundancy ensures reliability.
- Automatic go-around if landing conditions are unsafe.
- Continuous pilot supervision, even during automated landing.

Pilot Training for Autopilot and Autoland

Despite advanced automation, pilots undergo rigorous training to operate and supervise autopilot systems safely.

Step 1: Ground School

- Learn the theory of automation.

- Study FMS, VNAV, LNAV, and ILS procedures.
- Understand system limitations and potential failures.

Step 2: Simulator Training

- Full-motion Level D simulators replicate aircraft behavior.
- Practice low-visibility approaches, engine-out scenarios, and system failures.
- Train in go-arounds, diversions, and manual override operations.

Step 3: Check Ride

- Practical exam with an instructor.
- Demonstrate full control of autopilot, Autoland, and manual flight.

Benefits of Autopilot in Aviation

- **Reduced Pilot Workload:** Essential on long-haul flights.
- **Enhanced Safety:** Minimizes human error during stable flight.
- **Operational Efficiency:** Optimizes fuel use and route accuracy.
- **Improved ATC Coordination:** Ensures precise adherence to assigned altitudes and speeds.

Autopilot systems are not about removing the pilot from the cockpit; they **amplify human capability**, allowing pilots to manage complex flights more safely and efficiently. Mastery of these systems, especially Autoland, requires training, discipline, and continual situational awareness.

MSFS 2024 – CESSNA 172 QUICK GPS & AUTOPILOT

This section walks you through flying a Cessna 172 in **Microsoft Flight Simulator 2024** using the **G1000 GPS** and **autopilot** to follow a course to any destination.

Step 1: Set Your Destination on the G1000

1. Access your **G1000** display.
2. Press the **Direct** button, then select the **keyboard icon**.

3. Enter your destination's ICAO code (e.g., **KSEA, KLAX**) and press **Enter**.

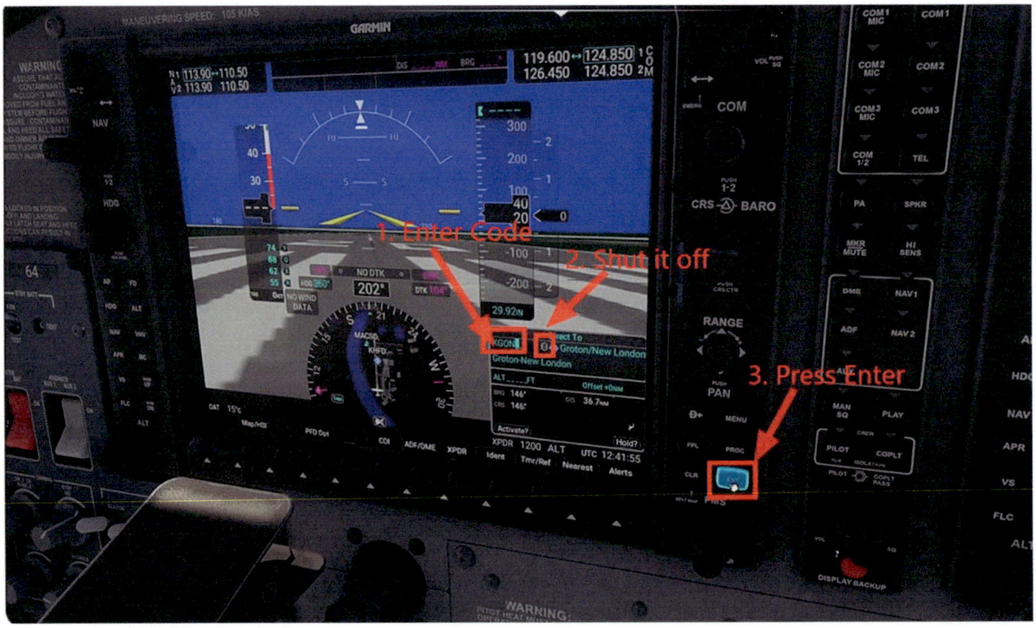

4. A **magenta line** will appear, showing the route to your selected destination.
5. Ensure the GPS is active by checking the CDI (Course Deviation Indicator). Press **CDI** until it reads **GPS**, and verify the destination, distance, and bearing on the top display.

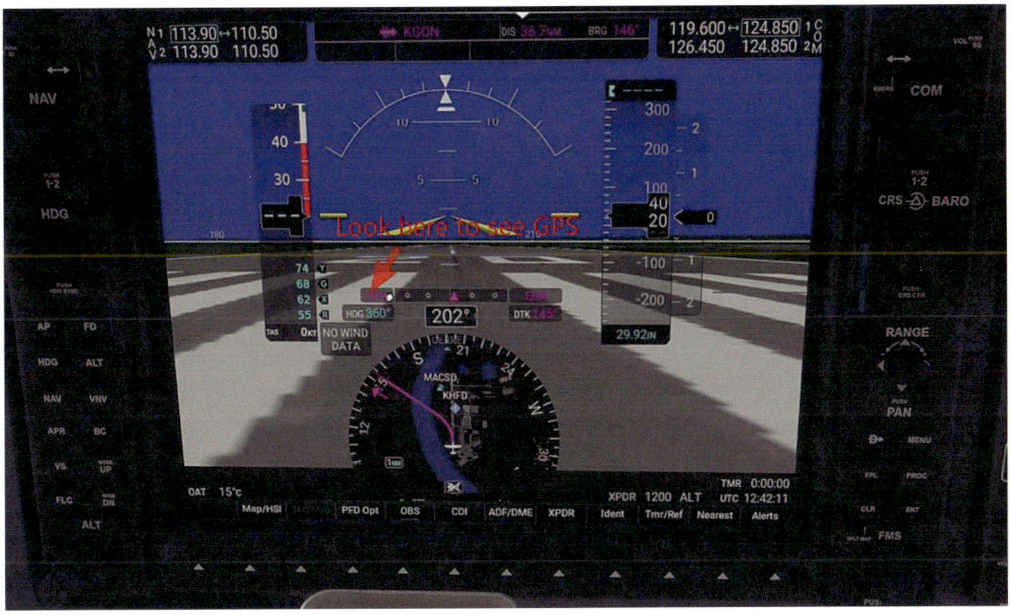

Step 2: Configure the Autopilot

1. Enable **NAV mode** on the autopilot panel.

- This allows the flight director to follow the GPS course.
- The panel will display **GPS**, confirming navigation is armed.

2. Ensure **pitch mode (PIT)** is active for controlled climbs.

Step 3: Set Target Altitude and Speed

1. Select your desired altitude; for example: **5,500 ft**.

2. Press the **FLC (Flight Level Change) button** to manage climb speed.

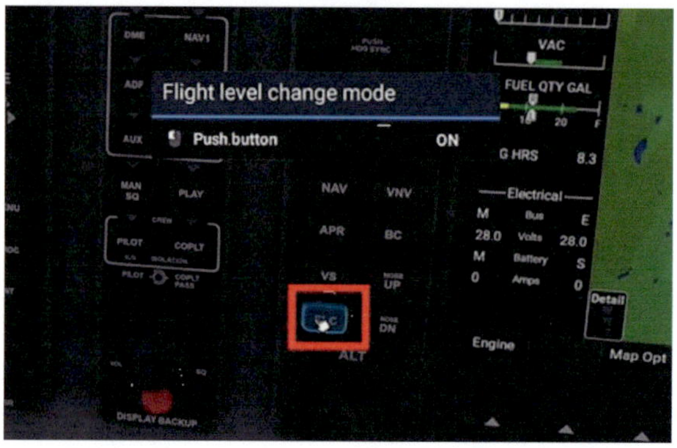

3. Set your climb speed using the **nose up/down controls**; e.g., **Vy = 74 knots**.

- Tip: Adjust speed after takeoff for smoother acceleration.

Step 4: Verify Autopilot Settings

Before applying power, ensure the following are armed and selected:

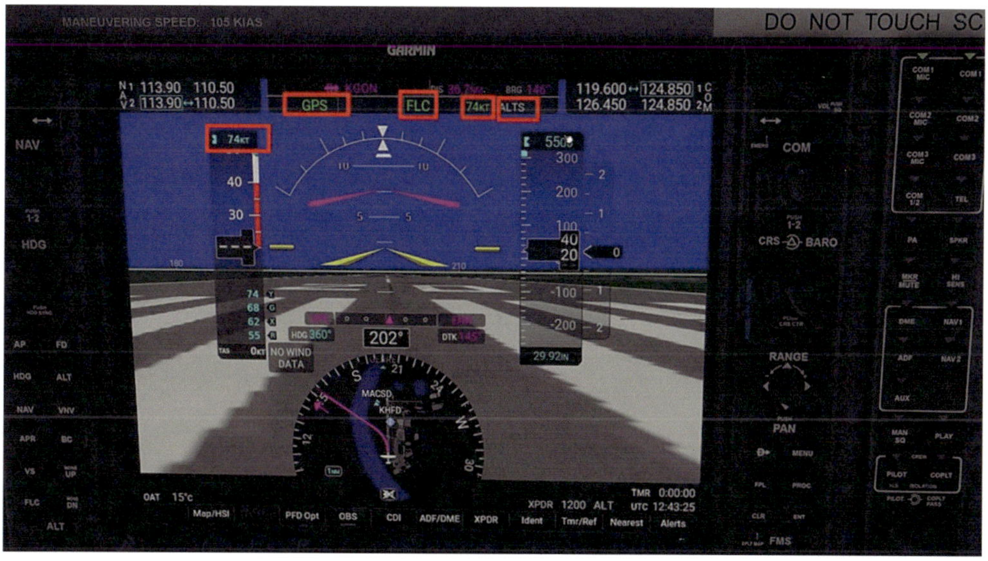

- **GPS course**
- **Flight Level Change (FLC) mode**
- **Target speed**
- **Altitude hold**

Step 5: Engage Autopilot

1. Give the aircraft power and begin your climb.
2. Press the **Autopilot Engage button**.
3. The aircraft will now fly automatically:
   - GPS hold active
   - Flight Level Change managing climb
   - Autopilot controlling heading and pitch

Note: FLC mode is often more reliable than vertical speed (VS) mode for climbs, reducing the risk of stalls.

Step 6: Observe the Flight

- The **flight director** guides the aircraft along the magenta GPS line.
- The aircraft will climb at the selected speed (**74 knots**) and target altitude (**5,500 ft**).

- Minor adjustments with trim may be needed during sharp maneuvers.

Tips & Tricks

- Always verify GPS and autopilot settings before takeoff.
- Use FLC mode instead of VS for safer climbs.
- Monitor the autopilot regularly, especially during turns, to ensure the aircraft follows the planned course.
- Practice in simulator scenarios to gain confidence with the G1000 and autopilot workflow.

This workflow allows a Cessna 172 pilot to efficiently follow a GPS course using **modern autopilot functionality**, improving situational awareness and reducing manual workload during climbs and cruise.

HOW TO ACTIVATE AUTOPILOT IN MICROSOFT FLIGHT SIMULATOR 2024

Microsoft Flight Simulator 2024 runs in real-world time, which means long flights can last hours. That's where autopilot becomes essential. Unlike arcade-style flight games, MSFS 2024 does not offer a single "AI take over" button. Instead, autopilot works much like it does in real aircraft—you must configure it correctly before it will engage.

If autopilot isn't working for you, don't worry. The steps below break the process down into simple, reliable actions you can use on almost any aircraft.

Basic Steps to Turn On Autopilot

1. **Take off manually.**

2. **Stabilize the aircraft** at a safe speed and climb.
3. **Press the AP (Autopilot) button** near the Primary Flight Display (PFD).
4. **Set your target altitude** using the ALT knob.
5. **Select a climb mode**: Vertical Speed (VS) or Flight Level Change (FLC).
6. **Choose a navigation mode**:
   - **NAV** to follow your flight plan
   - **HDG** to follow a manually selected heading

Once these steps are complete, autopilot should take control of the aircraft's pitch, roll, and navigation—while you monitor the flight.

Understanding Autopilot Modes

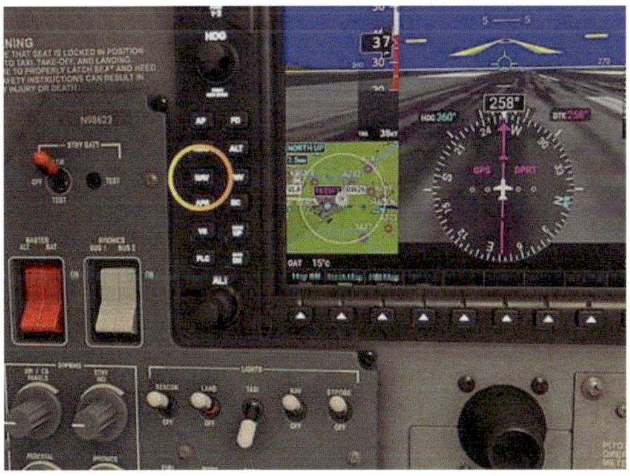

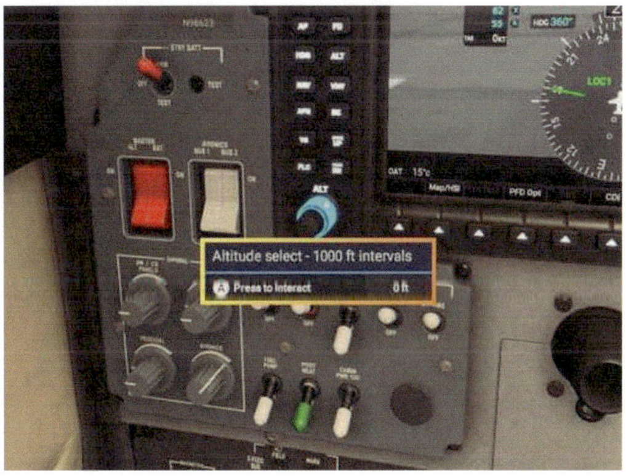

Autopilot panels vary by aircraft, but the core concepts are always the same. Master these three modes and you can fly almost anything on autopilot.

Heading Mode (HDG)

HDG mode keeps the aircraft flying in a specific direction.

- Adjust the heading using the **HDG knob**
- The aircraft will turn and maintain that heading automatically
- Useful when you don't have a flight plan or want manual directional control

You can change the heading at any time without disconnecting autopilot.

Navigation Mode (NAV)

NAV mode follows the programmed GPS flight plan.

- The aircraft automatically turns to stay on course
- Ideal for long-haul and IFR flights
- Requires an active flight plan

If you don't have a route, you can select a nearby airport using the **Nearest** function on the PFD to generate a basic GPS path.

Altitude Control (ALT, VS, and FLC)

Setting an altitude alone is not enough. Autopilot needs a *method* to reach that altitude.

Vertical Speed (VS)

- Controls climb or descent by pitching the nose up or down
- You manually select the climb or descent rate
- Simple, but can bleed airspeed if set too aggressively

Flight Level Change (FLC)

- Controls altitude using **airspeed**
- You set a target speed, and the aircraft adjusts pitch and power
- More realistic and safer for climbs

For best results, use the aircraft's recommended climb speed:

- Open the **TMR/REF** menu on the PFD
- Look for **Vy** (best rate of climb)
- Set FLC to that speed (e.g., 70 knots)

Common Reasons Autopilot Won't Engage (And How to Fix Them)

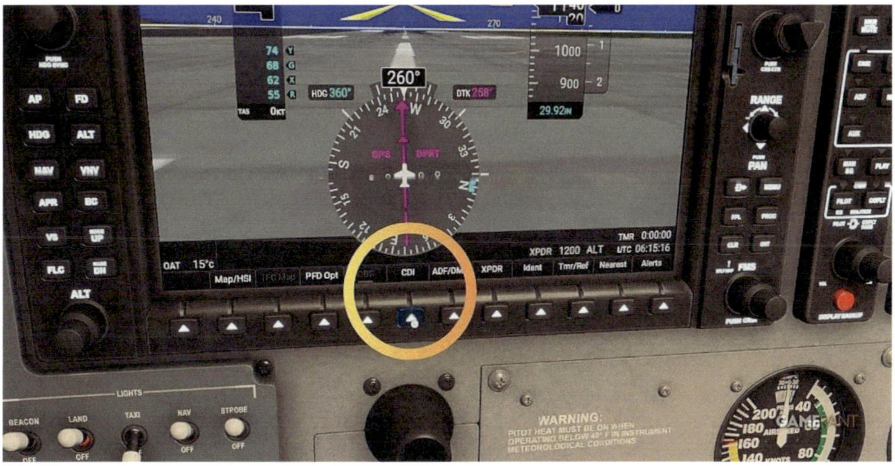

If autopilot refuses to turn on, check the following:

- **CDI not set to GPS:** Press the **CDI** button until it switches to GPS mode. You should see **magenta** guidance lines instead of green.
- **OBS mode is active:** Autopilot will not follow a route with OBS enabled. Turn OBS off.
- **Throttle not in the correct position:** Some aircraft—especially Airbuses—require the throttle to be set to **CL (Climb)** mode before autopilot will engage.

MICROSOFT FLIGHT SIMULATOR 2024 (PS5): FLIGHT PLANNING IN FREE FLIGHT

Let's jump into **Free Flight** and break down flight planning in *Microsoft Flight Simulator 2024*. There are several ways to create a flight plan, but we'll start with the **simplest and fastest method**. This approach is perfect for beginners or for anyone who just wants to get airborne quickly without building a detailed plan from scratch.

Basic Flight Planning (Fast & Simple)

We'll begin with an easy route:

- Select **Los Angeles International (LAX)** by clicking the airport icon and setting it as your **departure**.
- Select **San Francisco International (SFO)** and set it as your **arrival**.

That's it. The simulator automatically creates a flight plan for you.

At the top of the screen, you'll see the route details:

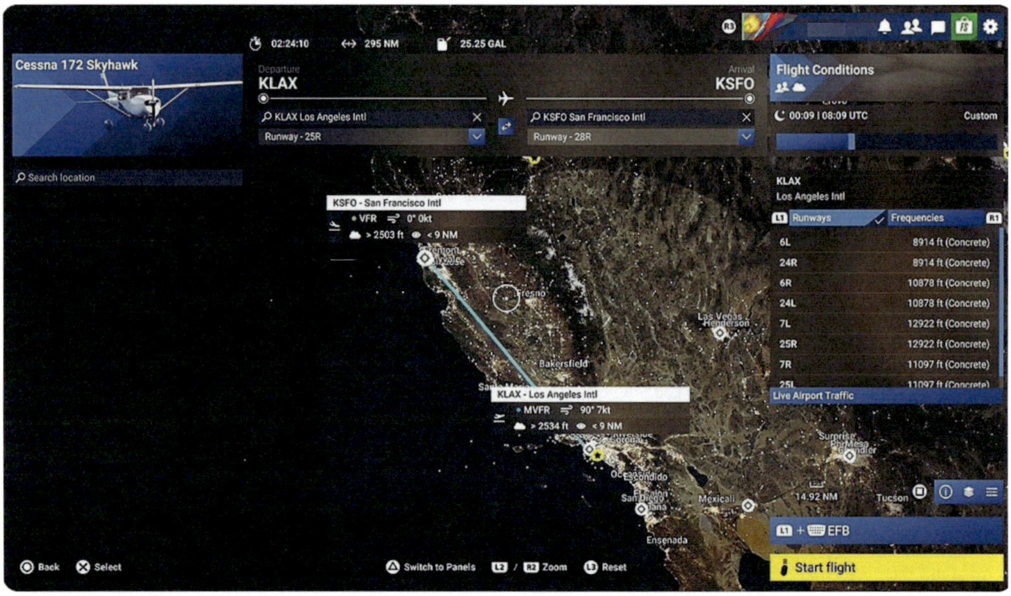

- **Flight time:** Approximately 2 hours and 24 minutes
- **Distance:** 295 miles

This method is straightforward and ideal if you just want to fly without worrying about advanced setup.

Important Note About Runway Spawns

When you create a flight plan by simply clicking airport icons, the simulator **spawns you directly on the runway**, fully powered and ready for takeoff.

This means:

- No cold-and-dark start
- No gate or parking setup

If you prefer realistic procedures, this method won't be ideal.

Changing Your Spawn Location (Runway, Gate, or Parking)

Before resetting the flight plan:

1. Press **Triangle** to highlight the top menu.
2. Move right to the **dropdown menu**.
3. From here, you can select a different runway, gate, or parking position.

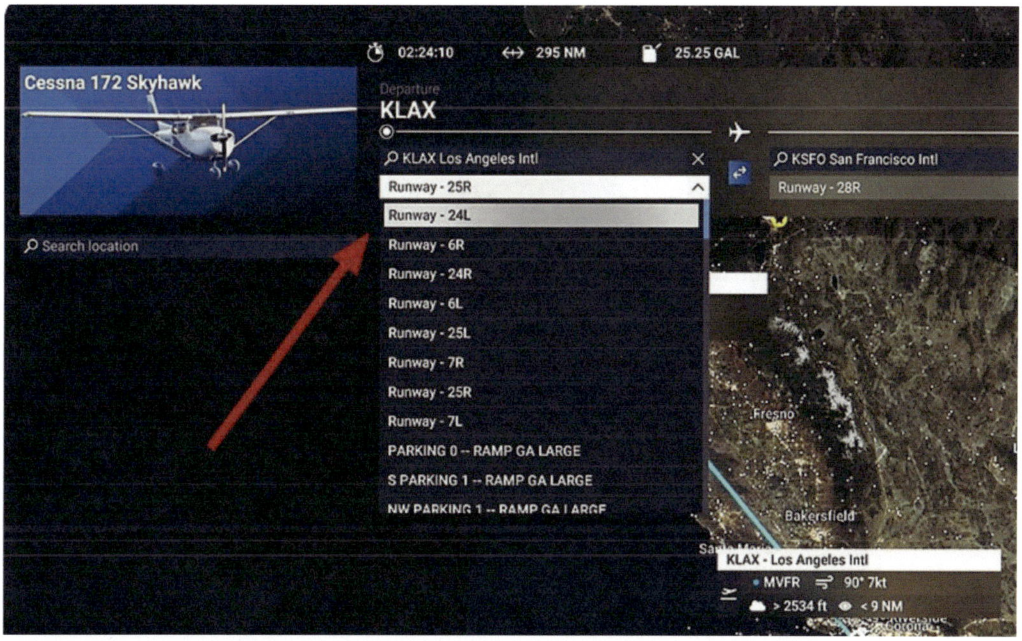

This works well at smaller airports, but at large airports like LAX, the list can be long and inconvenient to scroll through.

Spawning Cold and Dark at a Gate (Recommended)

A better method is to:

1. **Reset the flight plan** (left click on the left stick)

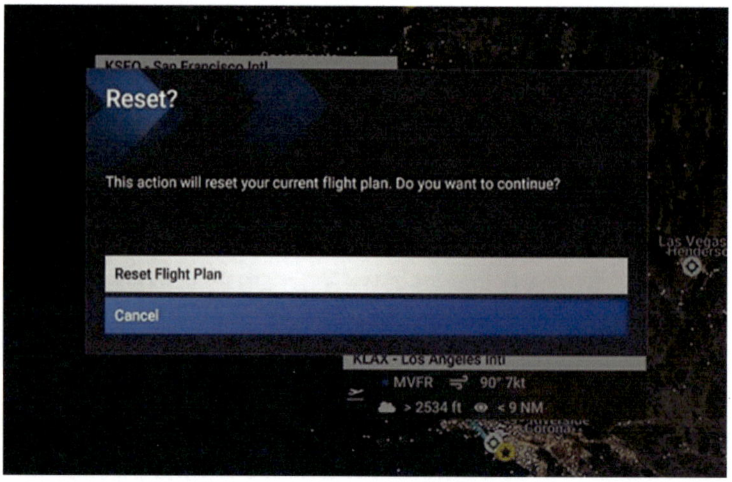

2. Zoom in closely on the departure airport.
3. As you zoom in, you'll see **multiple dots** appear. These represent gates and parking spots.
4. Select a gate or parking position (for example, **Parking 202D**).

5. Set it as your **departure**.

Now, instead of spawning on the runway, you'll start **cold and dark at the gate**, ready to perform a full startup sequence.

Custom Spawn Locations Anywhere in the World

You're not limited to airports:

- Click anywhere on the map, such as a desert, field, or forest.
- Set that location as your departure.

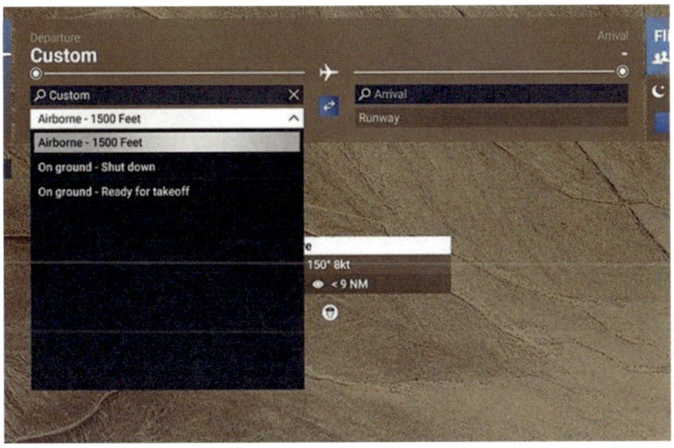

From there, you can choose:

- **Spawn in the air**
- **On the ground, engines off**
- **On the ground, ready for takeoff**

This is especially useful for:

- Bush flying
- Exploring remote areas
- Custom scenic flights

Just remember to use the **dropdown menu**, because the default option is always to spawn in the air.

Arrival Airport Setup

For arrivals, you can simply select the airport icon and set it as your destination. Once you land, **ATC will automatically assign you a gate or parking location**, so there's no need to manually choose one in advance.

In the end, the specific setting doesn't really matter. One major advantage of using this quick flight-planning method is that the plan is **automatically loaded into the aircraft**. There's no additional setup required.

Once you spawn into the simulator, you'll see that the flight plan is already active. Inside the **Cessna 172**, the route you created is fully programmed and ready to go, showing the full **292-nautical-mile** journey. You can view it both on the navigation display and on the main screen.

That's all there is to it. Creating a basic flight plan in Microsoft Flight Simulator 2024 is fast, seamless, and requires virtually no extra steps.

Now that we've covered the basics, let's head back to the **World Map** and create a flight plan **from scratch** using the **Electronic Flight Bag (EFB)**.

Opening the EFB and Flight Planner

We'll plan a short flight from **Zurich (LSZH)** to a scenic lakeside airport at **Altenrhein (LSZR)**.

To get started, open the EFB by pressing **L1 + the touchpad**, then launch the **Flight Planner app**.

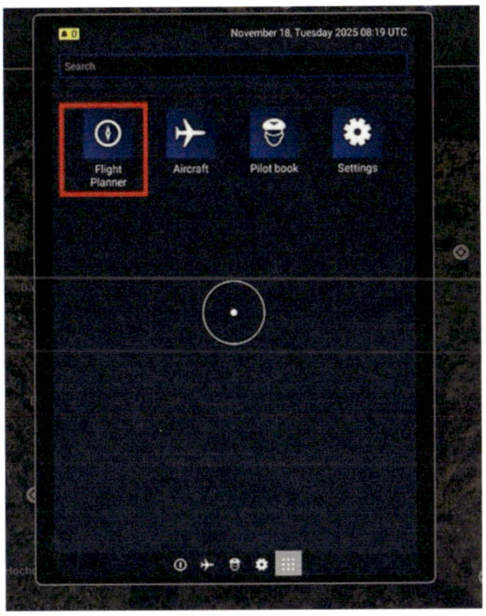

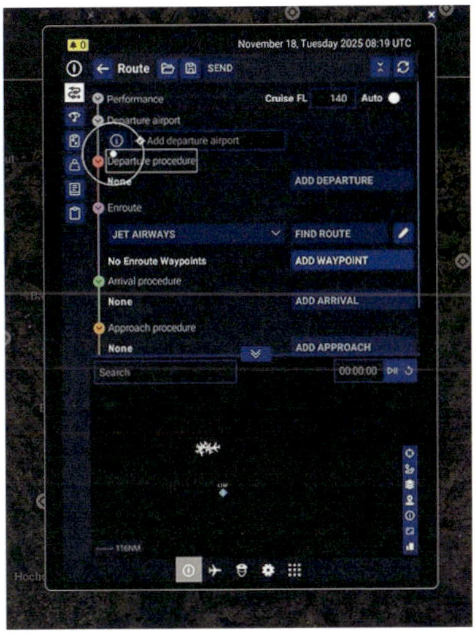

Once inside, close the map view so you can clearly see the **Route page**. This is the core of flight planning. From here, you can:

- Set **departure and arrival airports**
- Choose **departure, arrival, and approach procedures**
- Add **waypoints**
- Manage **altitudes and speeds**

Exploring the EFB Tabs

Across the top, you'll notice several useful tabs:

- **Performance**: Aircraft performance data
- **Flight Details**: Route overview and summary
- **Payload & Fuel**: Weight and balance setup
- **Navigation Log**: Distance tracking, stopwatch, and leg-by-leg details
- **Charts**: Automatically clipped airport and procedure charts

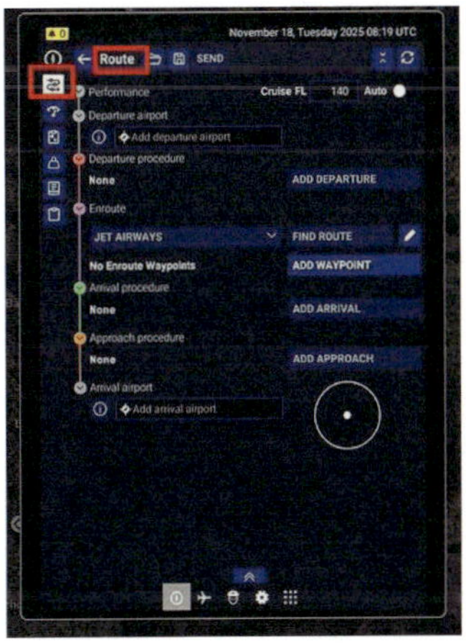

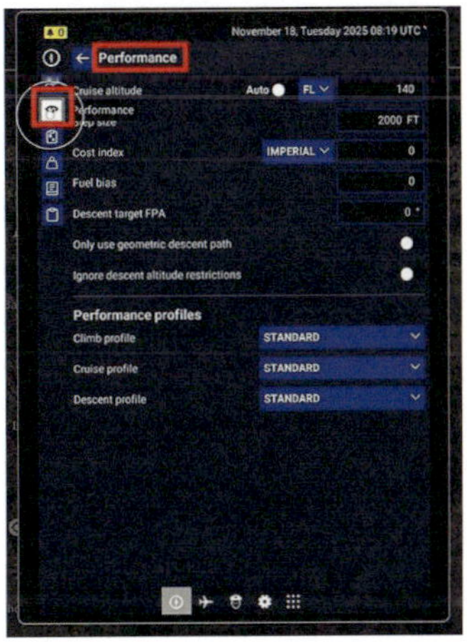

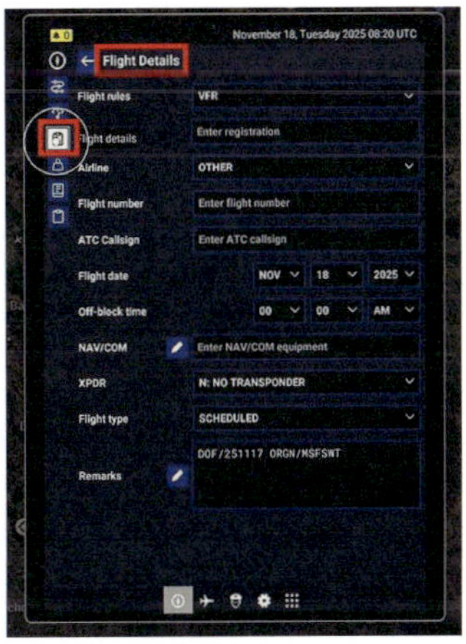

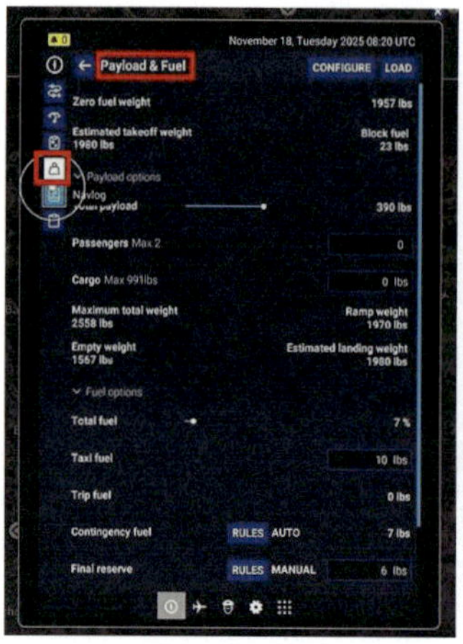

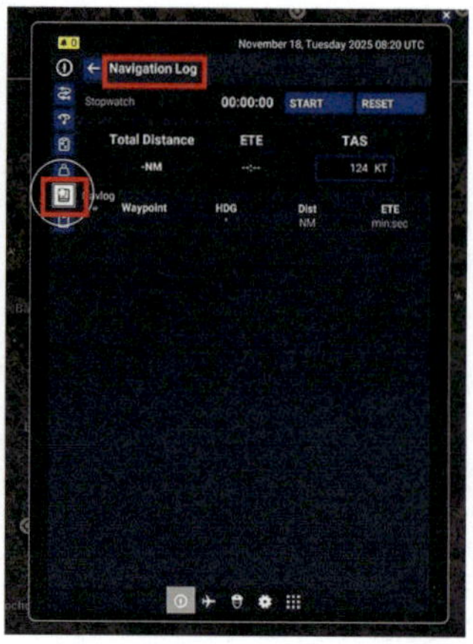

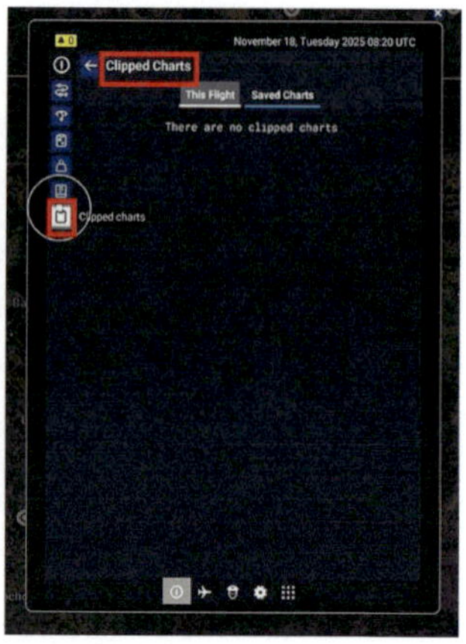

Once your departure and arrival airports are set, any available charts are automatically added here, especially if you select specific procedures. This gives you quick, in-sim access to critical information.

You can also customize the EFB itself. From the settings, you can:

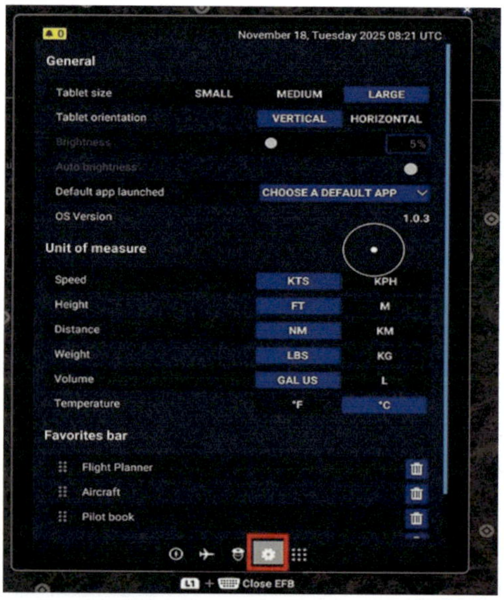

- Change **units of measurement** (knots, km/h, feet, meters, kilograms, liters, etc.)
- Adjust the **tablet size**
- Switch between **vertical or horizontal** orientation
  For this example, we'll keep the tablet vertical.

Setting the Departure Airport

Let's enter **Zurich (LSZH)** as our departure. As soon as you do, several options become available:

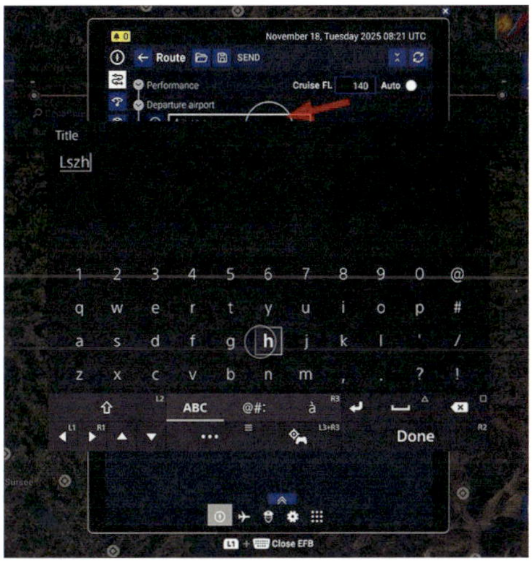

- Select your **departure runway**
- Add a **SID (departure procedure)** if desired
- Access quick airport information

This airport info panel includes:

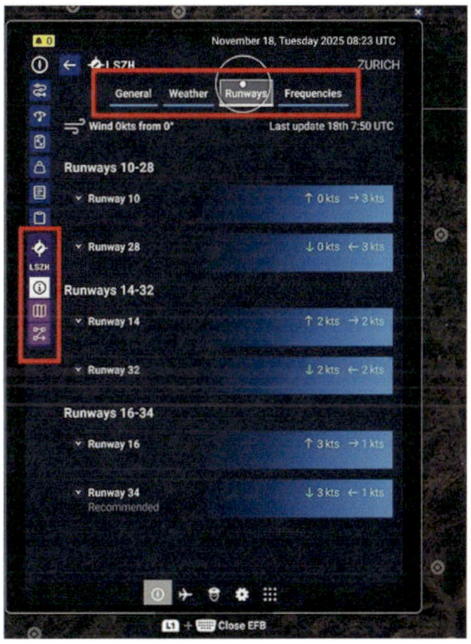

- General airport details
- Current **weather**
- **Runway data** and wind conditions
- **Radio frequencies** for ground, tower, and approach

Using Built-In Charts

Below the info tab is the **Charts** section. Here you'll find:

- Airport diagrams

- Taxi and parking charts
- Departure, arrival, and approach procedures
- Miscellaneous charts

For example, opening the **airport ground chart** shows all taxiways and radio frequencies.

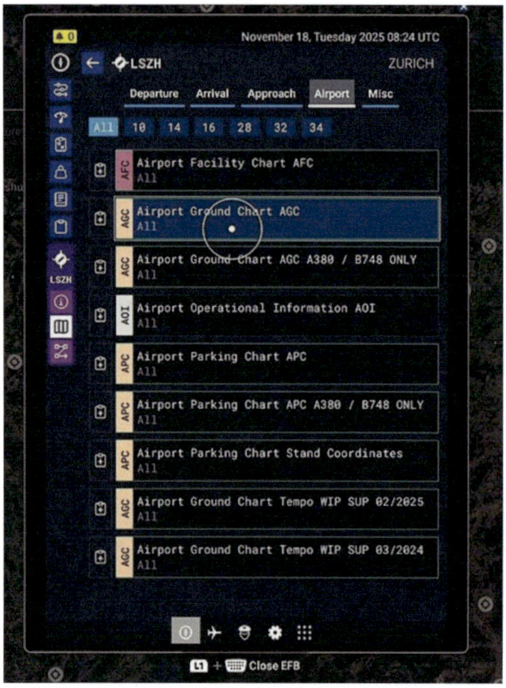

The **parking chart** displays gate numbers and concourses, making taxi planning much easier. The fact that all of this is included directly in the sim, without subscriptions or extra costs, is a huge advantage.

You can also view **airport procedures**, select a runway (such as Runway 10), and instantly see the highlighted taxi and routing paths. Switching runways updates the visuals automatically.

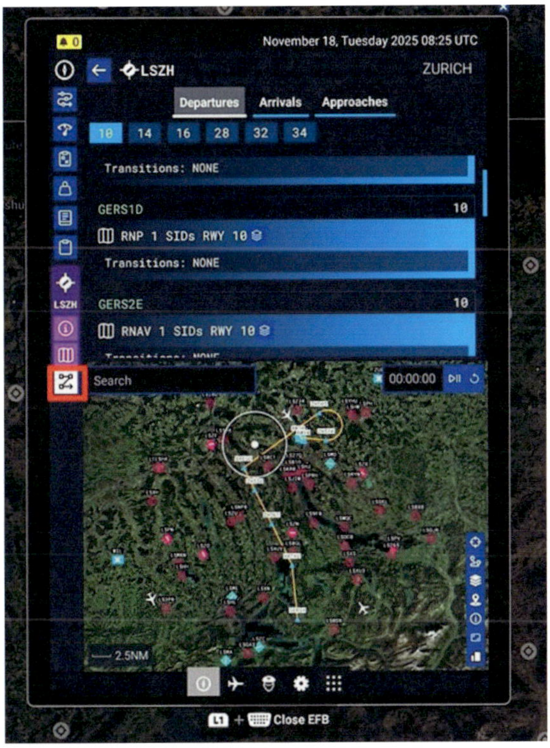

Automation and Ease of Use

One standout feature is the **Auto** option. Since the sim knows which aircraft you're flying—in this case, the **Cessna 172 Skyhawk**—it can automatically assign appropriate altitudes and profiles based on the aircraft's performance and ceiling. If you don't want to manually fine-tune everything, Auto handles it smoothly.

Overall, the EFB flight planner is incredibly flexible. You can keep things simple for a quick hop or dive deep into procedures and charts for a highly realistic experience. With that overview complete, we're back on the **Route page**, ready to finish building the flight.

Completing the Flight Plan in the EFB

Next, we'll add our **arrival airport**. With both the **departure and arrival airports** now set, we can finish building the route.

Adding Procedures

At this point, we can start adding procedures. I don't usually rely heavily on them, but for demonstration purposes, it's worth showing how they work. We'll add a

departure procedure, and as soon as we do, the planner nicely aligns the route toward our destination.

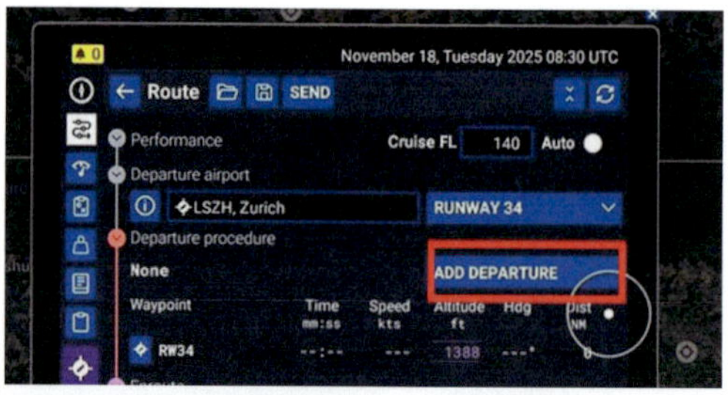

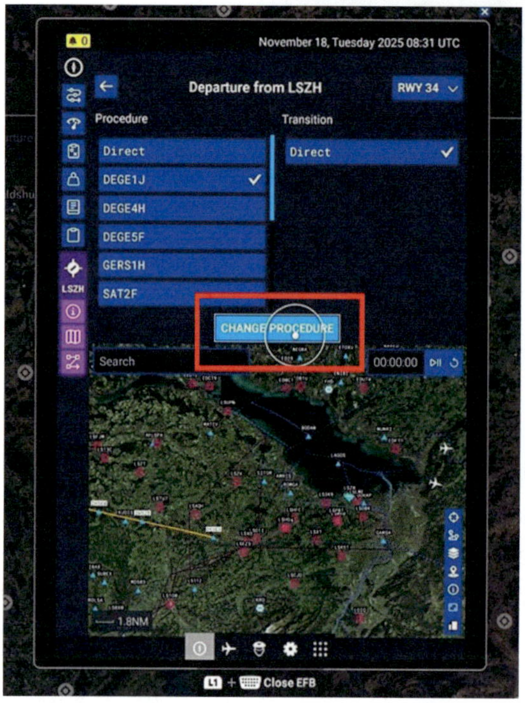

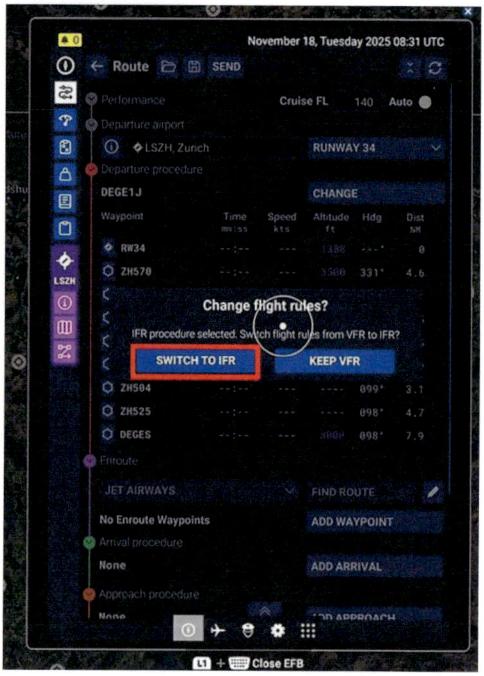

An **IFR procedure** is available, so we'll select that. Everything looks good so far, and we're already more than halfway toward the destination on the map.

Adding Custom Waypoints

From here, you have two main options:

1. Let the sim handle everything with procedures, or
2. Manually add your own waypoints for a more customized flight.

We'll add a waypoint to avoid flying straight into the airport. Let's choose **FILZE (Foxtrot India Lima Zulu Echo)** and insert it into the route. You can keep adding waypoints like this to shape your flight however you like.

Setting Up the Approach

Next, we'll look at the **approach options**. The planner already assumes we're landing on **Runway 10**, which is helpful. While there are several routing and VFR pattern options available, we'll go with an **approach procedure** that best aligns us with the runway.

To fine-tune the alignment, we'll add one final waypoint: **AMRIS (Alpha Mike Romeo India Sierra)**. Once added, the route lines us up perfectly with Runway 10. At this point, we have a clean, logical, and scenic flight plan.

This is generally how I like to plan flights: build a custom route, enjoy the scenery with hand-picked waypoints, and then smoothly transition into the final approach.

Adjusting Cruise Altitude

Before saving the plan, let's adjust the **cruise flight level**. It's important to understand how flight levels work:

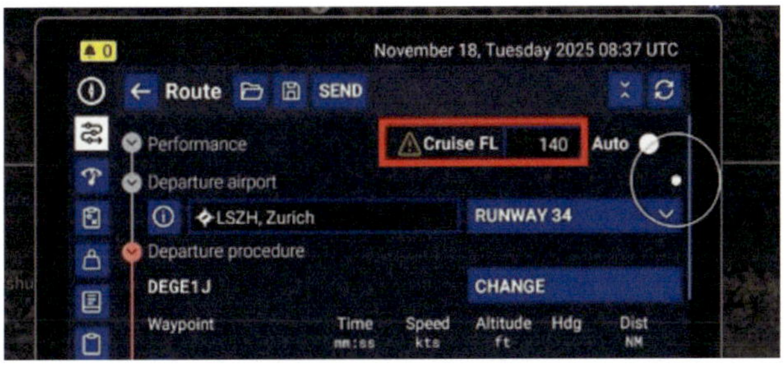

- **FL140** means 14,000 feet, not 140 or 1,400.
- **FL350** would be 35,000 feet.

For this flight, we'll set **FL080**, which equals **8,000 feet**. Once entered, the planner updates automatically. The aircraft will climb to 8,000 feet, then begin descending as we approach Altenrhein. The airport elevation is also visible in the flight details, which helps with descent planning.

Final Check

With everything set, the flight plan is complete. It's simple, well-structured, and exactly what we want. I'm happy with it—and yes, this one is definitely getting saved.

Saving, Loading, and Using Flight Plans in MSFS 2024

Once the flight plan is complete, it's a good idea to **save it for future use**. To do this, select the **Save** icon and choose **Save as Plan File**.

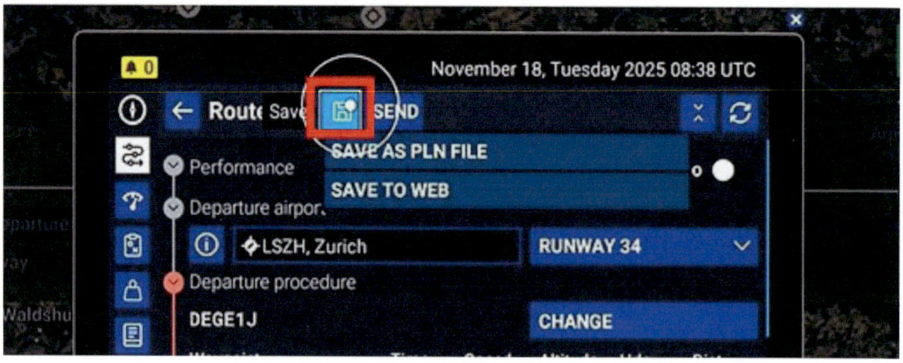

You'll also notice an option to **Save to Web**. This feature is tied to Microsoft's online flight planner (planner.flightsimulator.com), which allows users to create flight plans outside the sim and load them later. While this isn't currently usable on PlayStation, it's a promising feature that may become available in the future.

For now, we'll save the plan locally. Name it something recognizable, such as **ZurichFlight**, and confirm. The flight plan is now stored and can be reused anytime, regardless of which aircraft you choose.

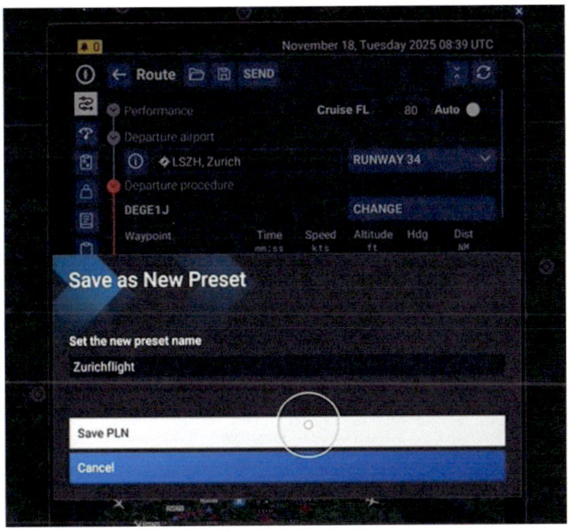

Reloading a Saved Flight Plan

To demonstrate, reset the flight and select **Import → Load Plan File**. Choose *ZurichFlight.pln* and confirm. Instantly, the entire route, including waypoints, altitude, and procedures, is restored exactly as before.

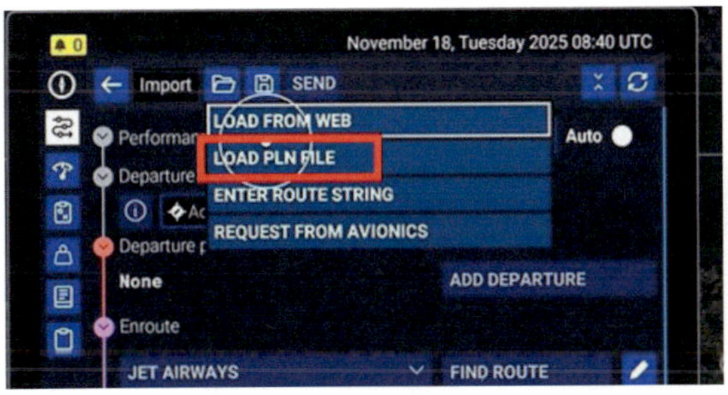

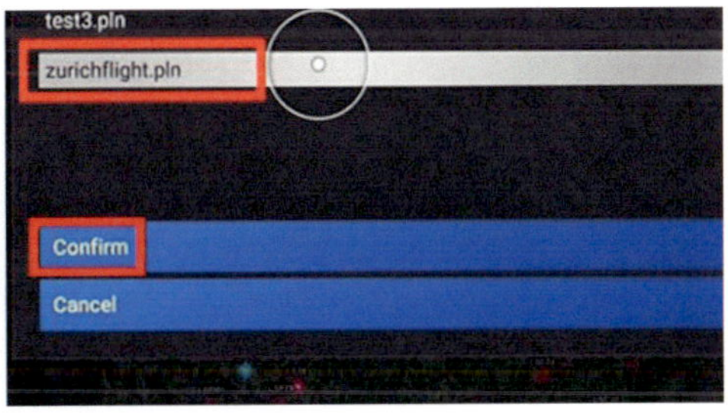

Sending the Plan to ATC and the Aircraft

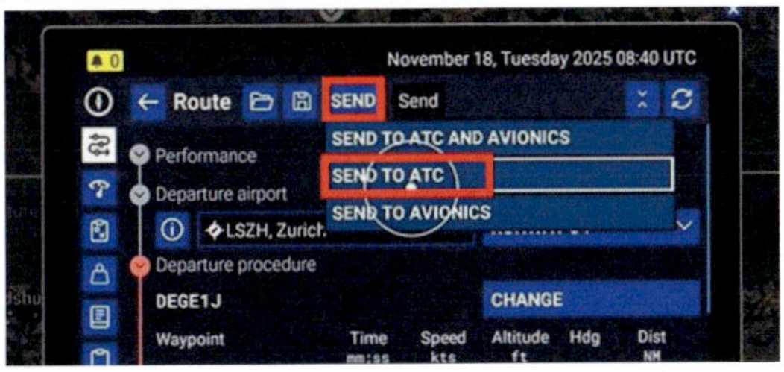

With the plan loaded, send it to **ATC**. You'll notice the world map updates immediately. Close the EFB, and you'll now see a **36-minute flight** from Zurich to Altenrhein in the Cessna 172, complete with all waypoints.

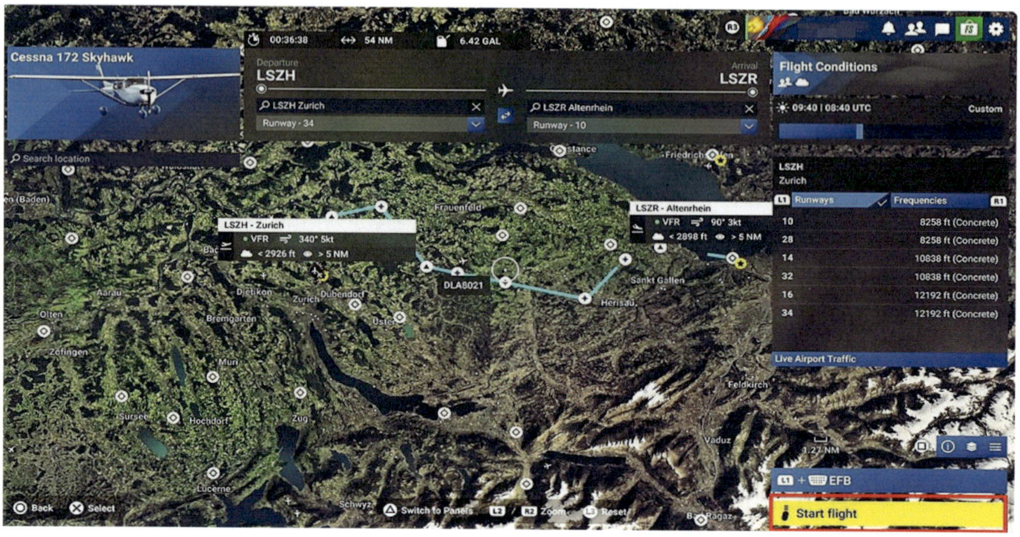

Start the flight, and once inside the cockpit, you'll see the **flight plan already loaded into the avionics**. In rare cases where it doesn't appear automatically, simply open the EFB again and select **Send → Send to Avionics**, and it will populate instantly.

With the flight plan active:

- Cruise altitude is already set to **8,000 feet**
- **NAV mode** is armed
- Engaging the autopilot will guide the aircraft along the entire route

At this point, everything is ready to go.

Airline-Style Flight Planning with Jet Airways

One of the most impressive features of the EFB is how it simplifies **airliner flight planning**. Open the Flight Planner again and enter:

- Departure: **EGSS**
- Arrival: **LXGB (Gibraltar)**

Instead of manually building the route, enable **Jet Airways** and press **Find Route**. In seconds, the sim automatically generates:

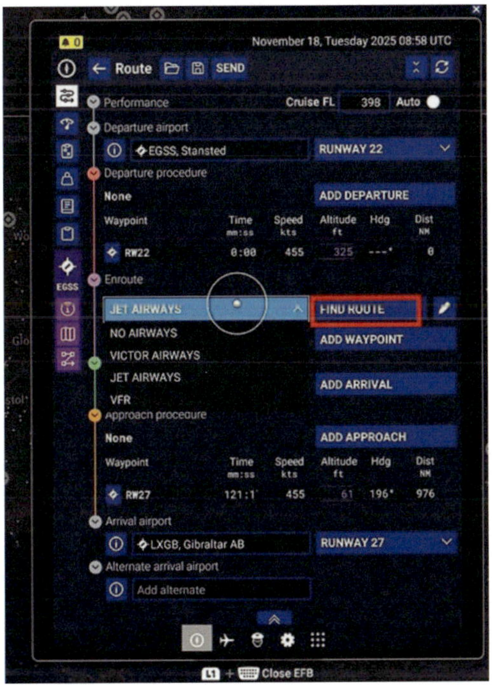

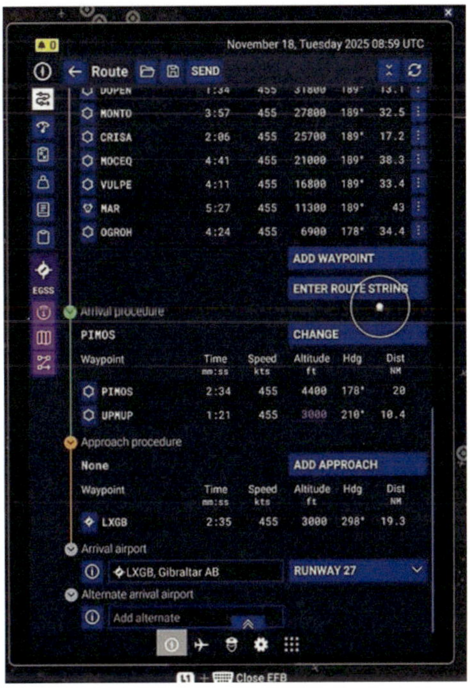

- Departure procedures
- Enroute waypoints
- Assigned cruise altitudes
- Arrival and approach procedures

All of this is done with a single button press. The complete airline-style route appears instantly on the map, including altitude constraints and terminal procedures.

If desired, send the plan directly to **ATC and avionics**, close the EFB, and the fully built flight is ready to fly.

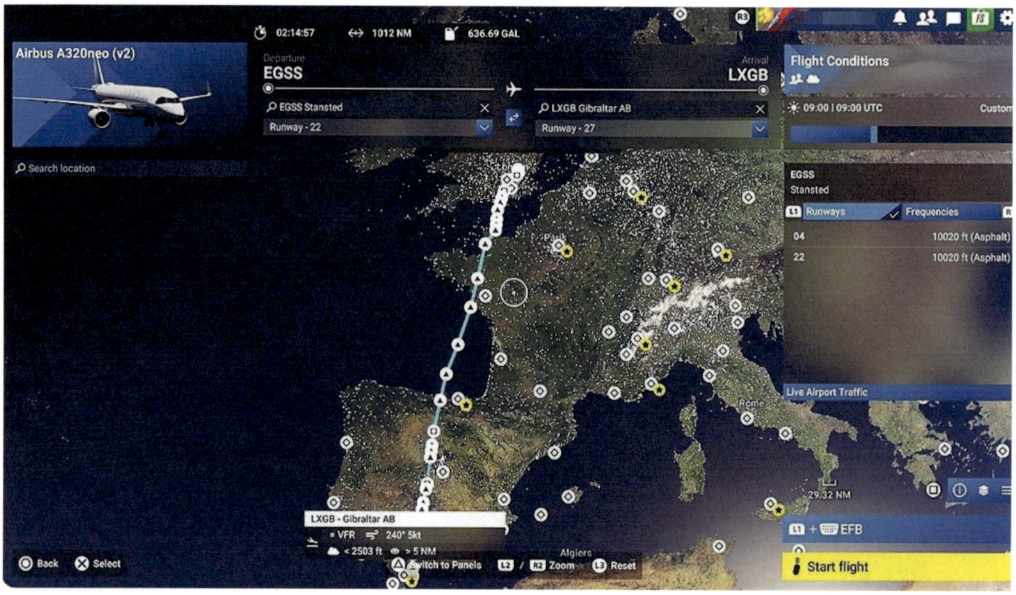

Final Thoughts

MSFS 2024 offers incredible flexibility in flight planning. You can:

- Create quick, simple routes in seconds
- Build detailed, custom plans waypoint by waypoint
- Instantly generate realistic airline routes using Jet Airways
- Save and reuse plans across any aircraft

Whether you want to jump in and fly quickly or meticulously plan every phase of flight, the tools are all there—powerful, intuitive, and impressively streamlined.

CHAPTER TWELVE

USING ATC AND GROUND SERVICES IN MICROSOFT FLIGHT SIMULATOR 2024 (PS5)

This section walks you through how to communicate with **ATC** and use **ground services** in Microsoft Flight Simulator 2024 on PS5, including pushback, fueling, catering, baggage handling, jetways, and passenger boarding.

USING ATC AND GROUND SERVICES

Although this demonstration uses a **Boeing 737 in Alaska Airlines livery**, everything shown here works with **any aircraft** in the simulator.

Opening the ATC Menu

Once your aircraft is powered on and parked at the gate:

1. Press **R1 + Left Analog Stick** to activate **cursor mode**.
2. Move the cursor to the **toolbar** at the top of the screen.
3. Select the **communications (messenger) icon** using **X**.

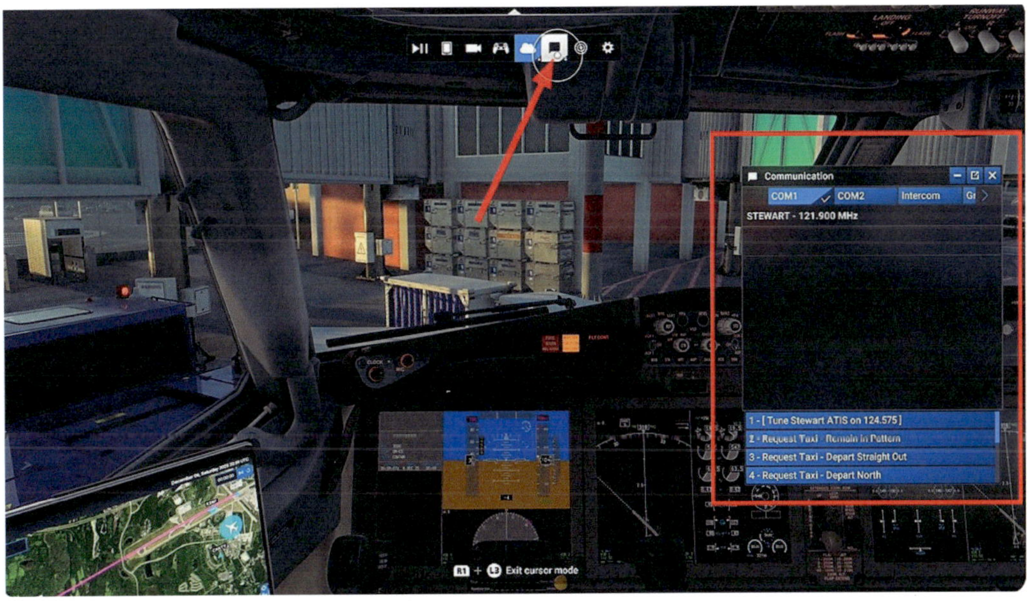

This opens the **ATC communication window**, where all radio interactions take place. While cursor mode is used here, there are other methods to access ATC, which will be covered later.

Listening to Weather Information (ATIS)

If you want airport weather and runway details, tune into **ATIS**.

ATIS continuously broadcasts information such as: Wind direction and speed, Visibility, Cloud cover, Temperature and dew point, Altimeter setting, Active runways and ILS approaches

Keep in mind: ATIS will **repeat endlessly** until you change frequencies. If it starts automatically when you spawn, simply open the ATC menu and switch to a different radio frequency.

Core ATC Ground Options

From the main ATC menu on the ground, you can:

- Request **taxi clearance**
- Remain in the **traffic pattern** (useful for touch-and-go practice)
- Request **departure clearance** based on your flight direction
- Access **ground services**, which is the focus here

Ground Services Explained

Select **Ground Services** from the ATC menu to access the following options:

- Pushback
- Fuel supply
- External power
- Passenger boarding
- Baggage service
- Catering service

Each service dispatches vehicles dynamically from around the airport rather than spawning instantly.

Requesting Fuel

Fuel trucks must physically drive to your aircraft:

1. Select **Request Fuel Supply**.

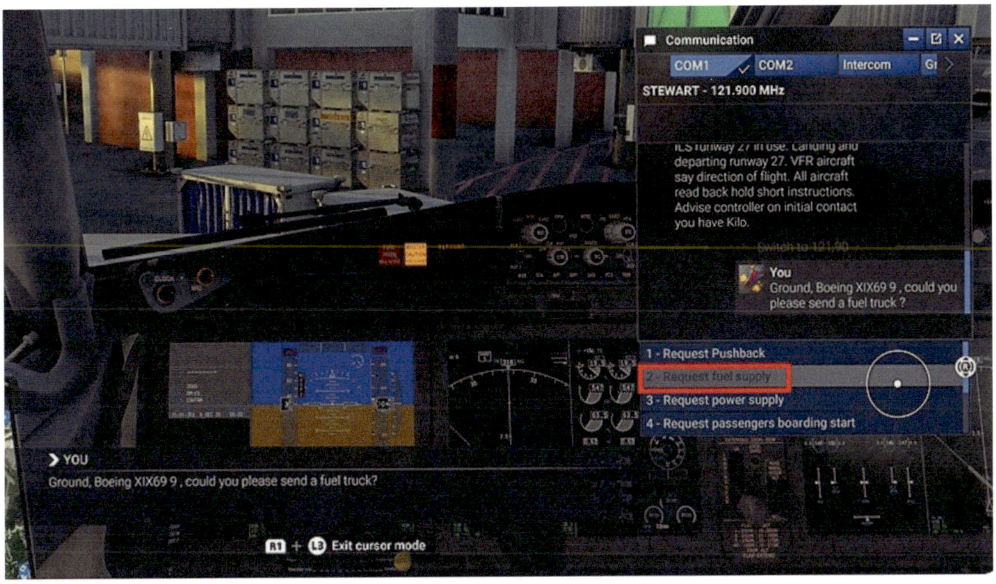

2. ATC confirms the request.
3. The fuel truck arrives after a short delay.

This adds realism and immersion, especially at larger airports.

Connecting the Jetway & Boarding Passengers

Next, request **Passenger Boarding**. When you do:

- ATC confirms the request
- The **jetway automatically connects**

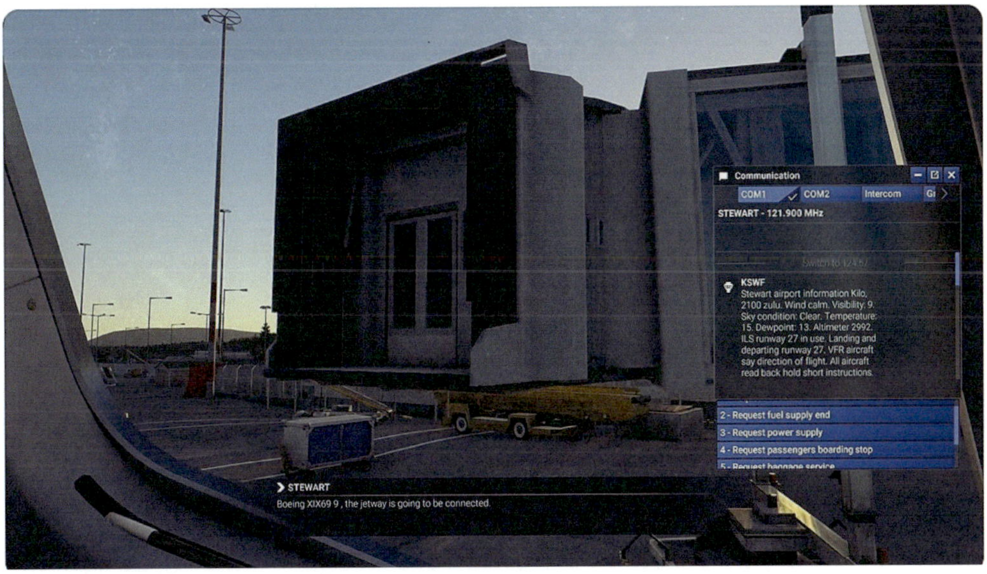

- Passenger boarding begins

Surprisingly, passengers are **fully animated**, walking through the jetway into the aircraft—something many players assume only exists in Career Mode. This works in **Free Flight** as well.

Enabling Passenger Boarding (Important Setup)

To see passengers board, you must configure them **before loading into the flight**:

1. Open the **Electronic Flight Bag (EFB)** with **L1 + Touchpad**
2. Go to:
   - **Aircraft**
   - **Flight Performance**
   - **Mass & Balance**
3. Under **Seats**, use **Quick Fill**
   - Example: 50–55% passenger load
4. Save the configuration

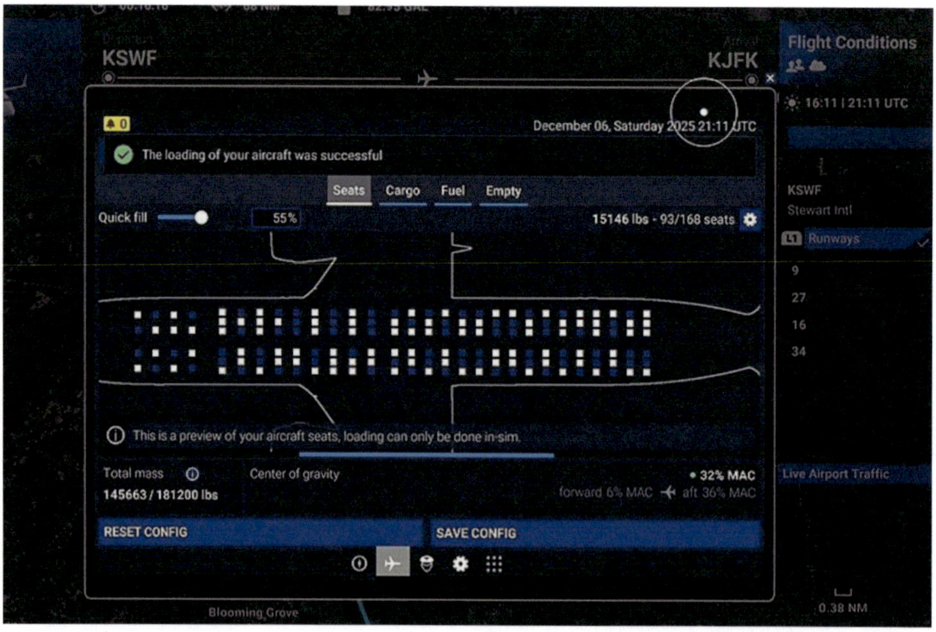

Once this is done, connecting the jetway triggers animated boarding automatically.

Passenger Boarding and Fueling in Action

Seeing **animated passengers walking through the jetway** is honestly surprising—and very cool. While boarding continues, the **fuel truck arrives**, connects to the aircraft, and shortly after, a **fuel management window** appears. Perfect timing.

What's especially impressive is that boarding doesn't pause during fueling. You can track the entire boarding process directly in the **EFB**, watching the seat indicators gradually fill. After countless hours in Free Flight, this was the first time seeing it fully animated—and it's a great immersion boost.

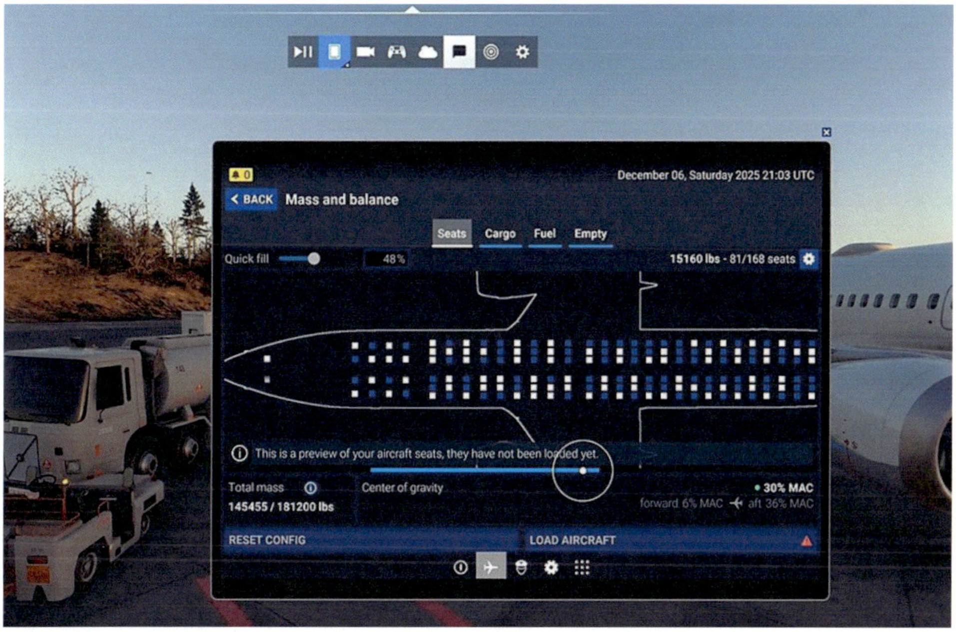

Refueling via the Fuel Truck

Once the fuel truck is connected:

1. Open the **EFB**
2. Select **Fuel**
3. Adjust the fuel quantity as desired

One important note: **engines must be shut down** for fueling to work properly. If the aircraft is powered on, the fuel options may not appear.

After shutting down the engines, the fuel truck completes its positioning. Even if it looks a little confused at first, it eventually connects correctly. In aircraft like the **Cessna 172**, you can actually see the **fuel hose connected to the wing**, which is a fantastic visual detail.

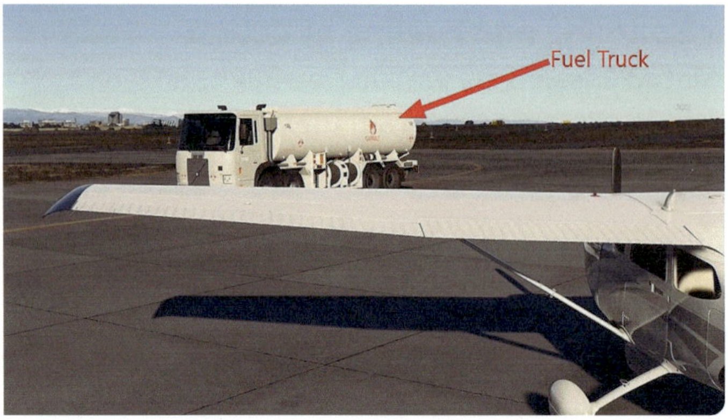

You can then set a specific fuel load—say **70% fuel**—and choose **Load Immediately**. Once fueling is complete, the truck disconnects and drives away automatically.

All the Ways to Refuel in MSFS 2024

Microsoft Flight Simulator 2024 gives you **three different refueling options**:

1. **Directly through the EFB**
   - Fastest and simplest method.
2. **Via ATC-requested fuel truck**
   - Fully animated and immersive.

3. **Using on-airport fuel stations**
   - Available even at very small airports.

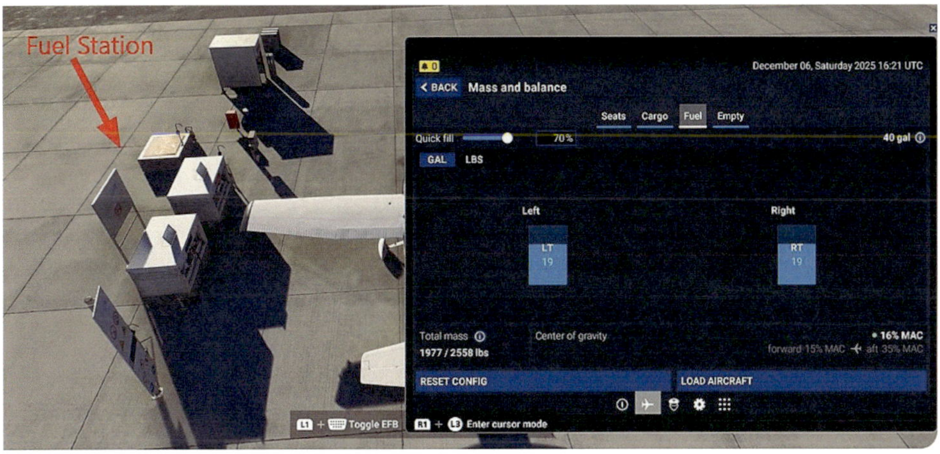

When parked near a fuel station, the refueling menu pops up automatically. You can shut down the aircraft if needed and refuel instantly—no ATC interaction required.

Wrapping Up Ground Operations

Once passenger boarding is complete:

1. Open the **ATC menu**

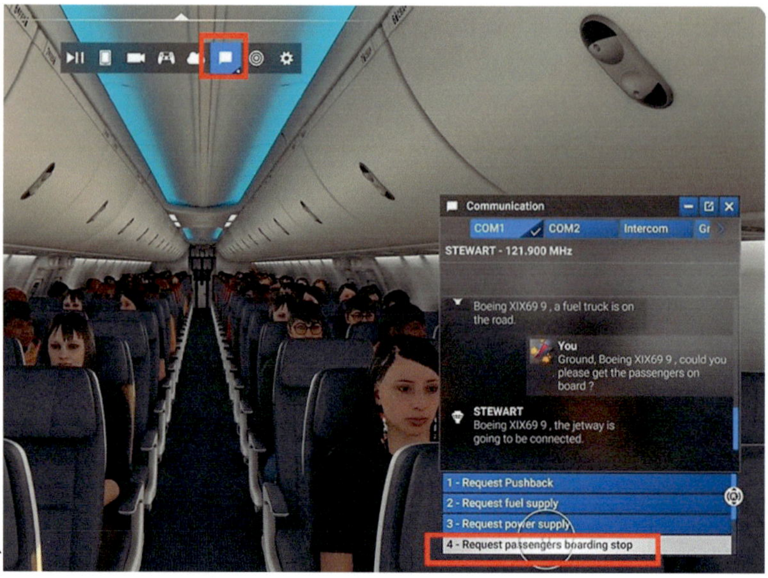

2. Select **Stop Passenger Boarding**
3. Request the **jetway to disconnect**

The jetway retracts and resets, clearing the aircraft for pushback or taxi. Occasionally, minor visual quirks occur, but nothing that affects functionality.

Catering, Baggage, and Pushback Operations

The last ground services worth showcasing are the **catering truck** and **baggage handling**, both of which are now fully animated and surprisingly detailed.

To start catering, you can request it through ATC:

"Ground, Boeing X-Ray India X-Ray 699, request catering."

"Boeing X-Ray India X-Ray 699, catering truck is on the way."

Moments later, the catering truck arrives and deploys its **scissor lift**, aligning perfectly with the aircraft door. It's a small detail, but the animation adds a lot of realism to the turnaround process.

Next up is baggage service:

"Ground, Boeing X-Ray India X-Ray 699, request baggage."

"Boeing X-Ray India X-Ray 699, baggage service on the way."

From here, you can watch baggage being **loaded directly into the cargo hold**. This animation is consistent across aircraft types—including the **737, 747, and Airbus family**—and it's genuinely impressive to see it play out in real time.

What's even better is that the cargo hold is no longer empty. You can actually see items inside, which is a first for many of us. Normally, these compartments are completely blank, but once passengers and baggage are properly loaded, the aircraft finally looks and feels "alive."

At this point, everything is ready:

- Passengers are on board
- Fueling is complete
- Baggage is loaded
- Catering is done (or, at least, the classic half-bag of peanuts)

Requesting Pushback

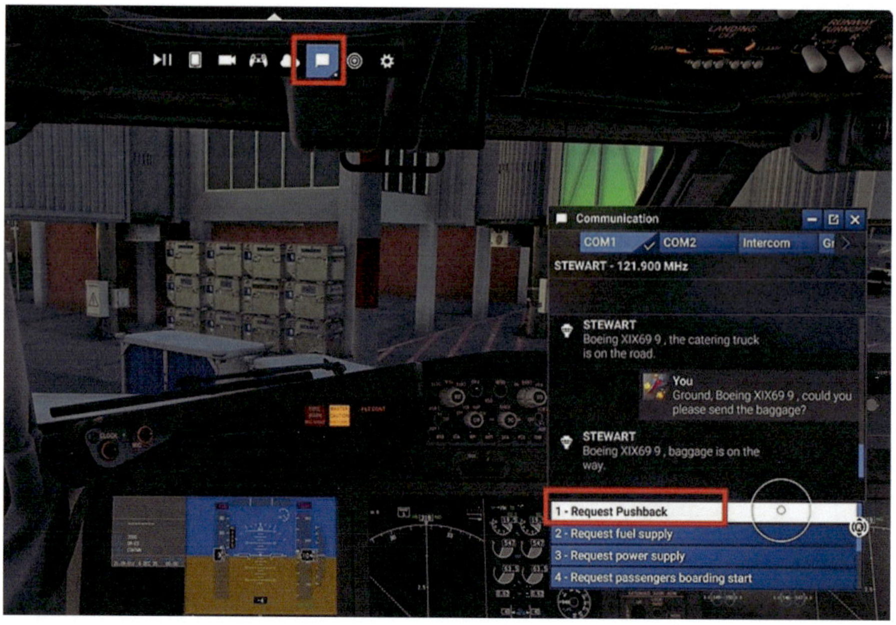

With ground services complete, the final step is **pushback**.

"Ground, X-Ray India X-Ray 699, requesting pushback."

"Boeing X-Ray India X-Ray 699, pushback request accepted."

Before pushback begins, it's critical to:

- **Release the parking brake**
- **Confirm all wheel chocks are removed**

If you miss either step, the tug won't move you—and you'll just sit there in a very awkward stalemate.

Once connected, you can open the pushback window. During pushback, you have the ability to:

- Steer left or right
- Request a stop at any time

Most of the time, you won't need to intervene—the ground crew usually positions the aircraft correctly and stops at the right location. Occasionally, things get a little... enthusiastic (maybe a gentle bump into nearby stairs), but overall, it works well.

Toggle Pushback (No ATC, No Tug)

One extra feature that's incredibly useful is **Toggle Pushback**, especially if:

- ATC is unavailable
- A pushback tug doesn't spawn
- You just want a quick, hassle-free solution

To enable it:

1. Pause the sim
2. Go to **Settings → Controls**

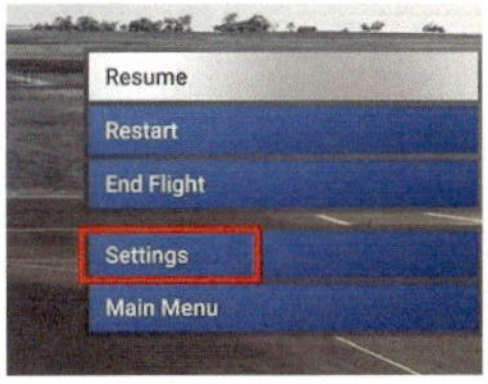

3. Search for **Pushback**
4. Assign a keybind to **Toggle Pushback**

Once mapped, activating it will **push the aircraft back invisibly**—no ATC interaction, no tug required.

For this setup, the command is bound to **Triangle + Up on the D-Pad**, though you can assign any control you prefer. Activating it instantly moves the aircraft back, and pressing the same command again stops the pushback.

This method works with **any aircraft**, including taildraggers, and is especially helpful when parked too close to buildings or in tight spaces.

Switching to the PC-12 and Pattern Operations

For the remainder of this section, we'll be flying the **PC-12**. I didn't want to stay in an airliner the entire time—I mainly wanted to showcase ground services and some of the newer features. Now, we'll shift focus to **ATC and pattern operations**.

The plan is simple:

- Take off
- Fly a traffic pattern
- Perform a go-around
- Land back at the same airport

This lets us explore more ATC interactions without committing to a full departure.

Accessing ATC Without Cursor Mode

This time, we won't rely on the traditional cursor method using **R1 + left stick**. Instead, we'll access ATC by **holding left on the D-pad**, which quickly opens the Communications tab.

Before we go any further, let's set the **parking brake**.

Even with the D-pad shortcut, you'll still need cursor mode—or a **mouse**, if you have one connected—for certain interactions. A mouse works especially well if you don't want to keep toggling cursor mode with the DualSense controller.

Requesting Taxi Clearance (Pattern Flight)

With the mouse active, let's contact ground and request taxi clearance. Since we're staying in the **traffic pattern**, ATC understands that we'll be operating locally rather than departing the area.

"Ground, Charlie Oscar Whiskey Tango Whiskey November, with Sierra, request taxi to the active, closed traffic."

"Charlie Oscar Whiskey Tango Whiskey November, taxi to and hold short of the runway via Taxiways Lima, Kilo, Alpha. Contact Tower on 12 when ready."

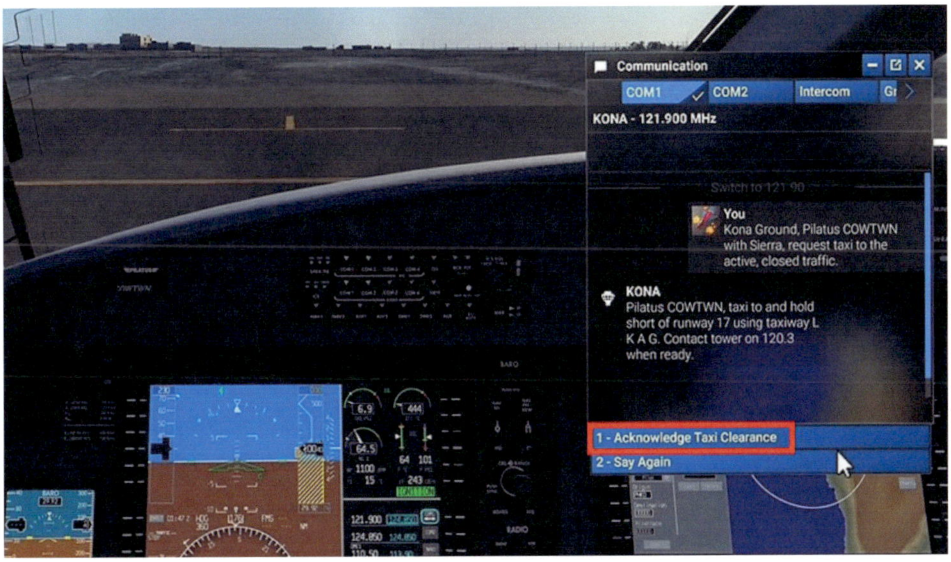

We acknowledge the clearance and begin taxiing as instructed.

Using the Taxi Ribbon Assist

If you have **Taxi Ribbon Assist** enabled—as I do—you'll immediately see the highlighted taxi path that matches ATC's instructions. This is incredibly useful, especially in **Career Mode**, and helps prevent wrong turns at unfamiliar airports.

You can:

- **Left-click the stick** to temporarily hide the ribbon
- Or permanently disable it by going to:
  Settings → Assistances → Visual Assistances → Taxi Ribbon

Other visual assists you can toggle here include:

- **Flight Path** (blue boxes in the sky from a flight plan)
- **Waypoint Markers**, which are mostly used in Career Mode

Taxiing and Traffic Awareness

As we taxi, you'll notice other aircraft appearing around the airport. It's great to see more and more live traffic populating the map—those green dots keep increasing as more players come online. And with additional editions releasing, airport activity is only going to get busier, especially on PlayStation.

Getting a Takeoff Clearance

Everything looks good, so let's open the **Communications tab**, tune in to the **tower**, and request **VFR takeoff clearance from Kona Tower**.

Tower responds with traffic information, so we acknowledge it. There's a **777 on approach**, but we'll be airborne and clear of the runway well before it becomes a factor. Once cleared:

- Parking brake released
- Gyro steering on

- A small amount of flaps set

And we roll.

Acceleration looks solid. At around **100 knots (V1)**, we're more than ready to lift off. Rotation is smooth, and we're airborne.

This puts us safely ahead of the **777 on final**, which is actually a great example of how **ATC interacts with AI traffic**. The system actively recognizes nearby aircraft and adjusts instructions accordingly. If traffic were closer, ATC would have delayed our takeoff until the runway was fully clear. Those little details add a lot to the realism.

We'll extend slightly on departure and fly a **simple traffic pattern**—nothing complicated. This video has already run long, but as always, I hope this walkthrough has been helpful for anyone learning how **ATC, ground services, and refueling** all work together in the sim.

Getting Copilot to respond to ATC

If you don't feel like handling **ATC communications manually every time**, there's a really useful feature built into the sim.

Pause the game, go to **Settings → Assistance**, and scroll all the way to the bottom. There you'll find **AI Radio Communications**. When this is enabled during free flight, your **AI co-pilot automatically handles ATC calls** for you—takeoff clearances, landing acknowledgments, frequency changes, and more. You still get full ATC functionality, just without constantly opening the menu.

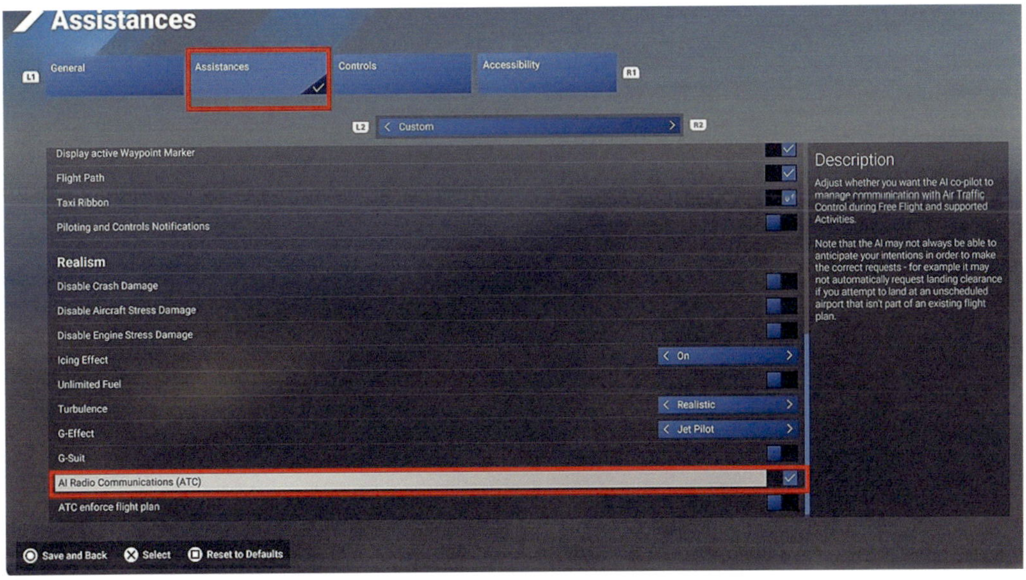

Let's turn it on and see how it works in real time.

As we continue around the pattern, ATC starts talking—but it cuts out briefly, likely due to other AI traffic on frequency. That happens occasionally. Normally, you shouldn't need to open the ATC window at all, but in this case, it looks like the system glitched, so I'll acknowledge it manually. A moment later, the AI co-pilot responds as expected.

This pretty much sums up ATC in the sim right now: **most of the time it works well, but it can be hit or miss**. Occasionally, especially in career mode, the quick-access ATC shortcut (left on the D-pad) doesn't register, and you'll need to open the full ATC window to move things along. Still, for the majority of flights, it functions smoothly.

There are also some promising improvements coming in future updates, with third-party ATC integrations reportedly in the works, which should make communications more reliable and realistic.

To demonstrate further, we'll perform another **touch-and-go** and let the AI co-pilot manage ATC responses automatically. Despite a few distractions from other players spawning nearby, everything works as intended.

This time, instead of another touch-and-go, we'll request a **full-stop landing**. Once again, the AI co-pilot handles the request and responds correctly when the tower issues landing clearance.

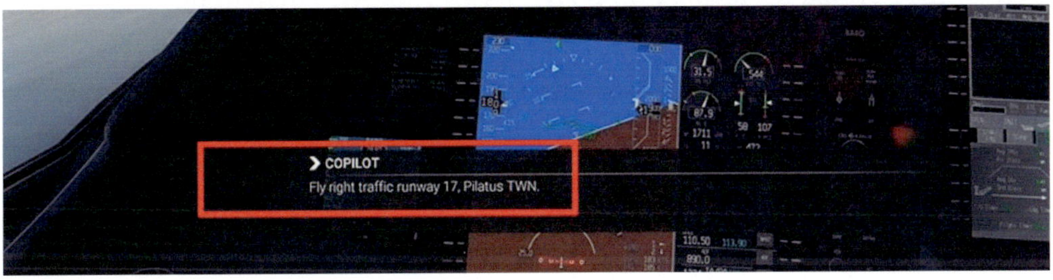

After touchdown, ATC provides taxi instructions and tells us to contact ground—and, just as expected, the AI co-pilot takes care of that communication too.

Overall, if you want ATC realism without constant menu interaction, **AI Radio Communications is a fantastic quality-of-life feature**, especially during longer or more relaxed flights.

Getting Taxi to Parking

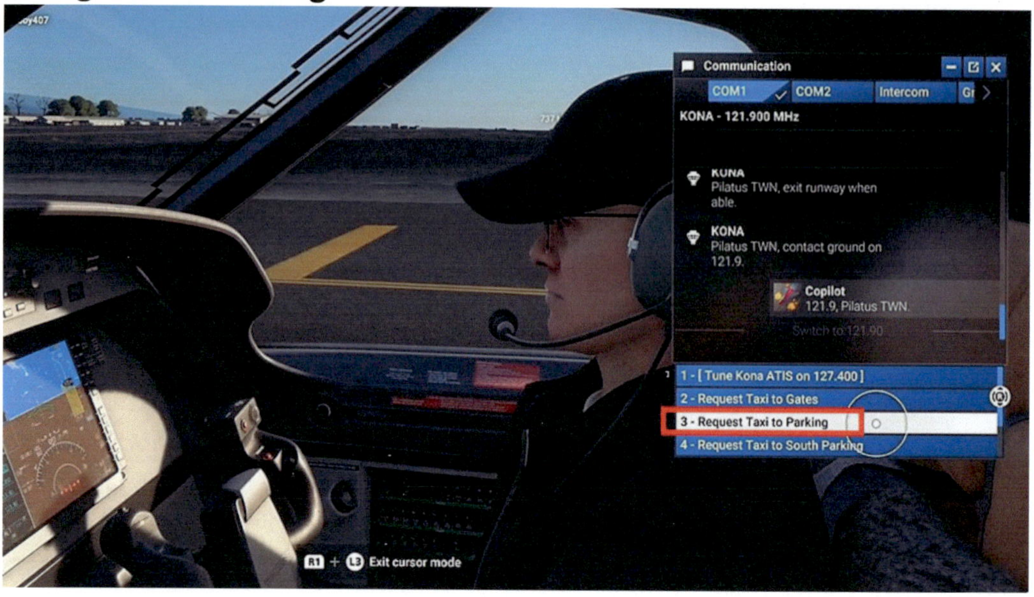

At this point, we *should* receive taxi clearance to parking automatically—but no luck. So, I'll handle it manually.

We request taxi to parking, and ATC responds with instructions to taxi to **General Aviation parking via Taxiway Hotel**. From here, the AI co-pilot steps back in and acknowledges the clearance for us—perfect.

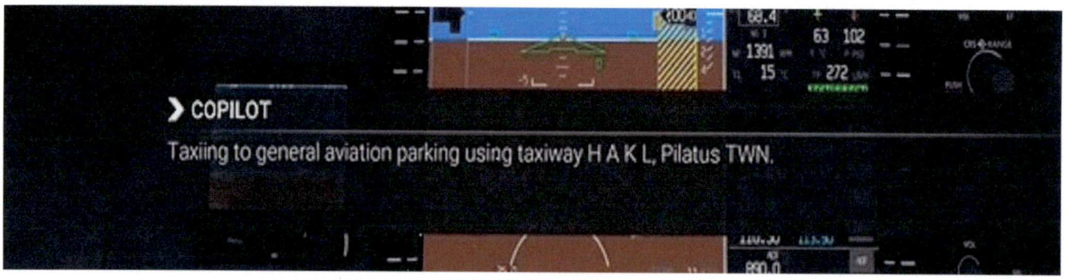

And just like that, we're on our way to parking.

Realistically, you probably wouldn't see someone take a PC-12 up for a quick loop, do a touch-and-go, and immediately call it a day—but for demonstration purposes, it gets the job done. Once ATC assigns parking, you may or may not see visual ground guidance. Sometimes there's no parking marker, and other times a **ground marshaller** appears to guide you into position, signaling if you're too far left or right and when to stop.

CHAPTER THIRTEEN

HOW TO MAKE A FLIGHT PLAN IN MSFS 2024

If you're new to aviation—or simply feeling overwhelmed by the redesigned flight planner in Microsoft Flight Simulator 2024—this guide is for you. In this section, you'll learn how the new system works and how to create both **VFR** and **IFR** flight plans, while getting familiar with the planner's most useful features.

TWO FLIGHT PLANNERS: WHICH ONE SHOULD YOU USE?

MSFS 2024 offers **two separate flight planners**:

1. Online Flight Planner (Recommended)

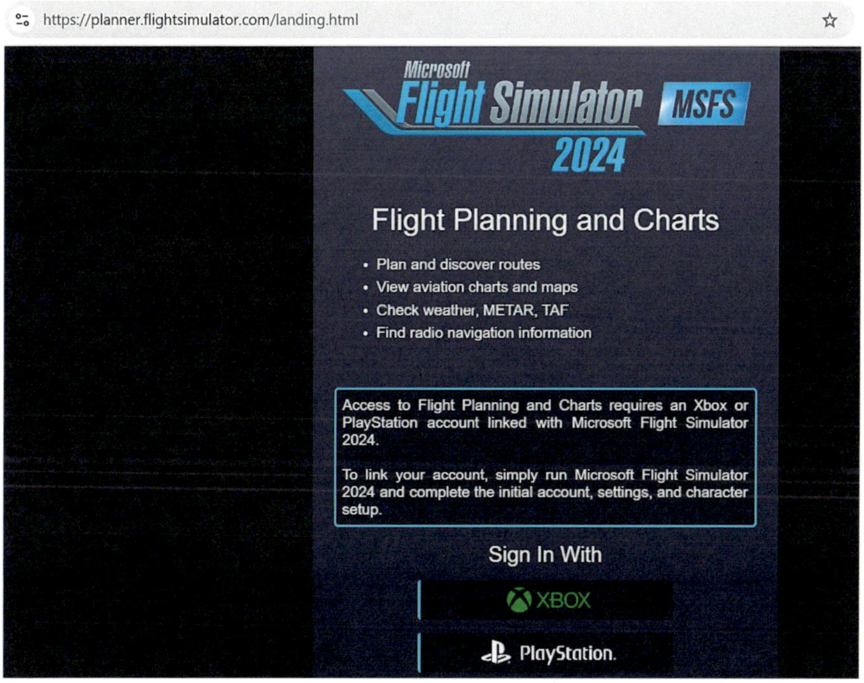

Available at https://planner.flightsimulator.com/ this is the most powerful and feature-rich option. It provides detailed routing tools, airspace visualization, weather overlays, and planning options suitable for both casual and advanced users.

2. EFB Planner (In-Sim)

The **Electronic Flight Bag (EFB)** planner is accessed inside the simulator. While convenient for quick routes, it lacks many advanced tools and is less intuitive. It's best used for simple planning or minor edits.

👉 **This section focuses primarily on the online planner**, with occasional references to the EFB where relevant.

UNDERSTANDING THE PLANNER LAYOUT

After signing in with the same Xbox account you use for MSFS 2024, you'll see an interactive world map surrounded by planning tools. Here's how everything is organized.

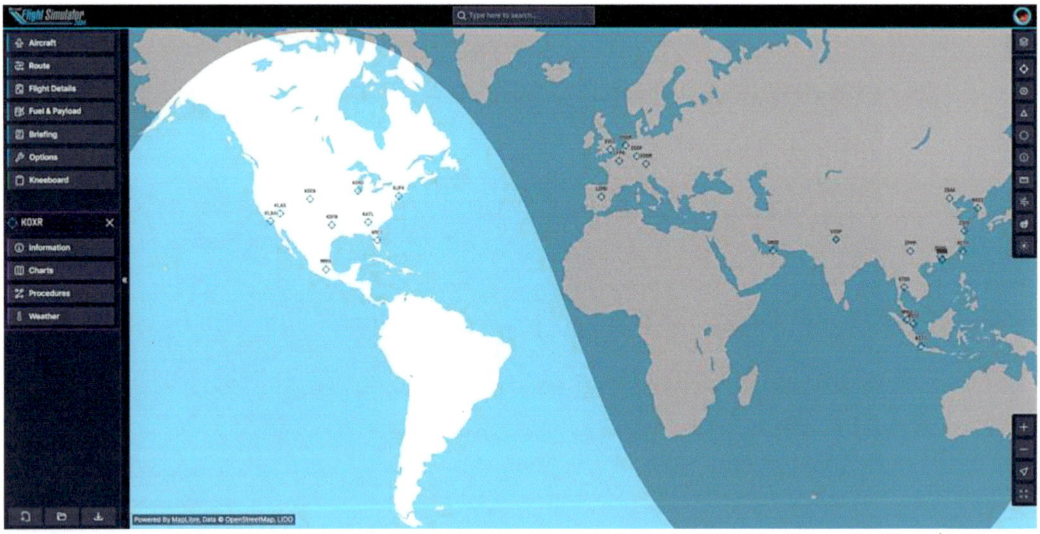

The Map (Center)

The map is where you build and visualize your route. It includes a **day/night terminator**, which is especially useful when flying with real-world time enabled. A **search bar** above the map lets you quickly find airports, waypoints, or navigation aids.

Map Options (Right Side Controls)

These tools allow you to customize what information appears on the map:

Map Presets 

Quickly tailor the display for your flight type:

- **IFR High** – Instrument flights above 18,000 ft
- **IFR Low** – Instrument flights below 18,000 ft
- **VFR** – Visual Flight Rules flying

Airports

Toggle airport icons on or off to declutter the map once your route is set.

Navigation Aids

Control the display of:

- Low or high airways (based on IFR preset)
- Radio navaids (VORs, NDBs)
- Landing aids (localizers)

Clicking a navaid reveals key details such as frequency, range, and coordinates.

Waypoints

Show or hide:

- **Terminal waypoints** (used in SIDs, STARs, and approaches)
- **Enroute waypoints** (used for general navigation)
- **VFR reporting points** (visual reference points for VFR pilots)

Airspaces & Restricted Areas

Essential for VFR planning:

- Toggle controlled and restricted airspace
- View **MORA (Minimum Off-Route Altitude)**
- Display **FIR boundaries** to know which ATC center you'll contact during cruise

Measurements

Measure distance and bearing between points:

1. Right-click any location on the map (without dragging)

2. Select the measurement icon

   You can later show, hide, or delete measurements as needed.

Weather 

Overlay real-time or forecasted:

- Cloud cover
- Precipitation
- Wind barbs

Time sliders allow you to see how conditions evolve, helping you plan more safely and realistically.

Landmarks 

Toggle visual references such as:

- Cities
- Roads and highways
- Railways and terrain features
  Useful for VFR navigation.

Day/Night Line 

Turn the day/night boundary on or off to improve visibility when planning flights in dark regions.

VFR PLANNING

VFR stands for **Visual Flight Rules**. These flight plans are commonly used in general aviation when weather conditions are clear enough to allow pilots to navigate primarily by outside visual references rather than instruments. Because VFR flights do not require strict routing, they are ideal for sightseeing, training, or relaxed recreational flying.

That said, airspace awareness is critical. Entering controlled airspace—such as **Class B, C, or D**—without authorization can cause issues, especially on online networks like **VATSIM**, where proper procedures are enforced.

Initial Setup

To begin a VFR flight plan, select the **VFR map preset**. This preset filters the map to display the most relevant information for visual flying, including terrain elevation, roads, landmarks, and reporting points.

Next, open the **Settings** panel on the left and confirm the correct configuration:

- **Altimeter:** inHg (U.S. standard)
- **Weight:** pounds (lbs)
- **Fuel:** gallons
- **Navlog type:** VFR

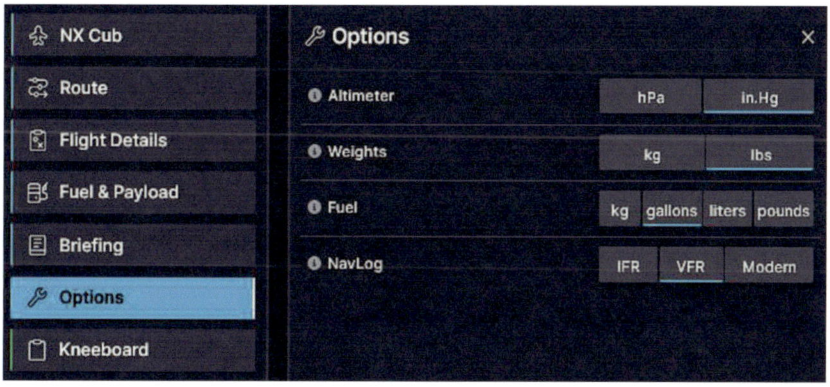

These settings ensure your navigation data and performance calculations align with real-world VFR operations in the United States.

Choosing a Flight Area

Once the setup is complete, choose a region to fly. For this example, a scenic coastal route along **Los Angeles** ending at **Catalina Island** makes for an enjoyable and beginner-friendly VFR flight.

Using the search bar to locate **Los Angeles International Airport (KLAX)** instantly zooms the map to the area, providing a convenient starting point for route planning.

Selecting an Aircraft

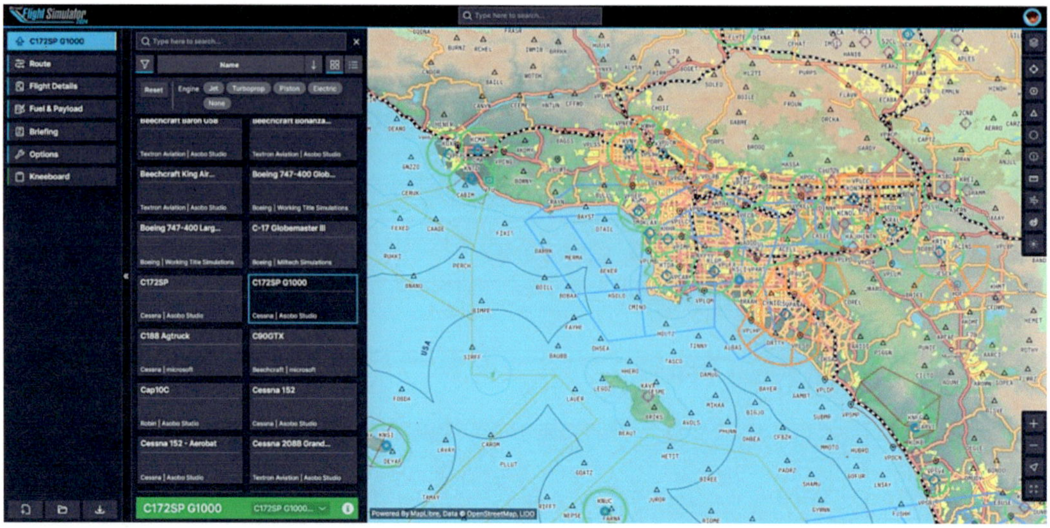

Click the **Aircraft** section on the left to view the available aircraft. For VFR flying, a slower aircraft with excellent visibility works best. A **high-wing Cessna 172** is an ideal choice, offering stable handling and unobstructed downward views—perfect for sightseeing and visual navigation.

At the moment, the flight planner supports only default aircraft. However, Working Title (the developer behind the planner) has stated that support for **custom and add-on aircraft** is planned for future updates.

Picking a Route

For this flight, I want to start just outside the Los Angeles area. **Oxnard Airport (KOXR)** offers good scenery and makes an excellent departure point, so I'll use it as my origin.

After zooming in on KOXR, I right-click the airport on the map to open the context menu. Clicking the **plus (+)** icon next to the airport adds it to the flight plan as the departure point.

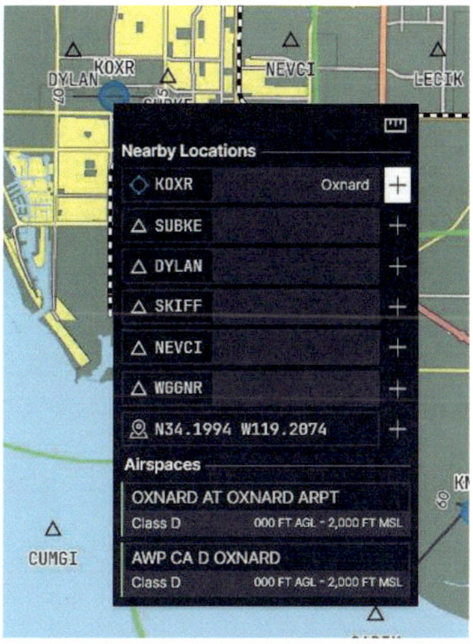

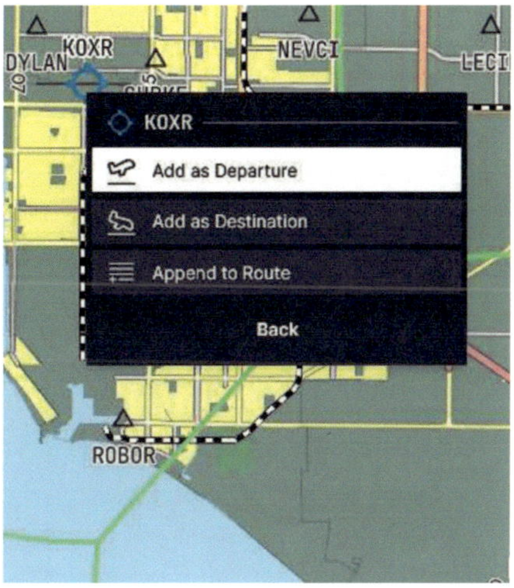

Adding Waypoints Along the Coast

To build a scenic coastal route, I add custom waypoints manually. This is done by right-clicking anywhere on the map, selecting the desired coordinate or waypoint, and choosing **"Append to Flight Plan."** Repeating this process lets me trace the coastline visually and shape the route exactly how I want it.

Understanding and Avoiding Airspace

As the route approaches the **Los Angeles Basin**, airspace management becomes critical. Under **VFR**, one of your primary responsibilities is avoiding controlled airspace unless you have authorization. Flying a small Cessna directly through busy arrival and departure corridors—especially near LAX—is a guaranteed problem.

Fortunately, the **VFR map preset** displays airspace boundaries by default. Clicking directly on an airspace label reveals detailed information such as altitude limits and airspace class. You can also right-click anywhere on the map to see airspace information listed at the bottom of the context menu.

Along this route:

- **Los Angeles North Class B** extends from **5,000 to 10,000 feet**
- **Santa Monica Class D** extends from the **surface to 2,700 feet**

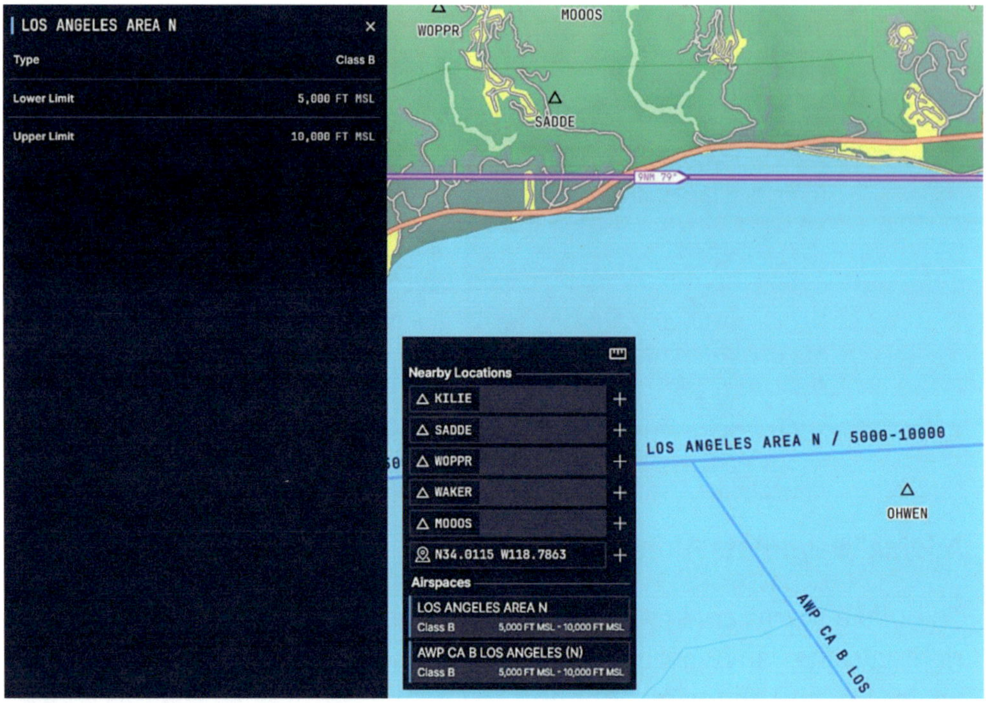

This leaves a usable altitude window between **2,700 and 5,000 feet**, which works—until reaching **LAX**, where **Class B airspace spans from the surface up to 10,000 feet**.

Navigating the LAX Area (SFRA)

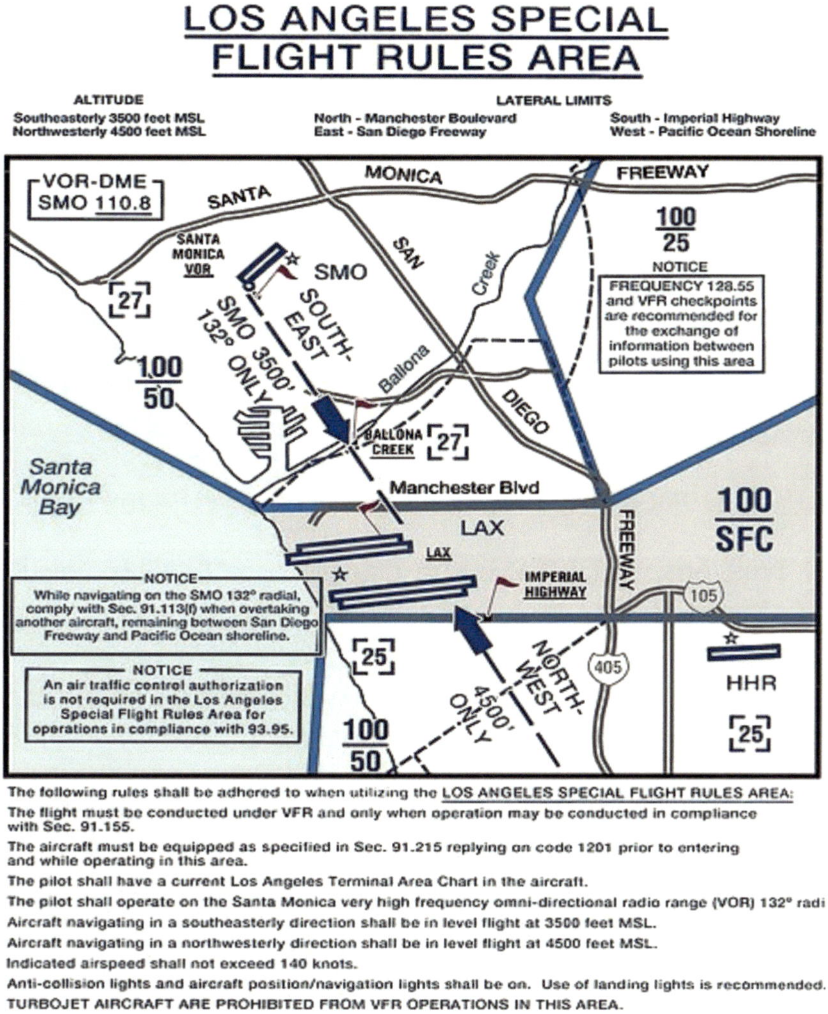

To legally pass through this congested area under VFR, we turn to the **Los Angeles Special Flight Rules Area (SFRA)**, which allows VFR aircraft to cross LAX without ATC clearance if specific procedures are followed.

According to the **Los Angeles Terminal Area Chart (TAC)**:

- Aircraft may fly **southeast on the 132° radial from Santa Monica (SMO)**
- At an altitude of **3,500 feet**

Unfortunately, MSFS 2024's flight planner does not include TAC charts and does not allow direct measurement of VOR radials—only bearings. Because of this limitation, accurately plotting the SFRA route in the planner can be tricky.

To keep things simple, I add a waypoint that visually crosses LAX and exits the Class B airspace, with the understanding that **VOR navigation will be used in the simulator** to fly this segment precisely.

Finalizing the Route

With the coastal waypoints and SFRA crossing complete, I add **Avalon Airport (KAVX)** on Catalina Island as the destination. That completes the enroute portion of the flight.

Switching to the **Route** page allows us to review the full plan, add procedures, and adjust aircraft performance settings.

Performance and Cruise Settings

Since this is a VFR flight, **VFR** should be selected at the top of the Route page.

- **True Airspeed (KTAS):** The planner uses KTAS to calculate flight time. Aircraft profiles do not automatically populate this value, so it must be entered manually.
  For the **Cessna 172**, a cruise TAS of **124 knots** is appropriate.
- **Cruise Altitude: 3,500 feet** is ideal for this easterly VFR flight and aligns perfectly with the SFRA requirements.
- **Fuel Burn:** Under **Performance Options**, the planner requires an average fuel burn value.
  MSFS 2024 lists the Cessna 172's fuel burn as **24.5 L/h (≈6.5 USgal/h)**, which is lower than real-world figures. In reality, a Cessna 172 typically burns closer to **9.3 gal/h** in cruise.

Because the planner only accepts whole numbers, I set fuel burn to **7 GPH** for this example.

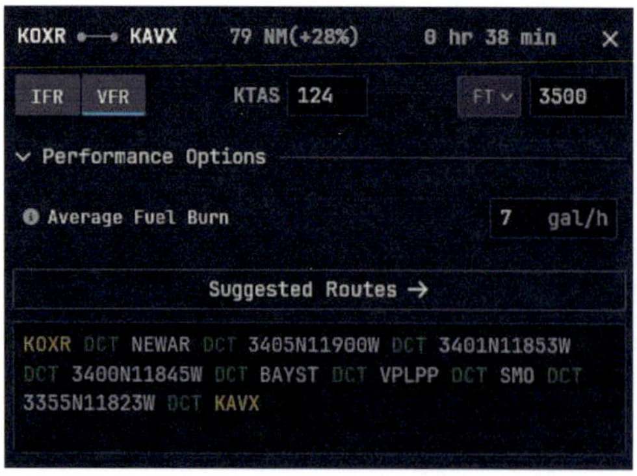

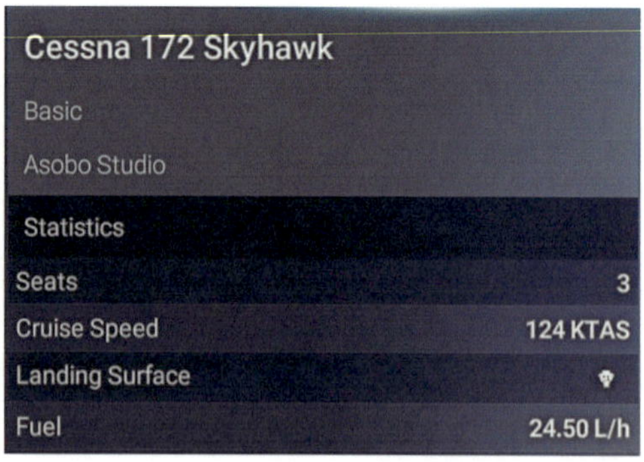

For greater accuracy, you can:

- Refer to the aircraft's **POH/AFM** (Pilot's Operating Handbook)
- Search online for *"aircraft type* POH"
- Or measure fuel burn experimentally during a cruise flight in the simulator

CESSNA
MODEL 172S

SECTION 5
PERFORMANCE

CRUISE PERFORMANCE

CONDITIONS:
2550 Pounds
Recommended Lean Mixture At All Altitudes (Refer to Section 4, Cruise)

PRESS ALT FT	RPM	20°C BELOW STANDARD TEMP			STANDARD TEMPERATURE			20°C ABOVE STANDARD TEMP		
		% BHP	KTAS	GPH	% BHP	KTAS	GPH	% BHP	KTAS	GPH
2000	2550	83	117	11.1	77	118	10.5	72	117	9.9
	2500	78	115	10.6	73	115	9.9	68	115	9.4
	2400	69	111	9.6	64	110	9.0	60	109	8.5
	2300	61	105	8.6	57	104	8.1	53	102	7.7
	2200	53	99	7.7	50	97	7.3	47	95	6.9
	2100	47	92	6.9	44	90	6.6	42	89	6.3
4000	2600	83	120	11.1	77	120	10.4	72	119	9.8
	2550	79	118	10.6	73	117	9.9	68	117	9.4
	2500	74	115	10.1	69	115	9.5	64	114	8.9
	2400	65	110	9.1	61	109	8.5	57	107	8.1
	2300	58	104	8.2	54	102	7.7	51	101	7.3
	2200	51	98	7.4	48	96	7.0	45	94	6.7
	2100	45	91	6.6	42	89	6.4	40	87	6.1

Adding Departure and Arrival Procedures

To complete the flight plan, I add departure and arrival procedures:

- **Departure:** The planner automatically selects the active runway. From Oxnard, I add a **visual departure**, choosing **right 45° from Runway 07**.
- **Arrival:** For Catalina, I select a **straight-in visual approach to Runway 22**, which fits the terrain and arrival direction well.

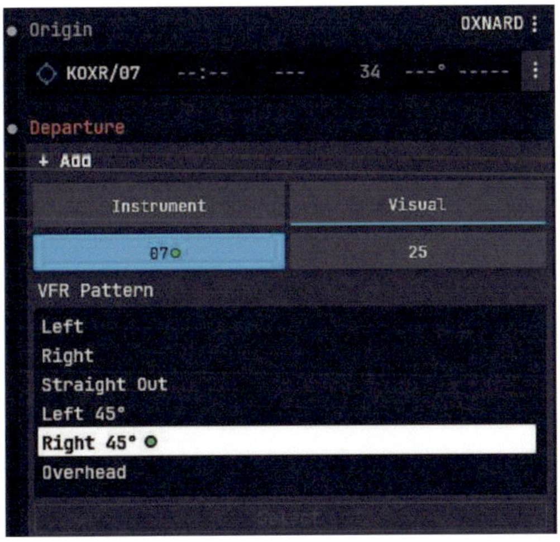

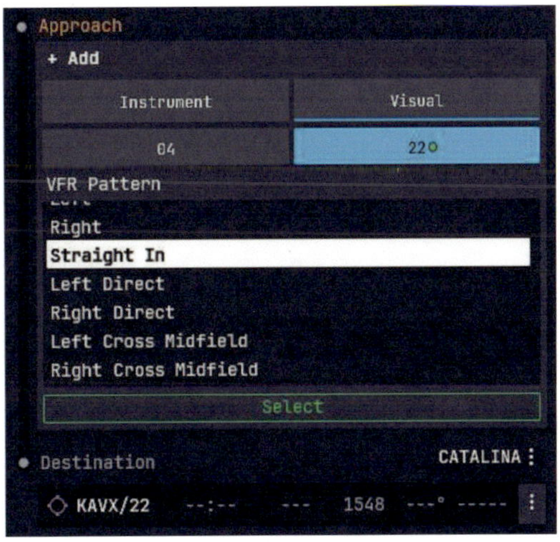

Weather

Weather is critical for **VFR flying**, so before committing to the flight, we must verify conditions at both the departure and arrival airports. VFR requires sufficient visibility and cloud clearance to operate safely without relying on instruments.

Clicking an airport on the map brings up detailed airport information. Selecting **KOXR**, opening the **Weather** tab on the left, and viewing the **METAR (Meteorological Aerodrome Report)** gives us our first reality check.

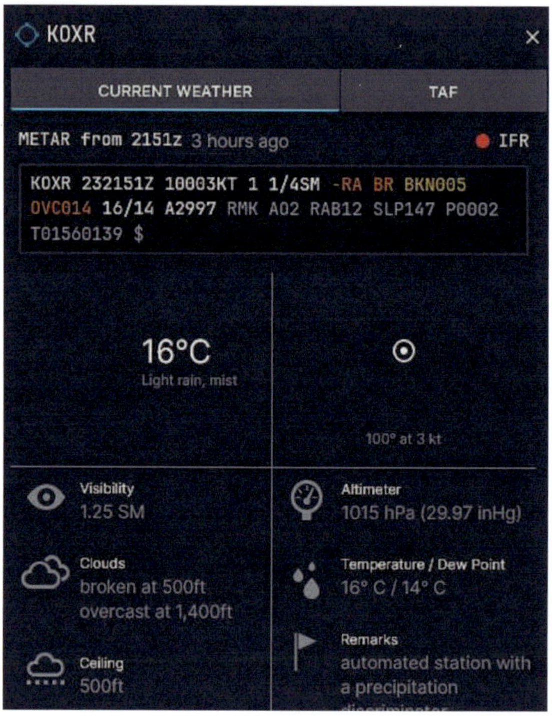

Unfortunately, conditions at Oxnard aren't suitable for VFR:

- **Ceiling:** 500 feet
- **Visibility:** 1.25 statute miles
- **Weather:** Light rain

These conditions make a VFR departure impossible. While disappointing, this gives us a perfect opportunity to use the **TAF (Terminal Aerodrome Forecast)** to see when conditions will improve.

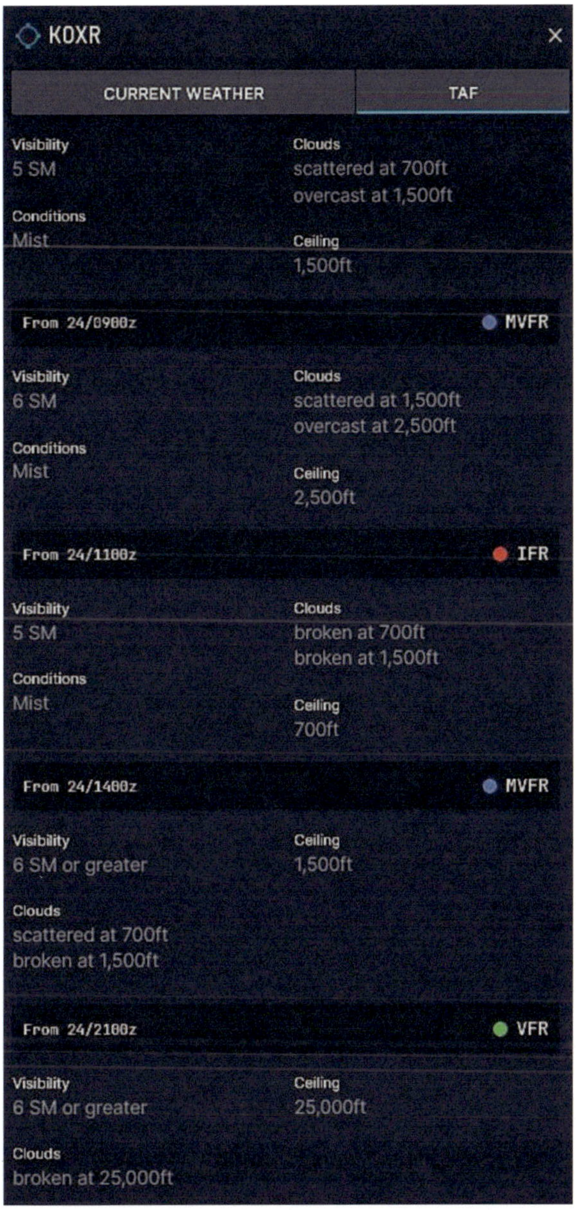

Opening the **TAF** tab next to "Current Weather" shows an easy-to-read forecast. The TAF indicates that conditions will soon improve to **Marginal VFR**, but if we want to climb out without entering clouds, we'll need to wait until **24/2100Z**.

That translates to:

- **Day:** 24th of the month (November)
- **Time:** 21:00 UTC
- **Local Time:** 12:00 PM (Los Angeles)

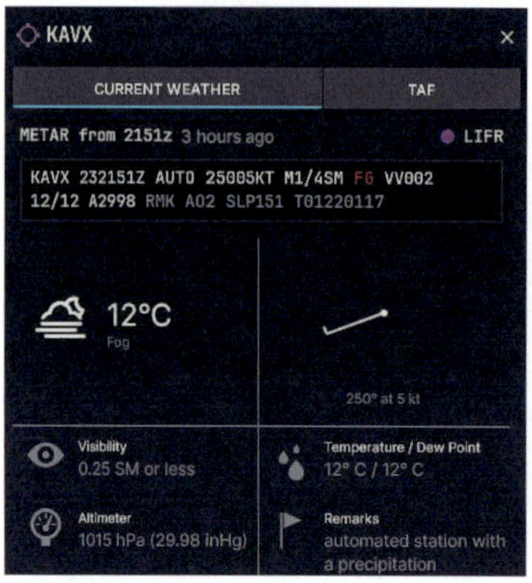

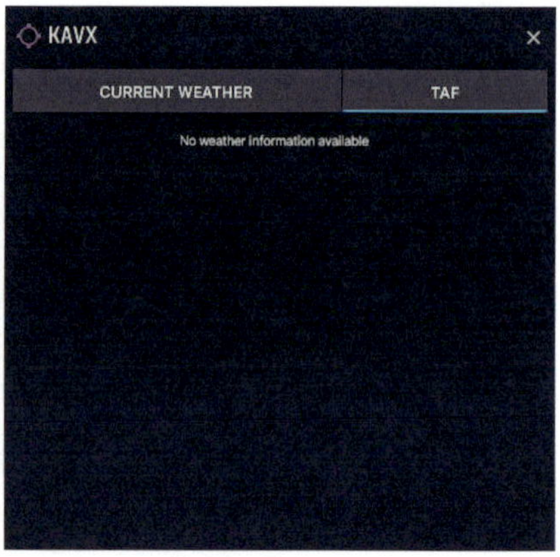

Catalina's weather is even less forgiving. The METAR shows **dense fog with visibility below ¼ mile**. Unfortunately, Catalina does not publish a TAF, so we'll need to recheck the METAR closer to departure time to confirm that conditions are safe for arrival.

Flight Details

The **Flight Details** section contains information primarily used by ATC and online networks.

For this flight:

- **Flight Rules:** VFR
- **Aircraft Registration:** Optional (user preference)
- **Airline:** Not applicable (General Aviation)
- **Flight Number & ATC Callsign:** Left blank

Since we determined earlier that departure must wait until **24/2100Z**, we set that as both the **flight date** and **off-block time**.

The **Equipment Builder** simplifies equipment code entry. For the Cessna 172, onboard equipment includes:

- Standard equipment
- DME
- ADF
- GNSS (GPS)
- ILS
- VOR
- VHF radio

The aircraft is equipped with a **Mode C transponder**, and the **flight type** is set to **General Aviation**.

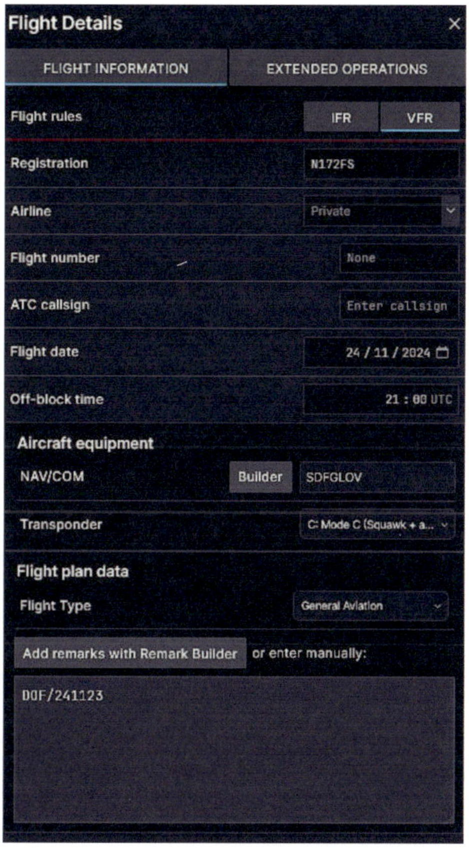

Fuel & Payload

If the average fuel burn is set correctly, the **Fuel & Payload** page automatically calculates a block fuel amount that includes reserves.

For this flight:

- **Planned Flight Time:** 39 minutes
- **Calculated Block Fuel:** 19 gallons

While this is reasonable, **Catalina does not have fuel available**, so it's wise to carry extra reserve. I switch the **Final Reserve** setting from *Auto* to *Manual* and increase it to **15 gallons** for added safety.

The **Payload** section allows you to configure aircraft loading:

- Set a percentage load
- Randomize passenger weights

- Or manually define passengers and cargo

For this flight, I manually configure:

- **Two passengers at 180 lb each**
- **No cargo**

These weights can then be matched in the simulator using the EFB to ensure consistency between planning and execution.

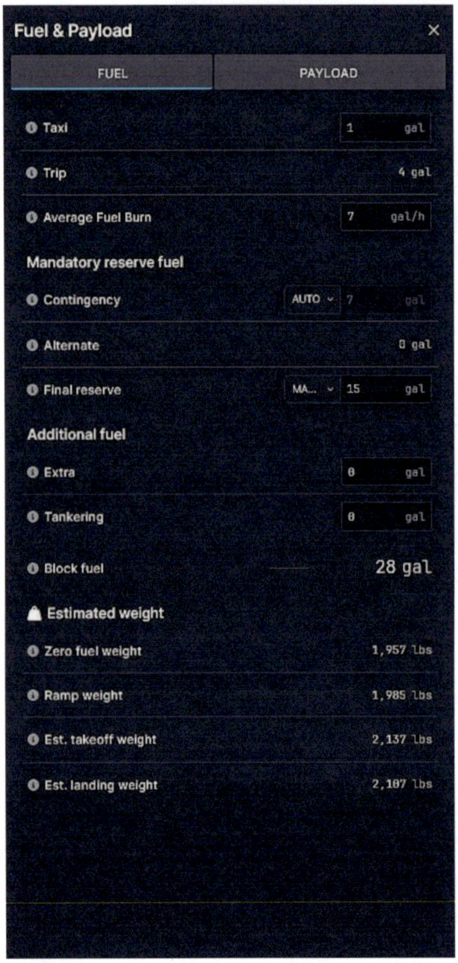

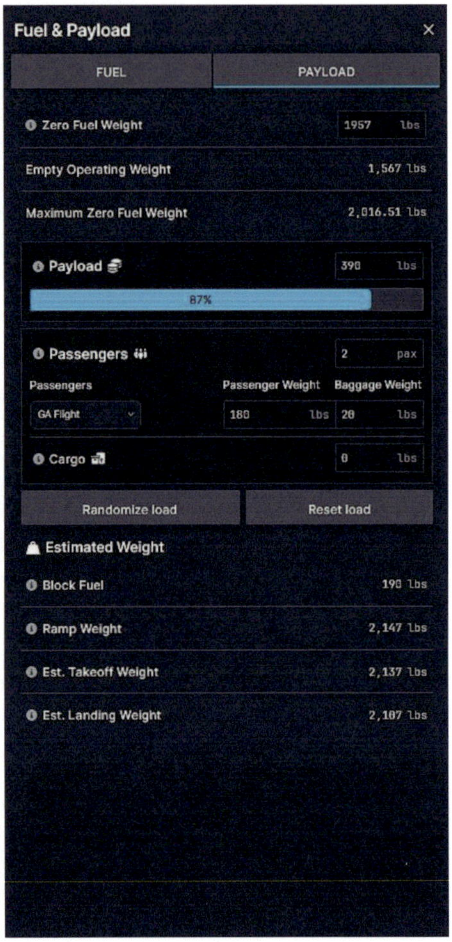

Briefing

The **Briefing** section contains two key elements: the **Operational Flight Plan (OFP)** and the **Navigation Log (Nav Log)**.

An **OFP** is a highly detailed document used mainly in airline operations. It includes payload and fuel weights, departure and arrival times, route waypoints, alternates, and performance calculations. Since this is a **general aviation VFR flight**, the OFP isn't necessary, so we'll focus solely on the **Nav Log**.

Briefing

OFP | NAV LOG

UNITS: knots, feet, °C, nautical miles, gallons — hints

Waypoint	Airway		Track	TH	wDir	wSpd	Dist		ETE	ATE	Fuel	Fuel
	Alt	MH	WCA	Var	Temp (dev)		GS	TAS	ETD	ATD	Rem.	Rem.
◇ KOXR OXNARD			134°	134°	0°	0°	4.6		08:03	unset	0.3	unset
△ NEWAR	0	122°	0°	+12°	0°(-15°)		124	124	16:58	unset	27.1	unset
			122°	122°	0°	0°	6		12:50	unset	0.3	unset
3405N11900W	0	110°	0°	+12°	0°(-15°)		124	124	05:49	unset	26.7	unset
			117°	117°	0°	0°	6.5		00:28	unset	0.4	unset
3401N11853W	0	106°	0°	+12°	0°(-15°)		124	124	06:18	unset	26.4	unset
			107°	107°	0°	0°	6.9		04:44	unset	0.4	unset
3400N11845W	0	95°	0°	+12°	0°(-15°)		124	124	11:03	unset	26.0	unset
			67°	67°	0°	0°	4.7		07:57	unset	0.3	unset
△ BAYST	0	56°	0°	+12°	0°(-15°)		124	124	19:00	unset	25.7	unset
			87°	87°	0°	0°	6.4		13:32	unset	0.4	unset
△ VPLPP	0	75°	0°	+11°	0°(-15°)		124	124	08:33	unset	25.3	unset
			111°	111°	0°	0°	4.2		03:25	unset	0.2	unset
SMO	0	100°	0°	+11°	0°(-15°)		124	124	11:59	unset	25.1	unset
110.8			147°	147°	0°	0°	6.3		10:04	unset	0.4	unset
3355N11823W	0	136°	0°	+11°	0°(-15°)		124	124	22:03	unset	24.7	unset
			235°	235°	0°	0°	1		12:05	unset	0.1	unset
◇ KAVX CATALINA	487	224°	0°	+11°	0°(-12°)		124	124	11:06	unset	22.9	unset

The **VFR Nav Log** provides valuable waypoint-by-waypoint data, including:

- Planned altitude
- Magnetic heading
- Distance between waypoints
- Estimated Time Enroute (ETE)
- Forecast winds

At the moment, some values—such as altitude and wind—may incorrectly show zero due to current planner limitations. During the flight, you can manually update the **ATE (Actual Time Enroute)** and **fuel remaining** fields to track progress and fuel usage in real time.

Loading the Flight Plan in the Simulator

Once planning is complete, the flight plan must be saved before it can be used in **MSFS 2024**.

To save the plan:

1. Click the **Save** icon at the bottom-left of the planner.
2. Name the flight.
3. Select **Save New Plan**.

From this same menu, you can also generate a shareable link for the flight plan.

To load the plan in the simulator:

1. Open the **EFB (Electronic Flight Bag)** from the top menu.
2. Launch the **Flight Plan** app.
3. Navigate to the **Route** page.
4. Select **Load Flight Plan**.

Once loaded, the route will appear in the EFB. At the bottom of the route page, you'll find options to:

- Load the plan into the aircraft's avionics
- File the flight plan with default MSFS ATC

(Note: I originally intended to fly this route using the steam-gauge Cessna 172, but it's currently not functioning correctly.)

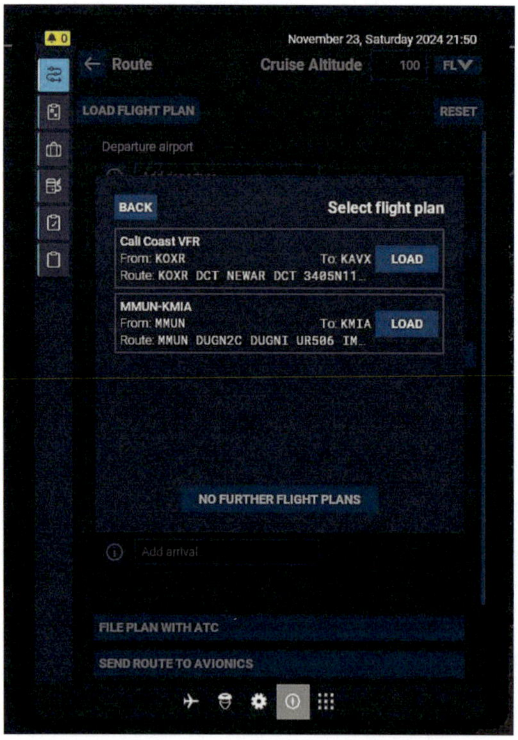

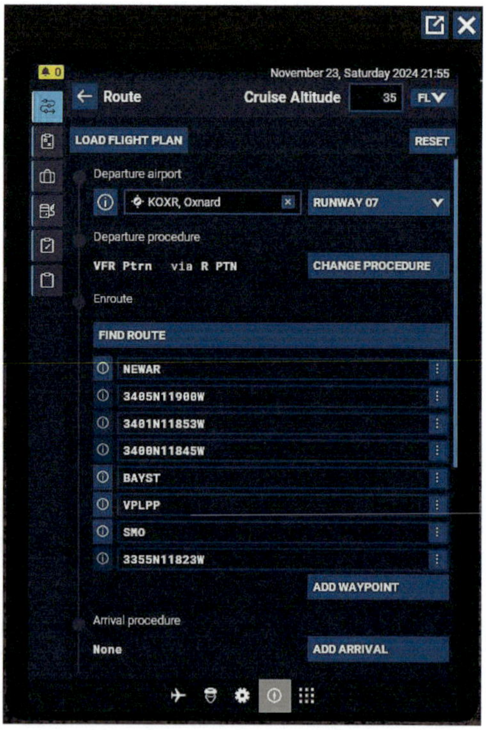

IFR PLANNING

IFR (Instrument Flight Rules) flight plans are commonly used by airliners and by general aviation pilots flying in poor weather or complex airspace. IFR flights require:

- A filed, structured route
- Continuous ATC communication
- Instrument-based navigation

While flying IFR is more demanding, **planning IFR flights is often simpler than VFR**, as routes, altitudes, and airspace considerations are largely handled automatically.

IFR Setup

To begin IFR planning, select the appropriate **IFR map preset**:

- **IFR Low** for flights below 18,000 feet
- **IFR High** for flights above 18,000 feet

For this example, we'll recreate a flight from **Lisbon to Madeira**, which means configuring settings suitable for European operations:

- **Altimeter:** hPa
- **Weights:** kilograms (kg)
- **Fuel:** kilograms (kg)
- **Nav Log:** IFR or Modern

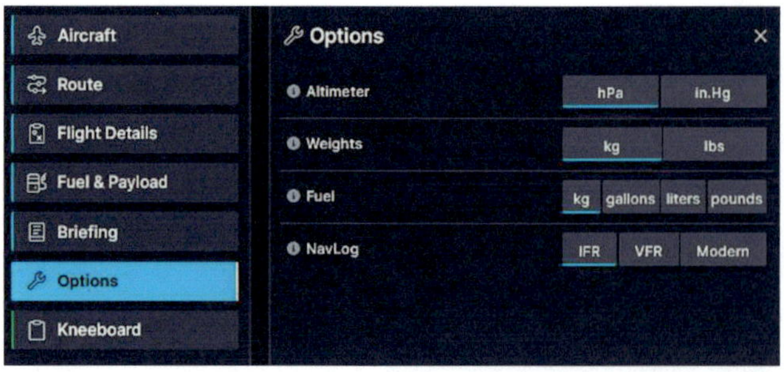

Next, select the aircraft. Since this is a **Boeing 737 MAX 8** flight, choose that model from the aircraft list. Be sure to select the **correct variant**.

By default, the planner selects the **737 MAX BBJ**, which is configured for private use. Because this is a commercial passenger flight, the variant must be changed to **737 MAX 8 Passenger**. This ensures accurate fuel, payload, and performance calculations.

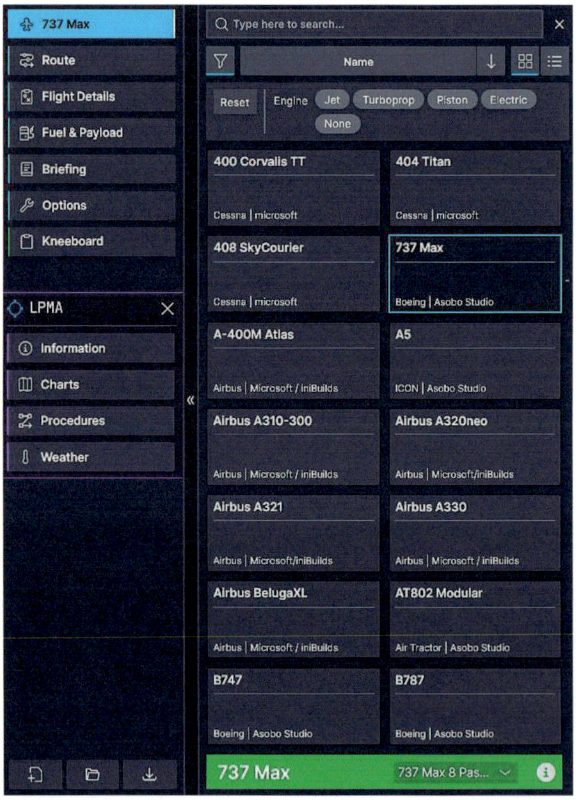

Route Planning (IFR)

Creating an IFR route in the MSFS 2024 flight planner is straightforward.

Start on the **Route** page and click **Add** under **Origin**. Search for your departure airport—either by name or ICAO code. In this case, enter **LPPT** for Lisbon. Repeat the process for your destination, **Madeira (LPMA)**.

Once both airports are entered, click **Auto-Route**. The planner will automatically generate a suitable IFR route and select departure and arrival procedures based on runway availability and current weather at both airports.

Reviewing and Correcting the Route

Always review the generated route, especially near the departure and arrival phases.

The departure from Lisbon looks correct, but the arrival into Madeira needs adjustment. The planner routes us to **PILIM**, then oddly turns the aircraft back toward **FUN12**, creating an unnecessary conflict between the STAR and the approach.

In addition, the planner selected a **VOR/DME approach to Runway 05**. While this approach is perfectly valid, **RNAV approaches are generally easier to fly and offer better guidance**, and Runway 05 has an RNAV option available.

Click **Change Procedure** to view all available approaches. After reviewing them, the **RNP 05 Z** approach stands out—it connects cleanly with the **PILIM** waypoint and provides a direct, stable path to the runway. Select this approach to resolve both issues.

Adding an Alternate Airport

An IFR flight always requires an alternate in case landing at the destination becomes impossible.

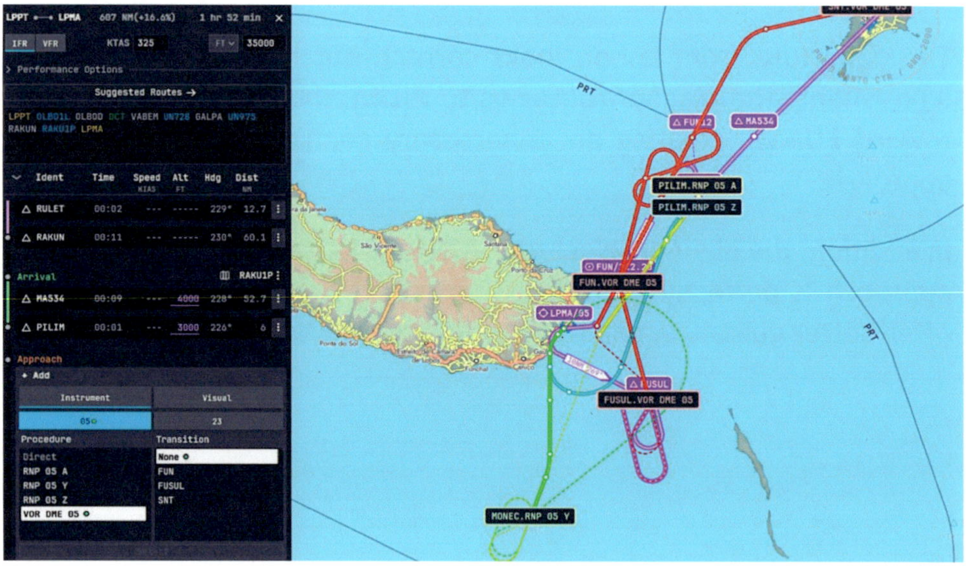

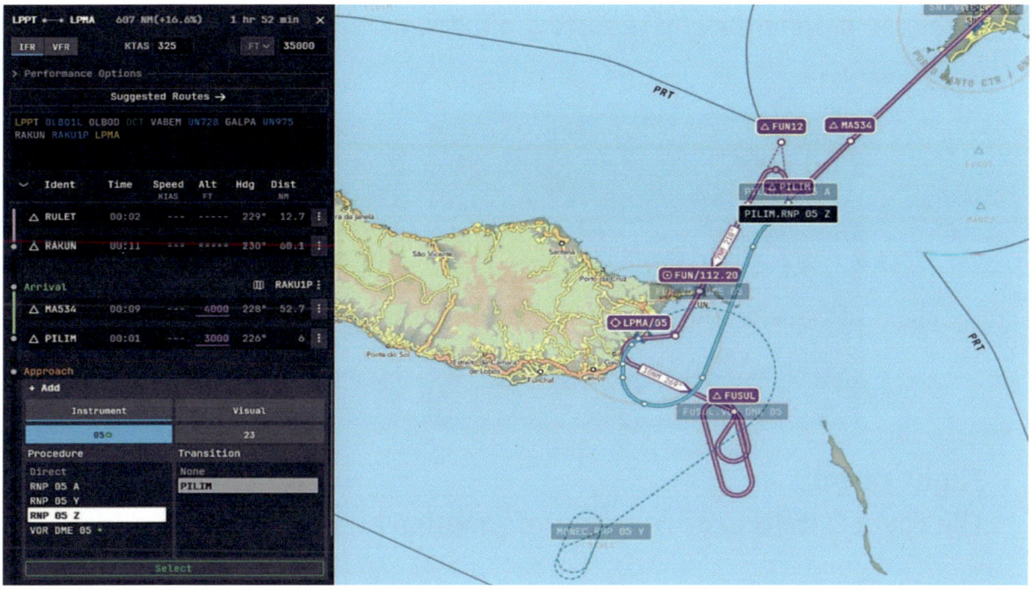

For this flight, **Gran Canaria (GCLP)** is a solid choice. It's far enough from Madeira to avoid sharing the same weather system, yet close enough to be operationally practical.

Scroll to the bottom of the **Route** page, search for the alternate airport, and add it. The planner will automatically generate a diversion route to use if needed.

Performance Planning

With the route finalized, it's time to configure **speed, altitude, and fuel burn**.

As with VFR planning, you can find rough performance estimates in the MSFS aircraft selection menu:

- **Cruise Speed:** 455 KTAS
- **Fuel Burn:** 2,268 L/h (≈ 1,821 kg/h)

Choosing Cruise Altitude

Selecting the right cruise altitude for a jet depends on several factors, including aircraft weight, wind, temperature, and performance limits. Direction of flight also matters due to **semi-circular cruising altitude rules**:

- **Eastbound (000°–179°):** Odd flight levels (e.g., FL350)
- **Westbound (180°–359°):** Even flight levels (e.g., FL340)

To keep things simple, **FL360** is a suitable choice for this route. It aligns with the direction of travel and is well within the aircraft's capabilities.

(Why the planner briefly reports a maximum altitude of 12,999 feet is anyone's guess.)

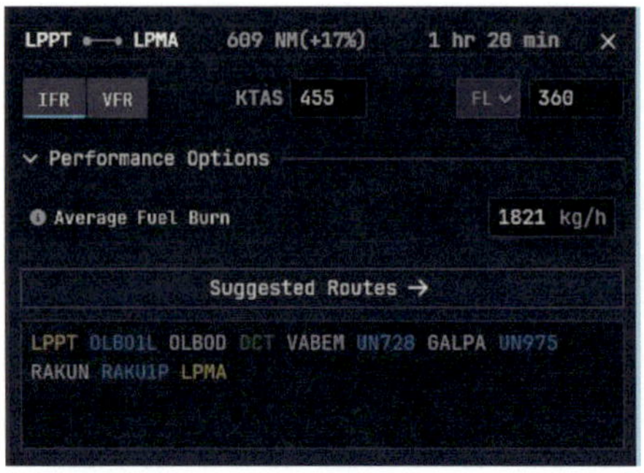

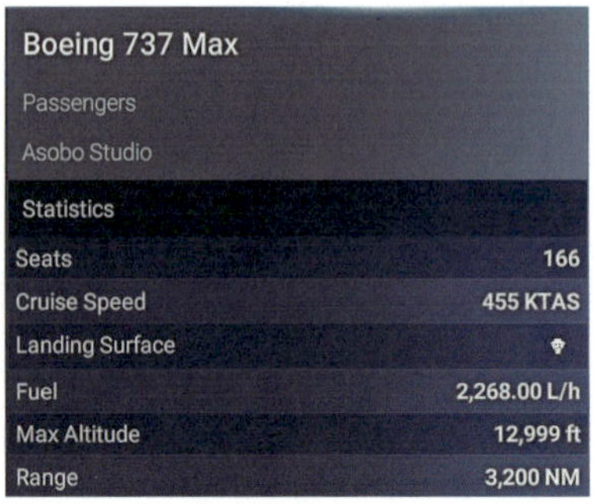

Flight Details

The **Flight Details** page contains information primarily used by ATC.

For this flight:

- **Flight Rules:** IFR
- **Airline:** Ryanair
- **Flight Number:** FR385
- **ATC Callsign:** RYR385
- **Flight Date & Off-Block Time:** Your choice

Use the equipment builder to configure onboard systems. The correct transponder code for the 737 MAX is **Code L**, which includes **Mode S with aircraft identification, altitude reporting, ADS-B, and enhanced surveillance**. Set the flight type to **Scheduled**.

EDTO Compliance Check

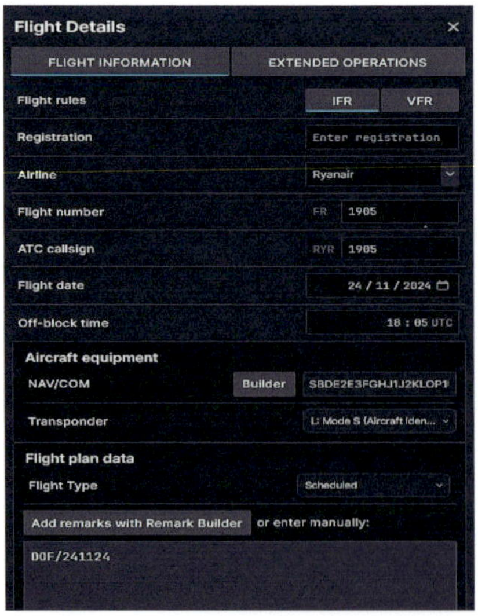

Twin-engine aircraft like the 737 MAX must comply with **EDTO (Extended Diversion Time Operations)** rules when flying long overwater routes. These rules ensure the aircraft remains within a safe diversion distance of suitable airports in case of an engine failure or emergency.

To verify compliance:

1. Click **Extended Operations**
2. Select **EDTO**
3. Click **Check Route**

In this case, the planner confirms that **EDTO compliance is not required**, meaning the route is fully acceptable without additional restrictions.

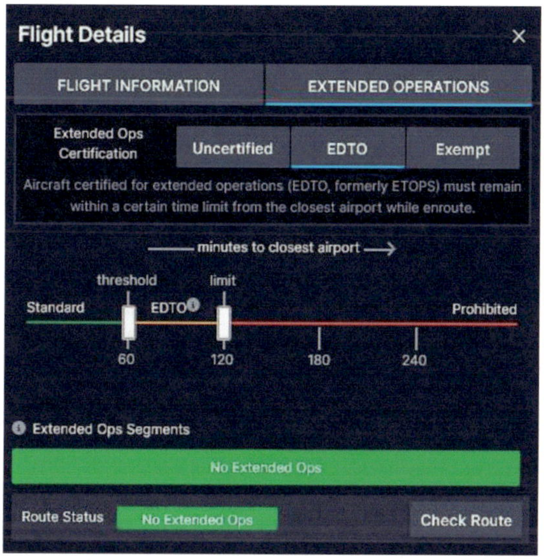

Fuel & Payload

Once you enter an accurate **fuel burn rate**, the flight planner automatically calculates the **block fuel**, which includes trip fuel, reserves, and additional fuel for the alternate airport. In this case, the planner calculates **5,578 kg**, which is reasonable for a **1 hour and 20-minute flight** in a Boeing 737 MAX.

On the **Payload** page, click **"Click to set payload"** to assign a payload percentage. The planner will automatically distribute passenger and cargo weights. Be sure to verify the **passenger weight setting**—mine was initially set to an unrealistic **165 kg per passenger**.

After finalizing the payload, note the **Zero Fuel Weight (ZFW)** displayed at the top of the page. You'll need this value when configuring the aircraft's **FMC** inside the simulator.

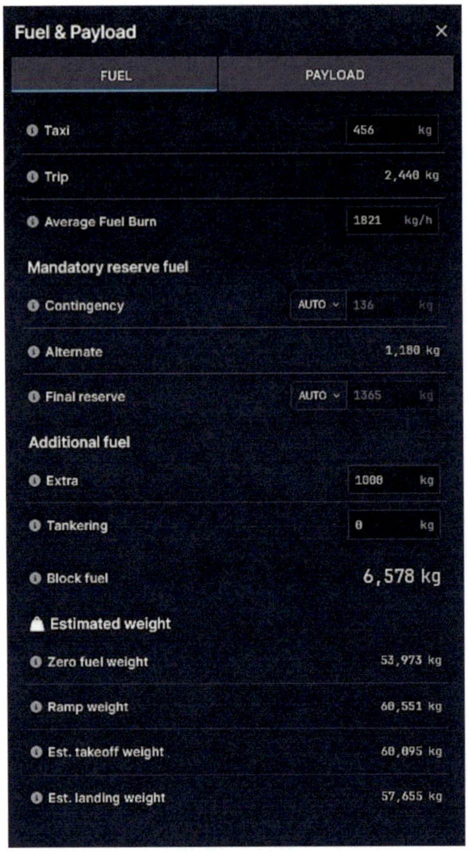

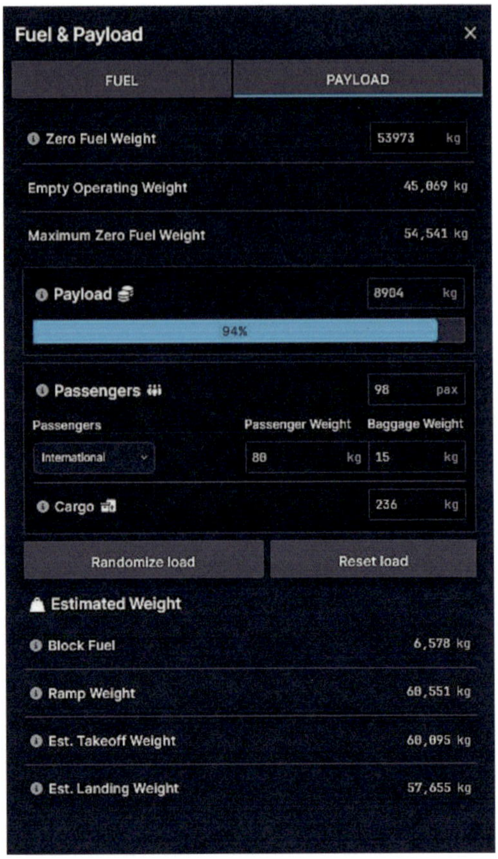

Briefing

The **Briefing** page provides access to two key documents: the **Operational Flight Plan (OFP)** and the **Navigation Log (Nav Log)**.

The **OFP** condenses the entire flight into a single document, including:

- Departure and arrival times
- Fuel and weight data
- Waypoints and routing
- Cruise speeds and altitudes

While OFPs can look overwhelming at first, the built-in **Hints** feature explains each section clearly, making it easier to understand.

The **Nav Log** lists every waypoint along the route, along with planned speeds, altitudes, distances, and expected winds. By default, the planner uses a standard IFR nav log, but you can switch to the **Modern Nav Log** in the settings for a cleaner, more customizable layout.

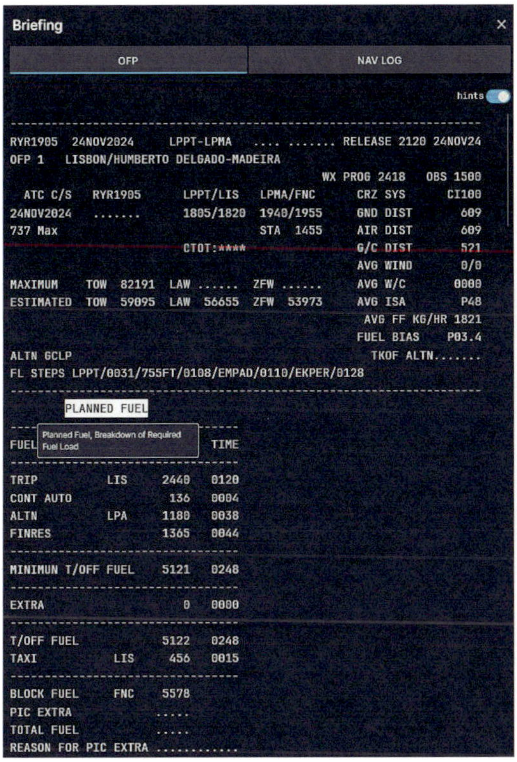

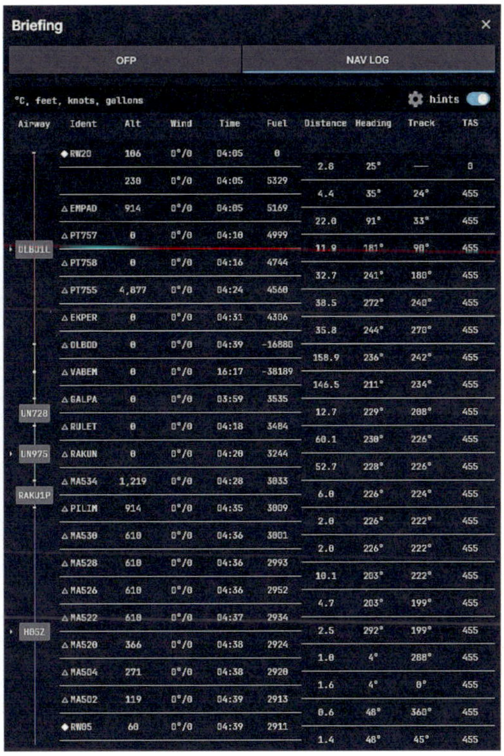

Weather Check

Before departure, always review the weather at both your **departure and arrival airports**.

Click on either airport in the map to open its information panel, then select the **Weather** tab. Here you'll find:

- **METAR** – current observed weather conditions
- **TAF** – forecasted conditions for the next 24 hours

For example, **"From 24/1800Z"** means *the 24th day of the month at 18:00 UTC.*

Checking both reports ensures that weather conditions remain suitable throughout your flight, especially during arrival.

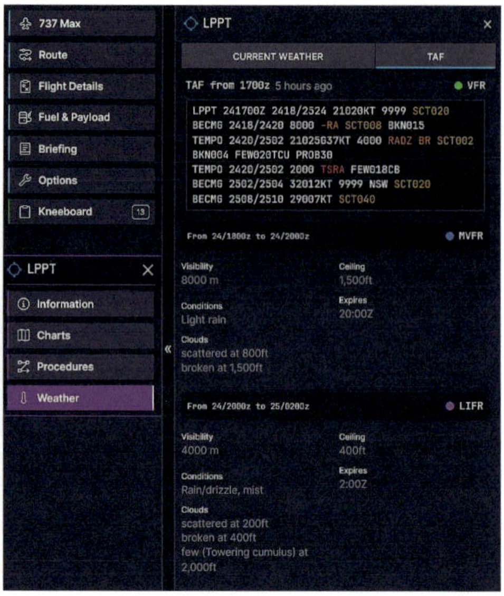

Kneeboard & Charts

Charts are essential for IFR flying. They provide precise guidance for **taxi routes, departures, arrivals, and approaches**.

One of the standout features of the MSFS 2024 flight planner is its integration of **LIDO charts** for most airports worldwide.

After creating a flight plan, the **Kneeboard** automatically displays all charts relevant to your route.

- Click **Preview Chart** to view it
- Click **Pin Chart** to save it for quick access

If you want to view **all charts for a specific airport**, or check charts outside your current flight plan, simply search for the airport or click it on the map. An information panel will appear on the left, giving you full access to the airport's chart library.

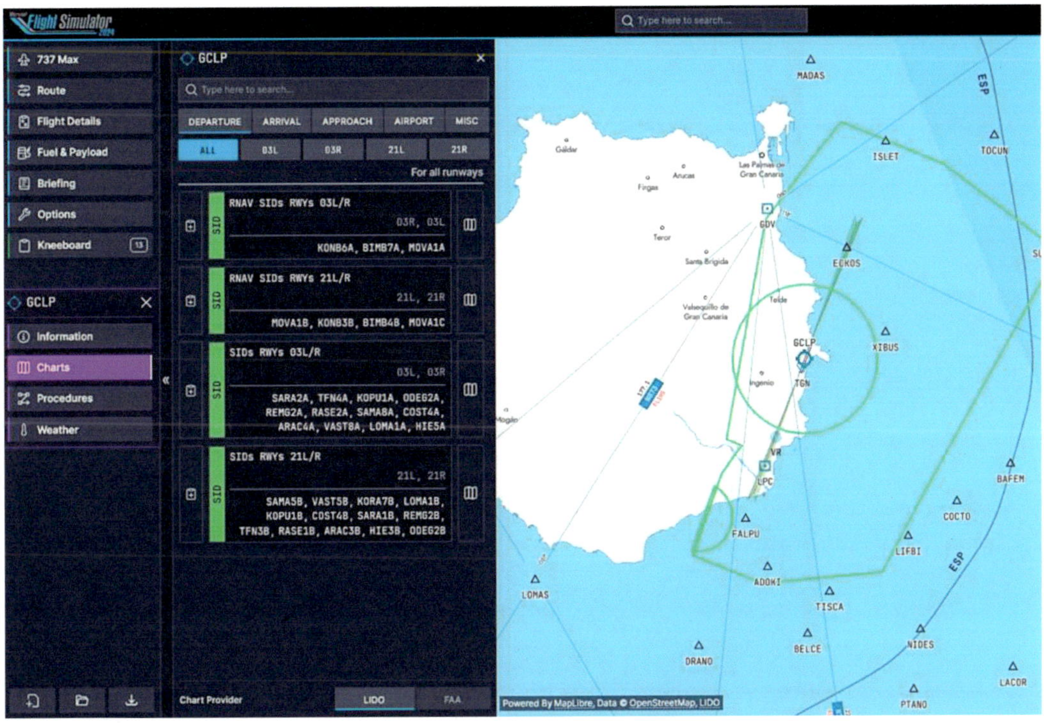

In the Simulator

Once your flight plan is complete, it's time to **load it into MSFS 2024**.

1. **Save the Flight Plan** – Click the **save icon** at the bottom-left of the planner and give your flight a name, such as *"LPPT-LPMA"*. You can also share your plan with others from this screen.
2. **Load via the EFB** – Open the **EFB tool** at the top of the screen, go to the **Flight Plan app**, and navigate to the **Route** page. Click **Load Flight Plan**. Your plan will appear in the EFB.
3. **Upload to Avionics** – Scroll to the bottom of the Route page to find buttons that allow you to **load the flight plan into your aircraft's avionics** and **file it with MSFS ATC**.

Note: For the 737 MAX, sending the flight plan to the FMC often only loads the departure airport, requiring you to manually enter the rest of the route.

Route
Cruise Altitude
BACK
Select flight plan
LPPT-LPMA
From: LPPT
To: LPMA
Route: LPPT OLBO1L OLBOD DCT V
LOAD
Cali Coast VFR
From: KOXR
To: KAVX
Route: KOXR DCT NEWAR DCT 3405
LOAD
MMUN-KMIA
From: MMUN
To: KMIA
Route: MMUN DUGN2C DUGNI UR586
LOAD
NO FURTHER FLIGHT PLANS
N
5NM

Route
Cruise Altitude
360
FL
LOAD FLIGHT PLAN
RESET
Departure airport
LPPT, Lisbon
RUNWAY 20
Departure procedure
OLBO1L
CHANGE PROCEDURE
Enroute
FIND ROUTE
OLBOD
VABEM
GALPA
RULET
RAKUN
ADD WAYPOINT
N
5NM

40 - 166K | 10 - 210K
230K ALT
FLAP EXTEND
BACKGROUND
AFDS FLOOD
OFF
INBD
RTE 1 LEGS
1/1
OLBOD
VABEM
ACTIVATE>
INIT REF
RTE
DEP ARR
ATC
VNAV
BRT
FIX
LEGS
HOLD
FMC COMM
PROG
EXEC
MENU
N1 LIMIT
PREV PAGE
NEXT PAGE
FUEL FLOW
RESET
RATE
USED
AUTO BRAKE
SELECTOR
MFD
ENG
SYS
Route
Cruise Altitude
LOAD FLIGHT PLAN
RESET
RULET
RAKUN
ADD WAYPOINT
Arrival procedure
RAKU1P
CHANGE PROCEDURE
Approach procedure
CHANGE PROCEDURE
Destination airport
LPMA, Madeira
Alternate destination airport
FILE PLAN WITH ATC
SEND ROUTE TO AVIONICS
REQUEST ROUTE FROM AVIONICS
LOAD / SAVE PLN FILE

Extras: Useful Planner Features

1. Adding Custom Waypoints

To insert a waypoint between two existing ones, **click and drag the connecting line**. Drop it where you want, and a **context menu** will appear with nearby waypoints to add to your plan.

2. Switching to FAA Charts

If you prefer **FAA charts** over LIDO charts (U.S. flights), click the airport, select the **Charts** button, and choose **FAA** at the bottom of the menu.

3. Viewing Airport Frequencies

Want to see all ATC frequencies for an airport? Click the airport, open the **Frequencies tab**, and view all listed frequencies. These are pulled from the sim, so they may not match real-life or VATSIM operations.

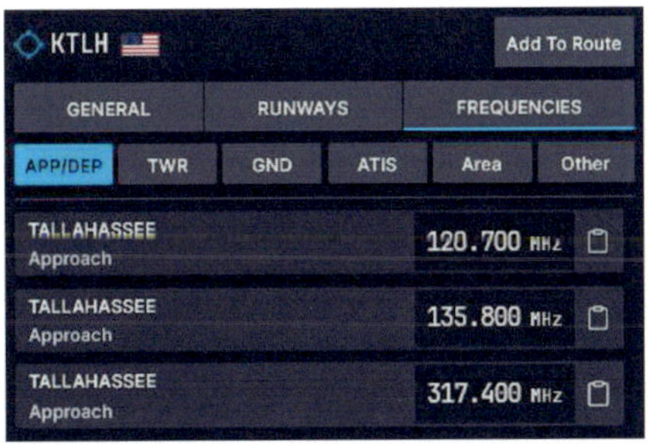

Note: Some UHF frequencies may also appear, even for civilian airports.

4. Checking Runway Winds

Although the planner selects the optimal runway automatically, you can view **wind direction and speed** by clicking the airport and selecting the **Runways tab**.

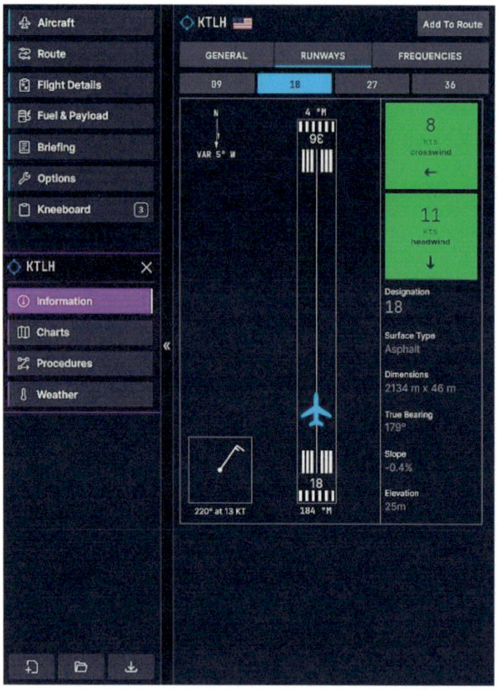

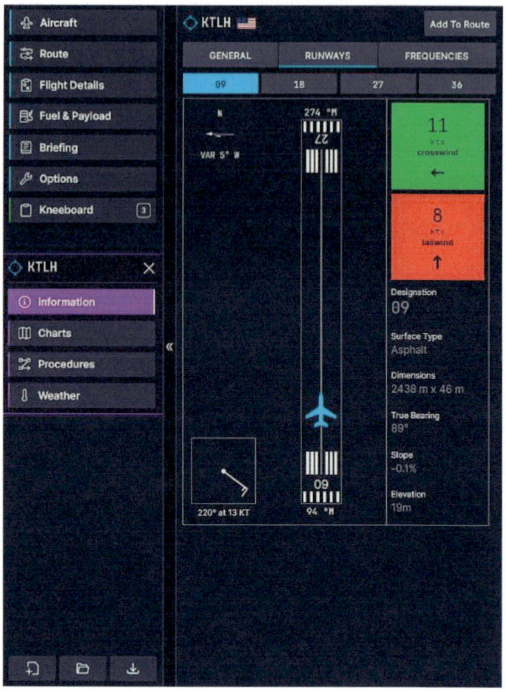

5. Importing Flight Plans from Other Planners

You can **import a route from another planner** (like SimBrief) by copying the text route and pasting it into the **Text Route box** on the MSFS Route page. This is useful for uploading complex plans while still taking advantage of the MSFS kneeboard charts.

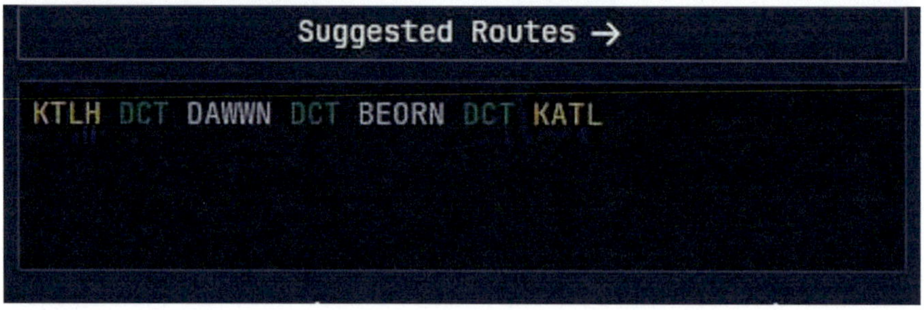

Reminder: Departures and arrivals may still need to be added manually in the default planner.

CHAPTER FOURTEEN

HOW TO TAKE OFF

To take off in Microsoft Flight Simulator 2024 (MSFS 2024), start by setting up your light aircraft (like a Cessna) with flaps and trim, then release the parking brake and add full throttle; use rudder pedals to stay centered on the runway as you accelerate, gently pull back on the yoke around 55-60 knots (rotation speed) to lift off, and maintain a gentle climb, gradually retracting flaps and adjusting power for a stable ascent, following the checklist for complex airliners.

BASICS OF TAKING OFF

To take off in **Microsoft Flight Simulator 2024**, follow this step-by-step guide tailored for a standard small aircraft like the Cessna 172.

1. Pre-Flight Preparation

If you start at a parking spot, you must first complete the new **Character Mode** walkaround before entering the cockpit:

- **Remove Exterior Obstacles:** Walk around the plane and click to remove wheel chocks, pitot tube covers, engine inlet covers, and tie-downs.
- **Enter the Cockpit:** Walk to the door and click it, or press **Shift + C** to jump instantly into the pilot's seat.
- **Engine Start:** For a quick start, press **Ctrl + E** to automatically start the engine and configure basic systems.

2. Takeoff Configuration

- **Flaps:** Set flaps to the recommended takeoff position (usually **Position 1** or 10 degrees) to increase lift.
- **Trim:** Ensure the pitch trim is set to the neutral or "Takeoff" position to help the nose lift naturally.
- **Parking Brake:** Release the parking brake by pressing **Ctrl + Space** or clicking the lever in the cockpit.

3. The Takeoff Roll

- **Apply Power:** Smoothly push the throttle to **Full/Max** power.

- **Stay Centered:** As the plane accelerates, it may drift to the left due to engine torque. Use the **rudder** (keyboard: **0** and **Enter** on the numpad; controller: **triggers**) to stay aligned with the runway centerline.
- **Monitor Airspeed:** Watch the airspeed indicator. Most light planes require reaching roughly **55–60 knots** before they can fly.

4. Rotation and Lift-Off

- **Rotate:** Once you hit the rotation speed (e.g., 60 knots), gently pull back on the yoke or joystick.
- **Climb Attitude:** Maintain a steady pitch up (nose above the horizon). Avoid pulling back too sharply, as this can lead to a stall.

5. Post-Takeoff Steps

- **Landing Gear:** If your aircraft has retractable gear, retract it once you have a "positive rate" (the altitude is steadily increasing).
- **Retract Flaps:** Once you reach a safe altitude and airspeed (typically above 70–80 knots), gradually retract the flaps to reduce drag.
- **Adjust Power:** Reduce power slightly from the maximum takeoff setting to a "climb power" setting as you continue to your desired altitude

MSFS 2024 WALK-AROUND GUIDE: HOW TO EXIT THE AIRCRAFT

Microsoft Flight Simulator 2024 introduces an immersive new feature that allows pilots to **exit the cockpit and walk around their aircraft**. This walk-around mode adds realism by enabling manual preflight inspections and even lets you explore airports and famous landmarks on foot.

In this section, you'll learn **how to exit and re-enter aircraft**, customize the controls, and understand the purpose of this feature—especially in Career Mode.

How to Exit and Enter Aircraft (and Other Vehicles)

Platform	Exit / Enter Shortcut
PC	Shift + C
Xbox	LB + B

To exit manually, locate the aircraft's nearest door—typically on the left side for left-seat aircraft. Click the door handle or press **A** on an Xbox controller. Aircraft with canopies use a latch along the seal, while some planes have rear or side doors behind the cockpit. You may need to move the camera around to locate them.

If you want a faster method, simply use the shortcut:

- **PC:** Press **Shift + C**
- **Xbox:** Press **LB + B**

Pressing the same shortcut again will instantly return you to the cockpit. *Note: The aircraft must be on the ground to exit.*

How to Rebind Boarding and Deboarding Controls

To customize the exit/enter shortcut:

1. Open **Settings**
2. Go to **Controls**
3. Select your keyboard or controller
4. Search for **"Take Control of Character"**
5. Remove the existing key bind and assign a new one

Tip: To avoid being prompted every time you change bindings, duplicate one of the default **MSFS 2024** control presets and apply your changes there. Avoid using the **2020 preset**, as it contains a known bug that removes the unbind shortcut.

On-Foot Controls and Interaction

Once on foot, you can interact with your aircraft's external components—an essential requirement for preflight inspections in Career Mode.

Basic Interaction

- **PC:** Left-click mouse
- **Xbox:** Press **A**

Your pilot automatically uses a flashlight at night for visibility. You can also crouch and sprint:

Action	PC	Xbox
Crouch	C	X Button
Sprint	Spacebar	RT

Why Walk-Around Mode Matters

While it's fun to explore airports and landmarks, the **primary purpose** of walk-around mode is realism. In Career Mode, you must physically inspect your aircraft before flight, including:

- Checking tires, wings, and control surfaces
- Removing chocks and engine covers
- Inspecting engine oil condition
- Confirming overall aircraft readiness

This feature adds depth, immersion, and a real-world pilot workflow that brings MSFS 2024 closer than ever to authentic aviation operations.

HOW TO INSTALL THE FLYBYWIRE A320 IN MSFS 2024

Before starting this series, it's important to choose which Airbus A320 to fly in Microsoft Flight Simulator 2024. Currently, there are **three main A320 options**, each designed for a different type of simmer.

A320 Options Explained

1. **Default (Vanilla) A320neo:** Included with the standard edition of MSFS 2024, this version is reliable and beginner-friendly. It's a great choice if you're just starting to learn airliners.
2. **FlyByWire A320neo (Freeware):** Developed by a passionate community, this aircraft significantly improves realism with better flight dynamics and more advanced systems modeling—all at no cost. It offers the best balance between realism and accessibility.
3. **Fenix A320 (Payware):** This is the most realistic A320 simulation available, with nearly every system modeled in extreme detail. However, it is a paid add-on and may be overwhelming for beginners.

For this section, we'll be using the **FlyByWire A320**, as it delivers excellent realism while remaining completely free.

Installing the FlyByWire A320

Installing the FlyByWire A320 is quick and straightforward:

1. Visit the **FlyByWire official website**.

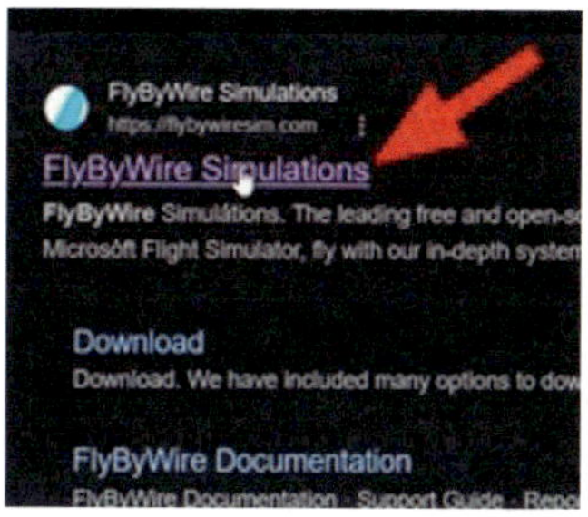

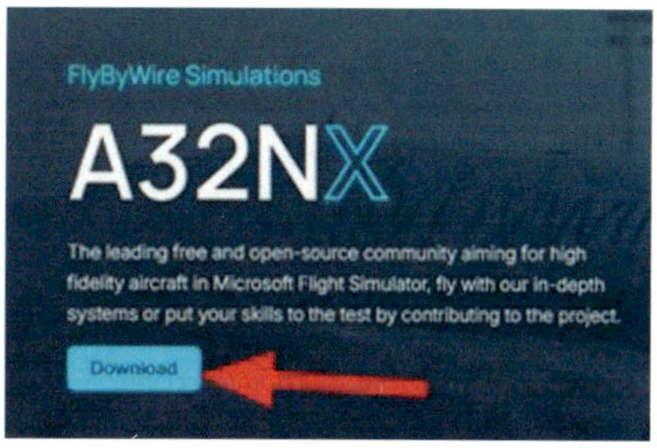

2. Click **Download**, then select the **Installer version**.
3. Download and install the **FlyByWire Installer App**.

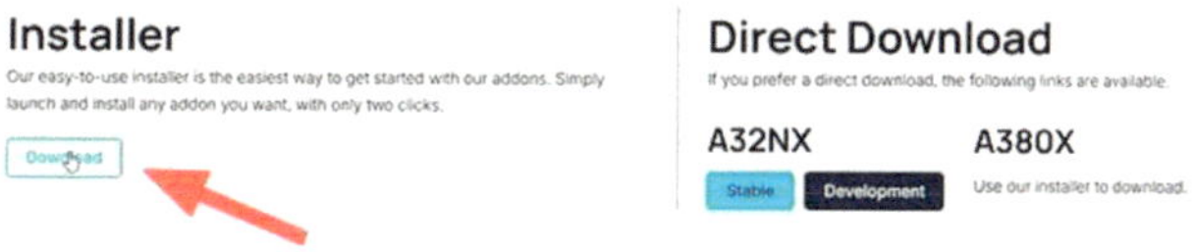

4. Launch the app once installation is complete.

Setting the Community Folder

When you first open the FlyByWire app:

1. Click the **Settings (gear icon)**.

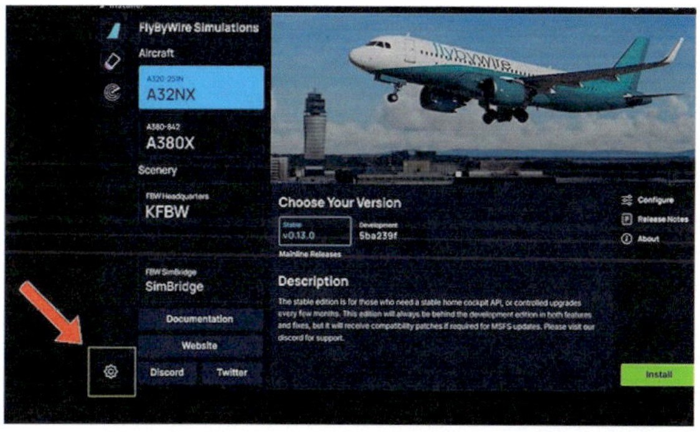

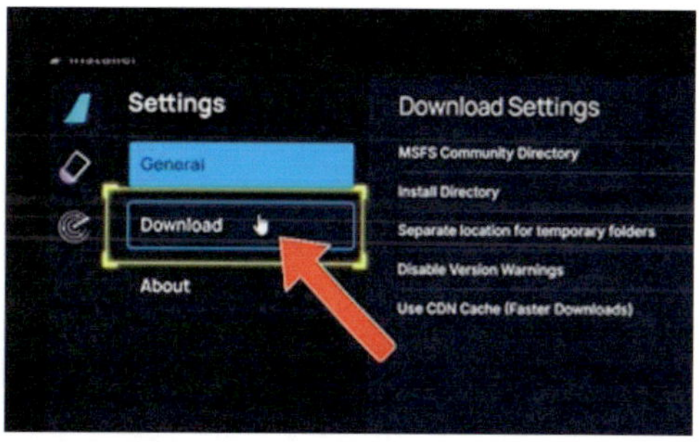

2. Navigate to the **Download** section.
3. Set your **Community Folder path**.

The Community Folder is where all MSFS add-ons and mods are stored and loaded during simulator startup.

- You may choose a **custom location** (recommended if you want to avoid cluttering your system drive).
- If you prefer the default location, the installer supports both **Microsoft Store** and **Steam** versions of MSFS 2024.

MICROSOFT / XBOX COMMUNITY FOLDER PATH:
C:\Users\<YourUsername>\AppData\Local\Packages\Microsoft.Limitless_<PlentyOfNumbersAndLetters>\LocalCache\Packages\Community

STEAM COMMUNITY FOLDER PATH:
C:\Users\<YourUsername>\AppData\Roaming\Microsoft Flight Simulator 2024\Packages\Community

Once a valid Community Folder is selected, the installer is ready.

Downloading the Aircraft

1. Return to the FlyByWire app's **main page**.
2. Select and download the **Stable version** of the FlyByWire A320.

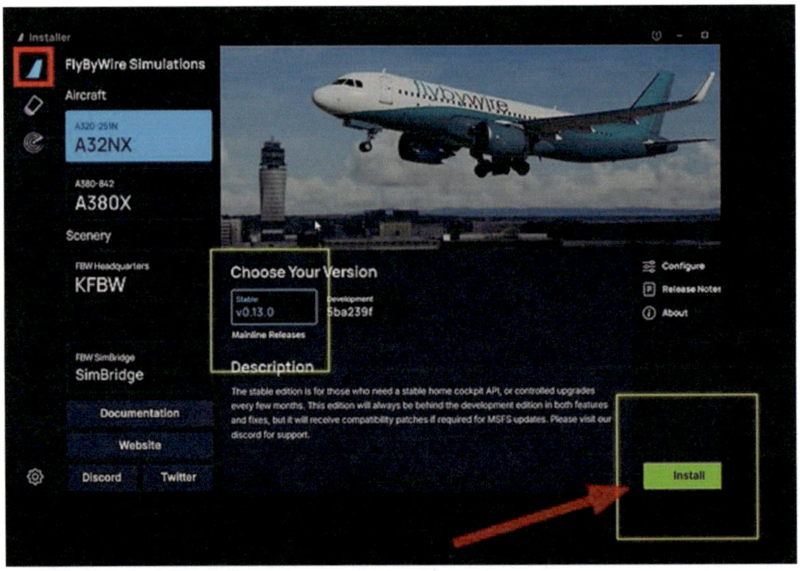

3. Wait for the installation to complete.

Launching the Aircraft in MSFS 2024

After installation:

1. Launch **Microsoft Flight Simulator 2024**.
2. Go to the **Aircraft Selection menu**.
3. You should now see the **FlyByWire A320neo** listed and ready to fly.

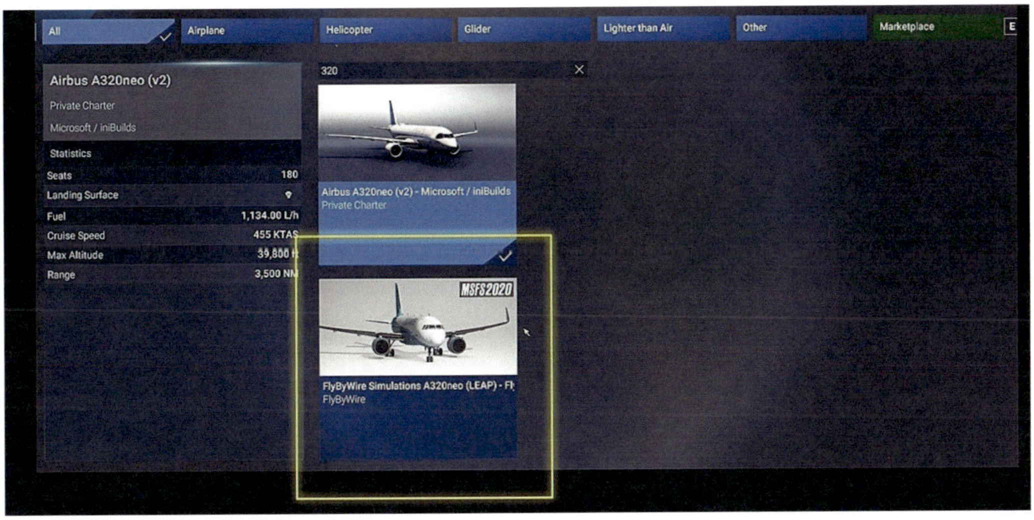

Additional Notes

- The FlyByWire A320 supports **hundreds of liveries**, available on third-party websites such as *flightsim.to*.
- Liveries are optional and do not affect aircraft performance.

HOW TO CONFIGURE THE MCDU IN THE FLYBYWIRE A320

You should now be fully ready to step into the FlyByWire A320 and begin cockpit setup. While on the ground, there's no need to remove the chocks manually—these are managed by the aircraft itself rather than Microsoft Flight Simulator.

To enter the cockpit, press **Shift + C**. Welcome aboard. Take a moment to appreciate the cockpit layout—this aircraft is both functional and visually impressive.

Powering Up the Aircraft

The first step is to supply electrical power:

1. Look up to the **overhead panel**.
2. Turn on the **two battery switches**.

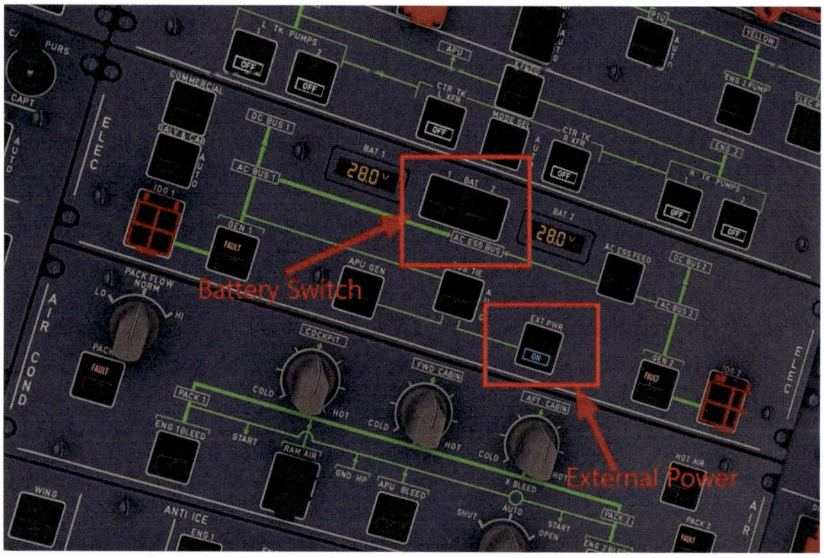

3. Activate **External Power** to connect the aircraft to the airport's power grid.

Once external power is online, you should hear the air conditioning systems start up, confirming the aircraft is receiving electricity.

Initial Systems Setup

Now that power is available, it's time to initialize the aircraft's navigation systems:

- Locate the **three Inertial Reference System (IRS) knobs**.

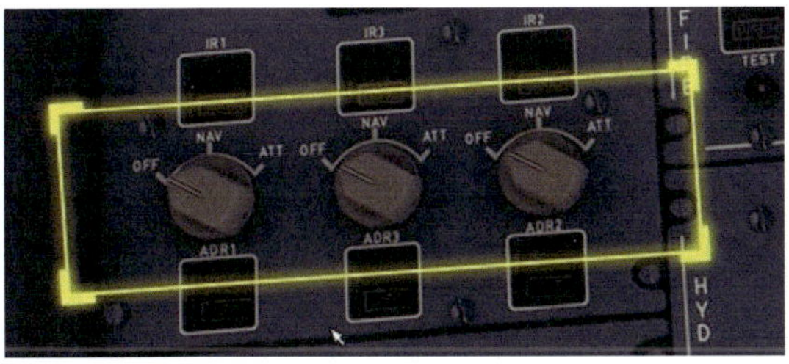

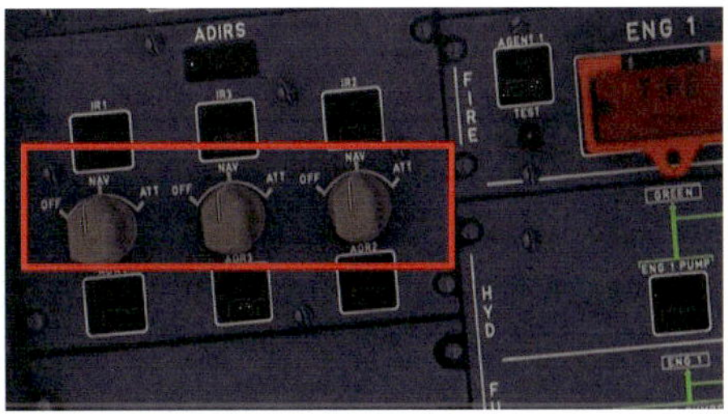

- Turn all three to the **NAV** position.

At this stage, you'll notice that the cockpit displays are showing red warnings. This is completely normal. The IRS systems require **approximately 5 to 8 minutes** to align and initialize.

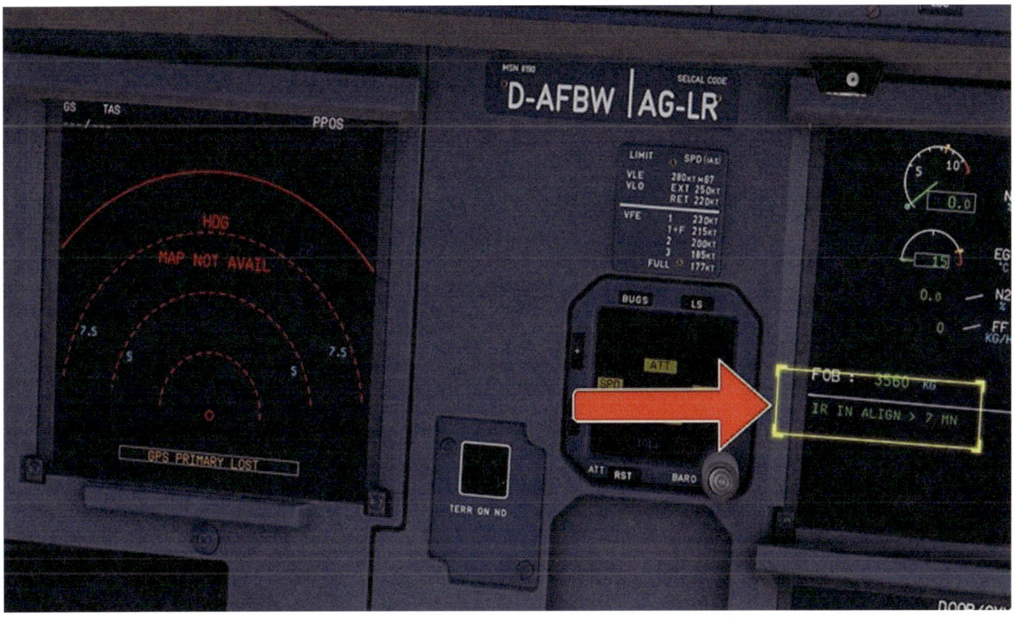

With the essential systems running, we can move on to configuring the aircraft tablet.

Configuring the FlyByWire Tablet

On your left side, you'll find the **FlyByWire Electronic Flight Bag (EFB)** tablet. This tablet allows you to manage several aircraft features and integrations.

1. Open the **Options menu**.

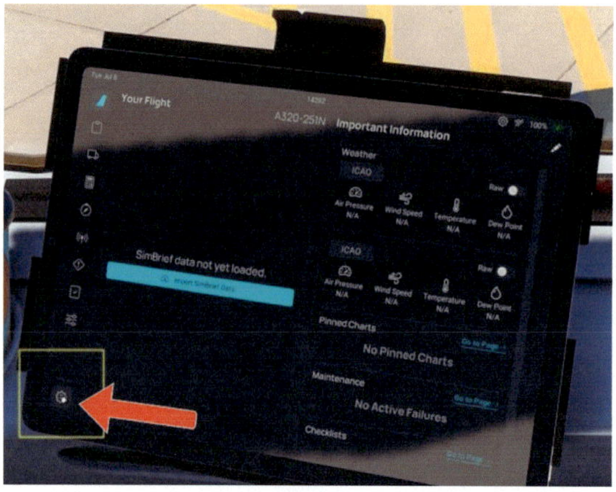

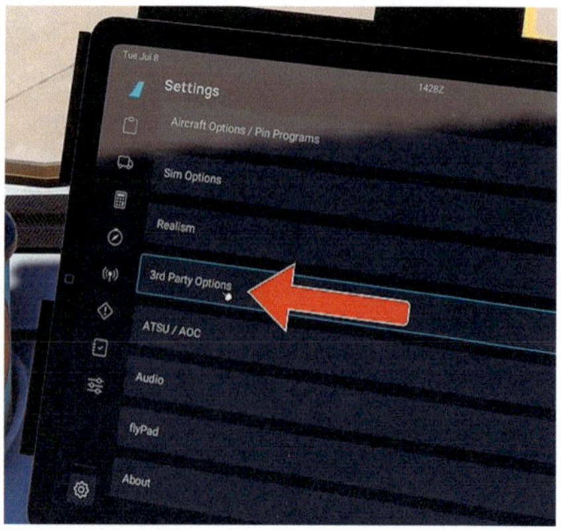

2. Navigate to **Third-Party Options**.
3. Enter your **SimBrief ID**.

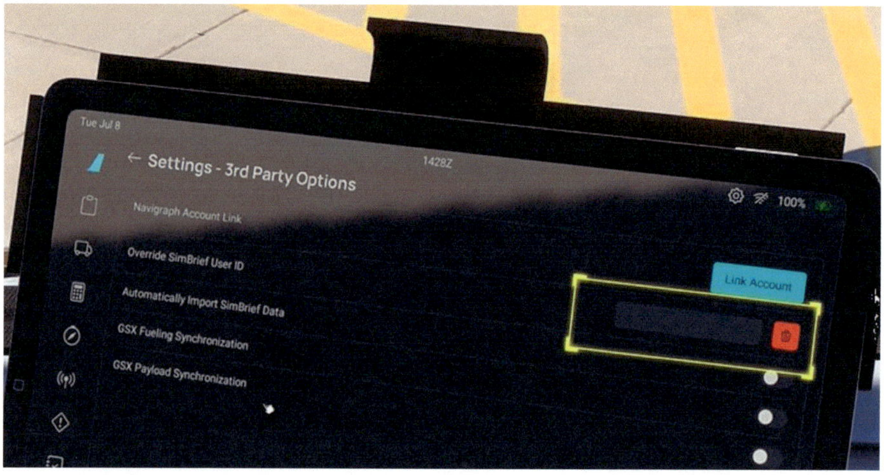

Your SimBrief ID can be found on your SimBrief account page. Once entered, the aircraft will be able to receive live flight-planning data directly from SimBrief.

Importing the Flight Plan

After entering your SimBrief ID:

1. Return to the tablet's **main menu**.
2. Select **Import SimBrief Data**.

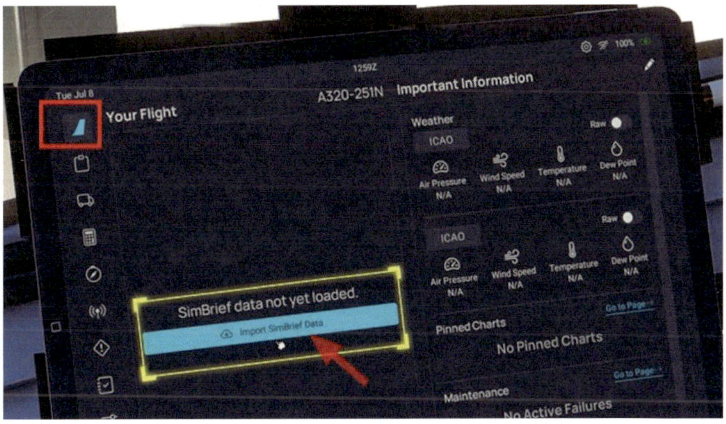

The tablet will now load your flight plan and display a visual overview, including:

- Route
- Weather
- Key flight details

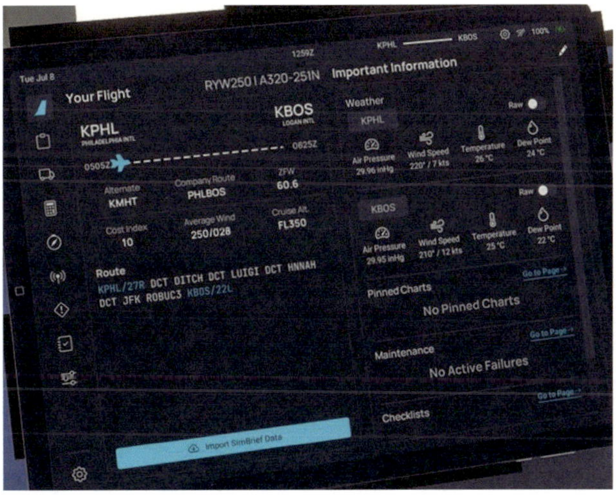

Keep in mind that this step only provides a **visual preview**. The flight plan has not yet been programmed into the aircraft's onboard computers.

Flight Plan Overview

For this flight, we'll be using a familiar route:

- **Departure:** Philadelphia (Runway 27R)
- **Arrival:** Boston

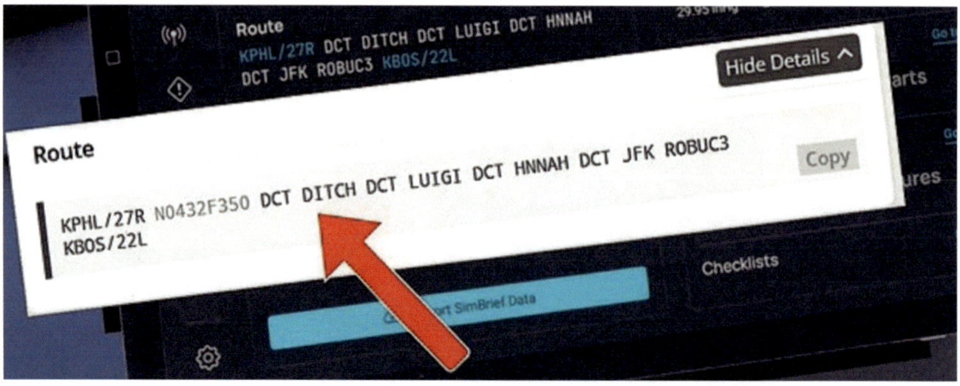

After takeoff, ATC will vector us until the **DITCH** waypoint, where we'll resume our own navigation. From there, we'll pass **Luigi** and **Hnnah**, then proceed to the **Kennedy VOR**, which serves as the transition point for the **ROBUC3 arrival** into Boston.

When creating the flight plan in SimBrief, make sure the aircraft type is set to **A320-251N**. Also, don't forget to click **Generate Flight Plan**, or the data will not sync to the tablet.

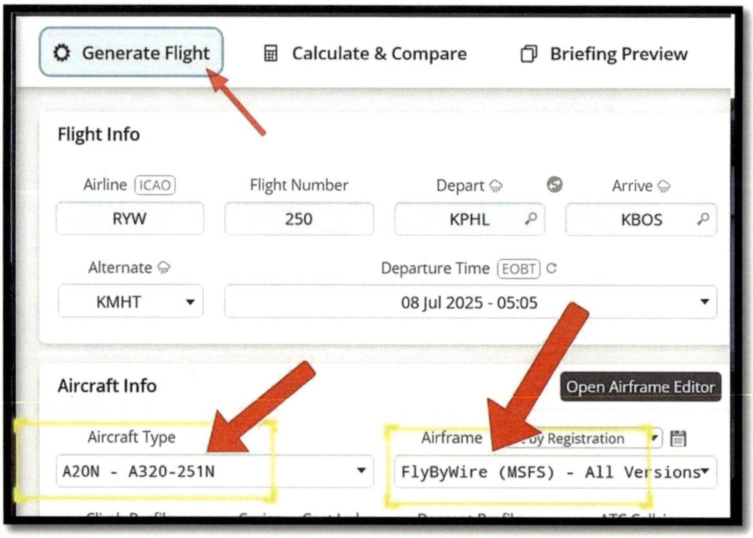

Passenger Boarding

With the setup complete, we're ready to begin boarding:

1. Open the **Ground** tab on the tablet.

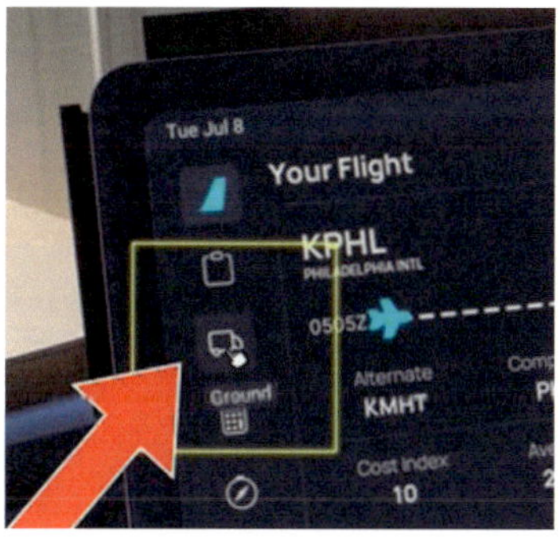

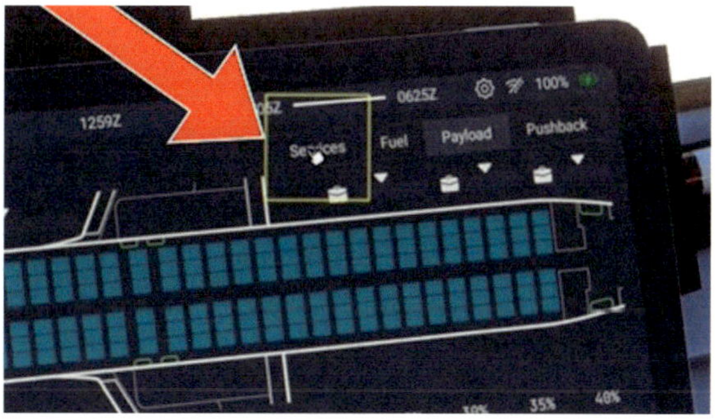

2. Select the **Services** menu.
3. Request the **jet bridge** to connect to the aircraft.

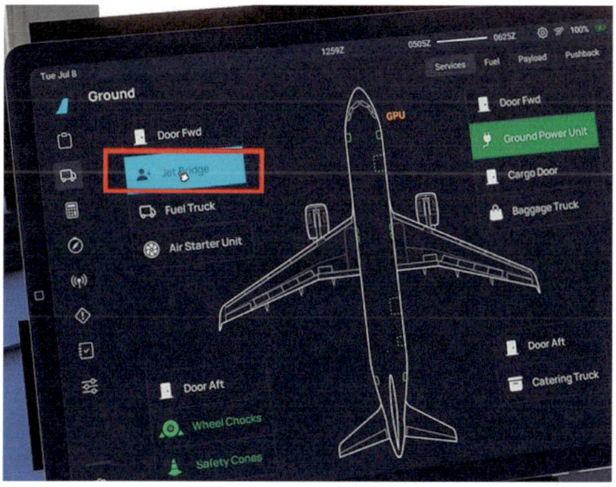

In this case, passengers appear to be boarding via stairs instead. This suggests that the feature may not be fully functional yet. Some ground-service behaviors are still being refined, so occasional inconsistencies are to be expected as development continues.

Setting Fuel, Payload, and Initial MCDU Configuration

Now it's time to load fuel into the aircraft. On the tablet, open the **Fuel** tab and click the **cloud icon** at the bottom of the screen. This synchronizes the fuel quantity calculated by SimBrief for your flight.

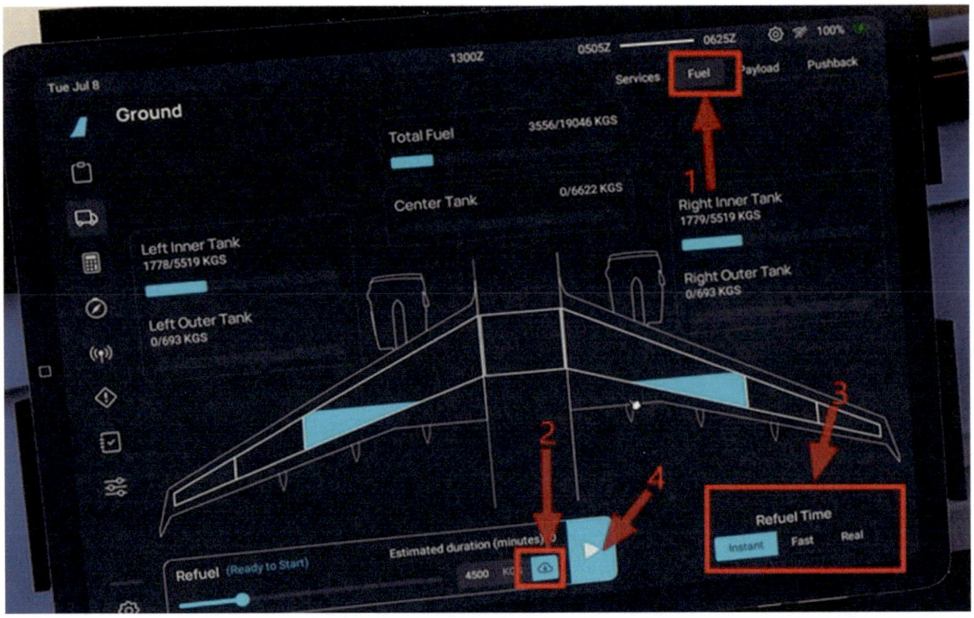

Choose how quickly you want the refueling process to occur: **Instant, Fast, or Real-time.** Once selected, press the **Play** button to begin refueling.

Boarding Passengers and Loading Cargo

Next, we'll load passengers and luggage. Open the **Payload** menu on the tablet. Because the aircraft is synchronized with SimBrief, the system automatically generates a realistic number of passengers and cargo.

- The **left side** shows passengers and cargo waiting at the terminal.
- The **right side** displays the current load inside the aircraft.

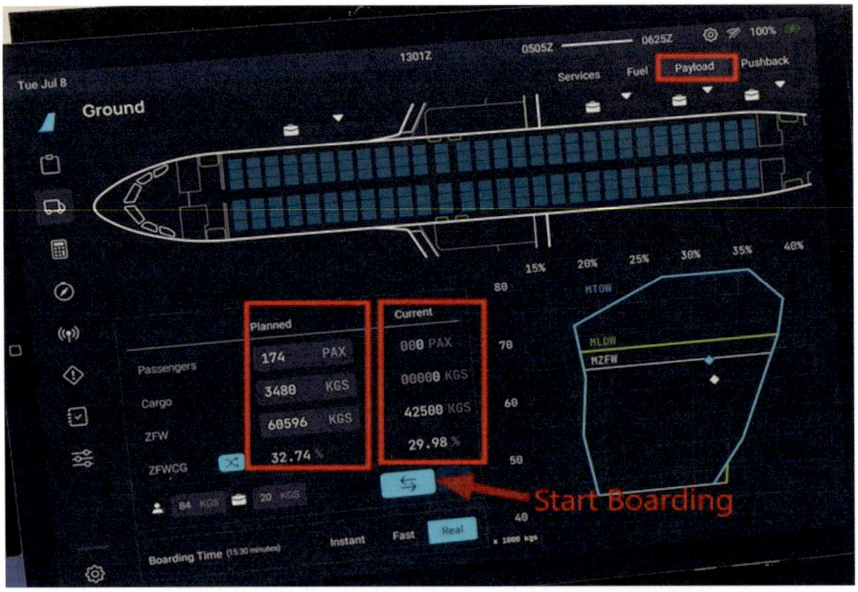

Click **Start Boarding**. As passengers board, you'll see seats gradually turn blue, indicating occupied seats.

With fuel, passengers, and cargo loaded, the aircraft's **weight and balance** are now correctly set.

Accessing the MCDU (FMGC)

We can now configure the aircraft's onboard computer. Press the **FMGC** button to access the MCDU.

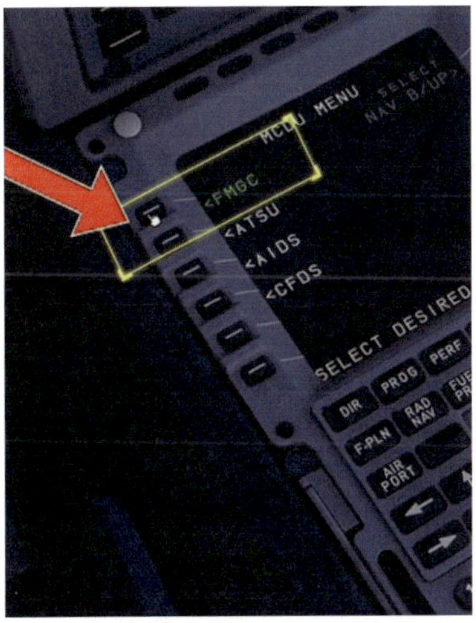
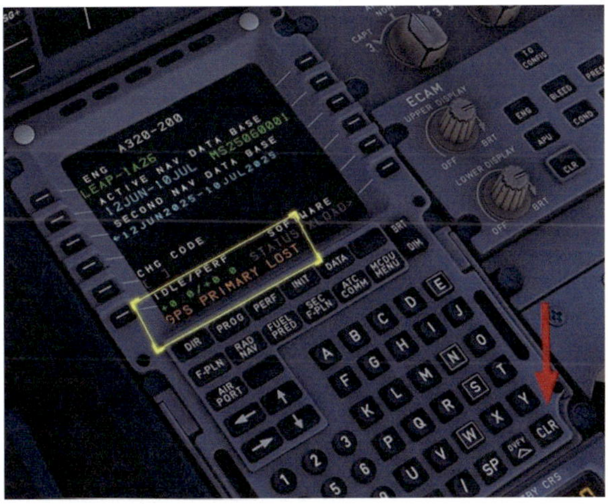

You may see a **GPS warning message** at this point. Don't worry—this is normal because the navigation system has not fully aligned yet. Simply clear the message by pressing the **CLR** button in the lower-right corner.

INIT Page: Basic Flight Information

Navigate to the **INIT** page. This is where you'll enter essential flight data.

The MCDU works as follows:

- Letters and numbers are entered using the keypad at the bottom.

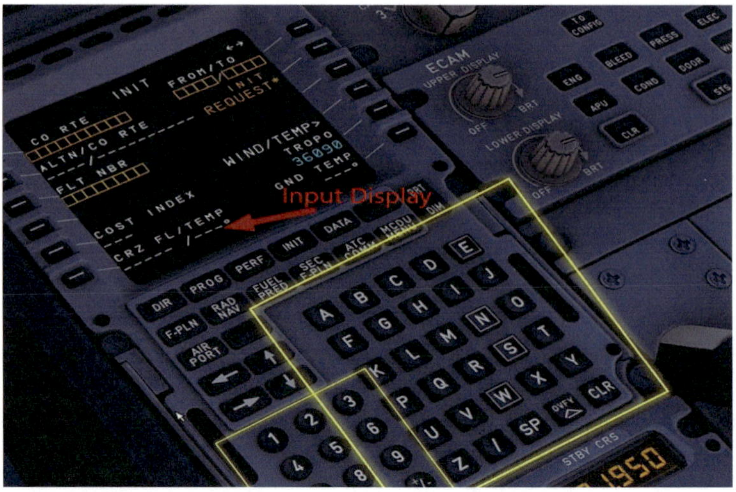

- Your input appears in the scratchpad.
- To assign the entry, press one of the **line-select keys (LSKs)** next to the corresponding field.

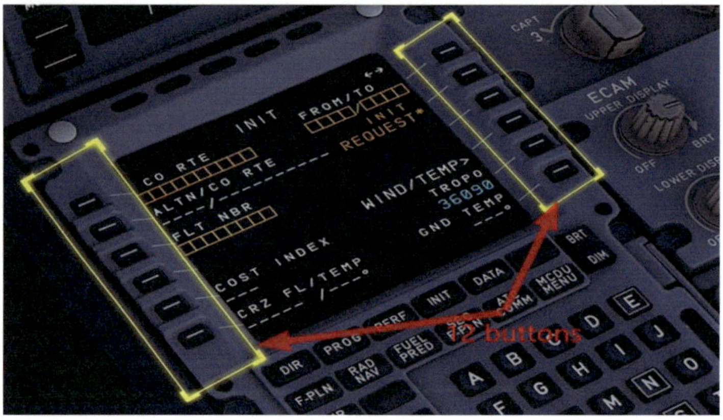

Origin and Destination

From our flight plan, we're flying from **Philadelphia (KPHL)** to **Boston (KBOS)**. Type the route into the keypad, then assign it using the **top-right line-select key**.

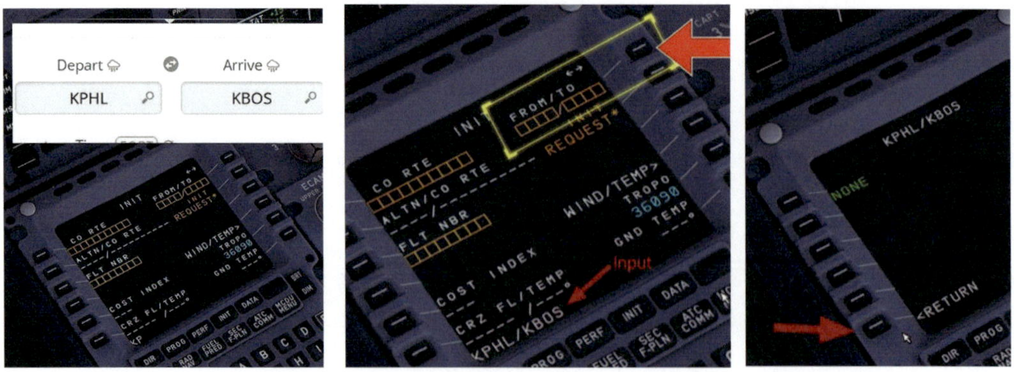

After entering this information, select **RETURN** to continue.

IRS Alignment

Next, we need to confirm the aircraft's position:

1. Select **IRS ALIGN**.

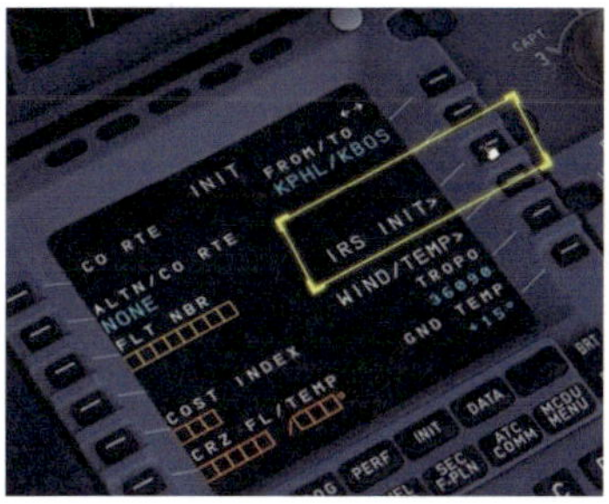

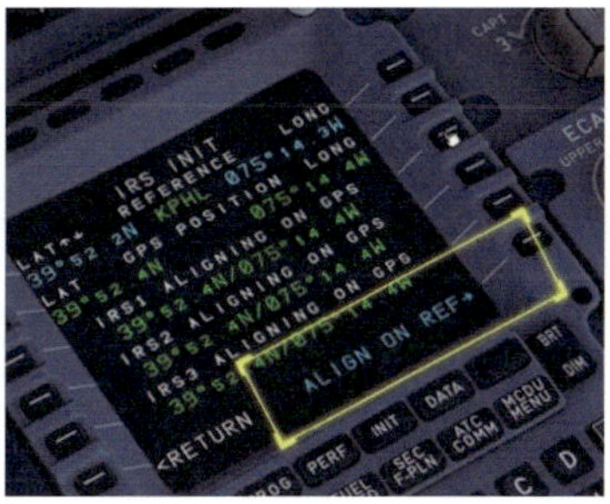

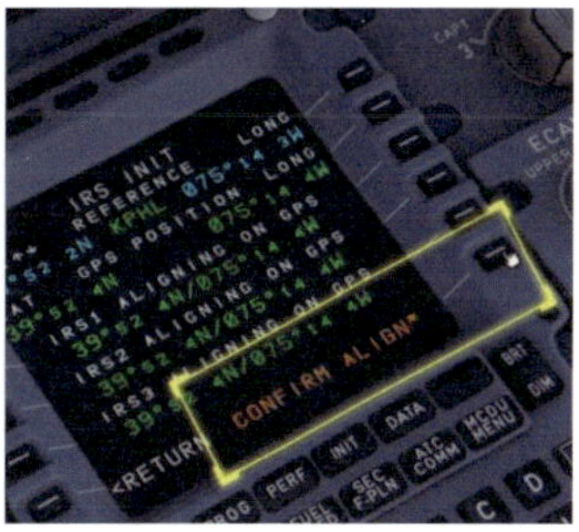

2. Choose **ALIGN ON REF**.
3. Confirm the action.

This synchronizes the inertial navigation system with the aircraft's current position.

Flight Details

Now enter the remaining flight data:

- **Flight Number:** Rock Your Wings 250

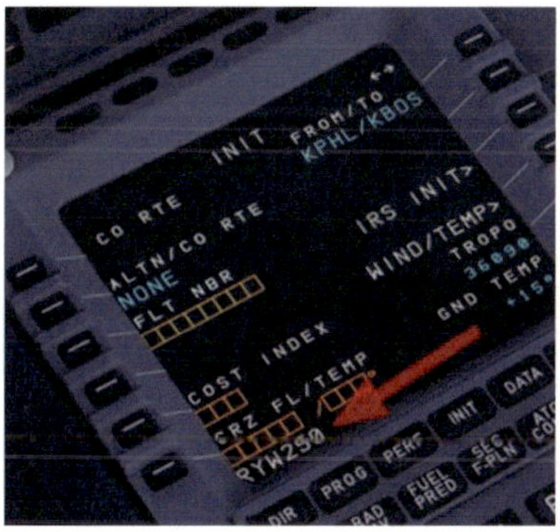

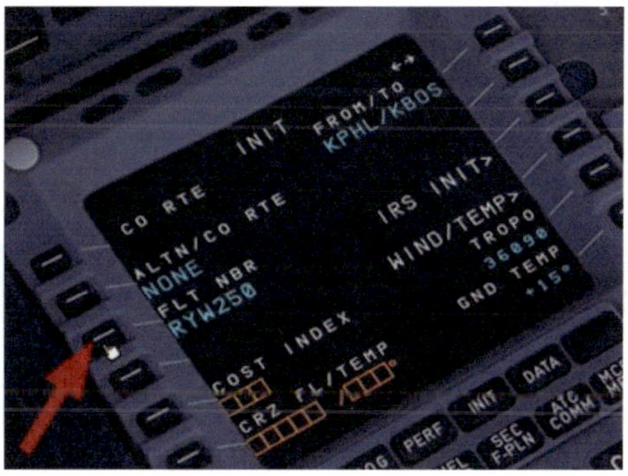

- **Cost Index:** Found in SimBrief or on the tablet

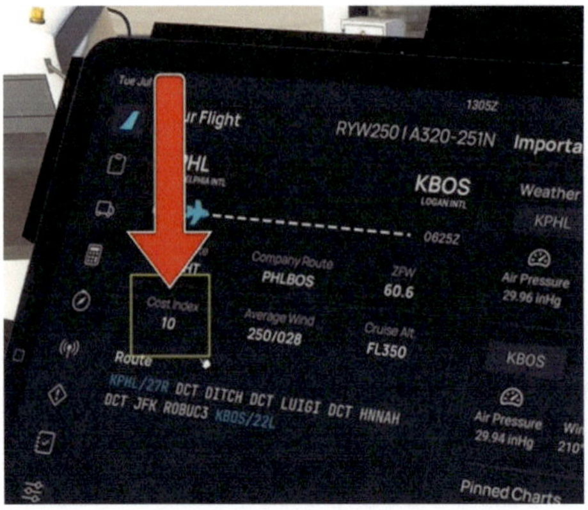

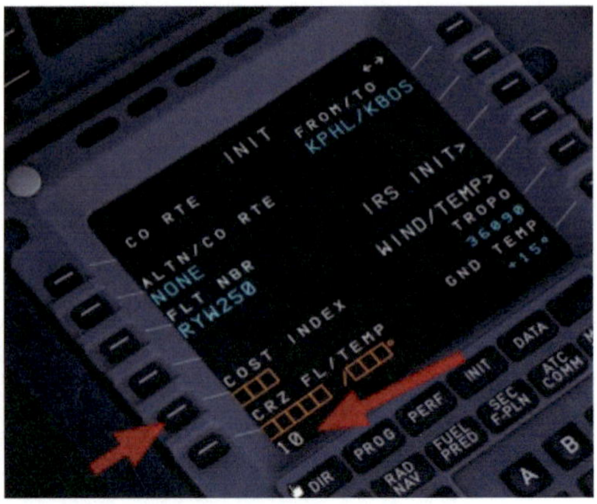

- **Cruise Altitude:** Flight Level **350**

That completes the basic INIT setup.

Weight and Fuel Prediction

The INIT page contains multiple subpages, which you can navigate using the **left and right arrows**.

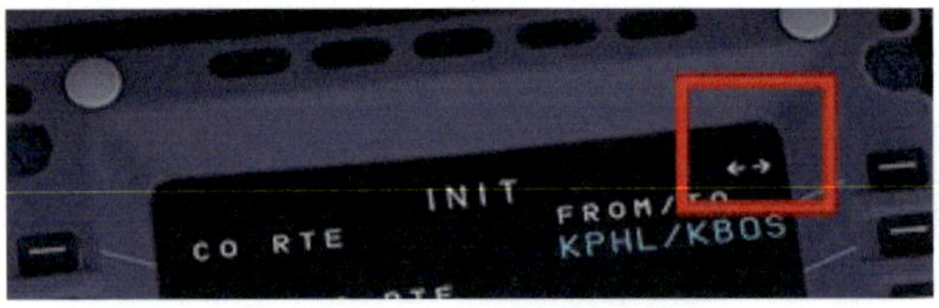

On the **Fuel Prediction** page, the aircraft requires:

- **Zero Fuel Weight (ZFW)**
- **Zero Fuel Weight Center of Gravity (ZFW CG)**

Simply select each line twice, and the correct values will automatically populate.

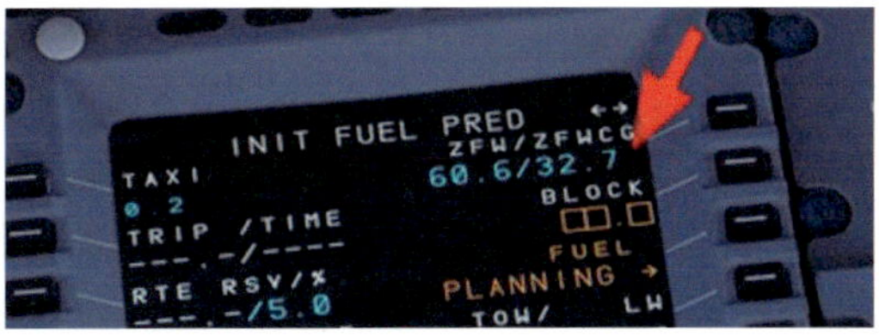

Finally, select **Fuel Planning**. The aircraft will calculate the expected fuel remaining at the destination. For this flight, the estimated fuel on arrival in Boston is approximately **2.6 tons**.

Entering the Flight Plan in the MCDU

Now let's program the flight plan. Press the **Flight Plan (F-PLN)** button. You'll notice that the **departure and arrival airports are already pre-filled**, thanks to the INIT page setup.

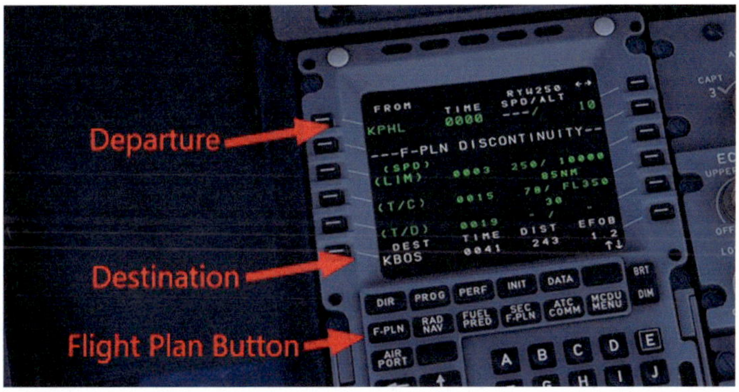

Setting the Departure

1. Select the **origin airport**.
2. Choose **Departure**.
3. Scroll using the **up or down arrows** until you find the correct runway.
4. Select **Runway 27L**.
5. Choose the **PHILLY 4 (PHL4)** departure.
6. Press **Insert** to confirm.

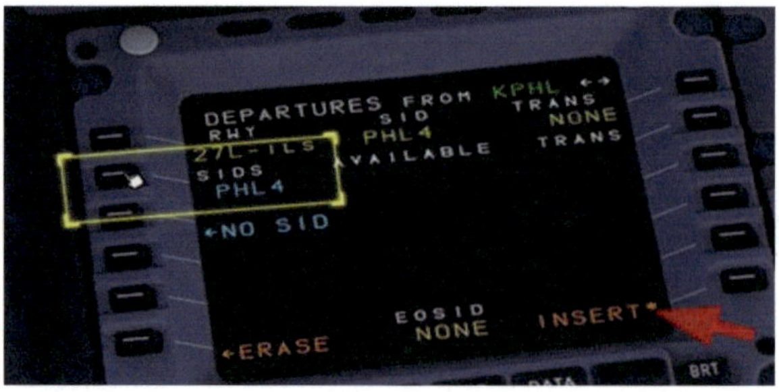

Setting the Arrival

Next, configure the arrival:

1. Select **Boston (KBOS)**.
2. Click **Arrival**.
3. Choose **Runway 22L**.
4. Select the **ROEBUCK 3 (ROB3)** arrival.
5. Choose **JFK** as the transition.
6. Verify the selections, then click **Insert**.

Verifying the Route

Scroll through the flight plan using the **up and down arrows**. You should now see all the departure and arrival waypoints correctly inserted.

You can also confirm this visually on the **Navigation Display (ND)**:

- The **straight line after departure** indicates where ATC will vector us.
- On the arrival side, you'll see the **ROEBUCK 3 arrival path**, guiding the aircraft safely into Boston.

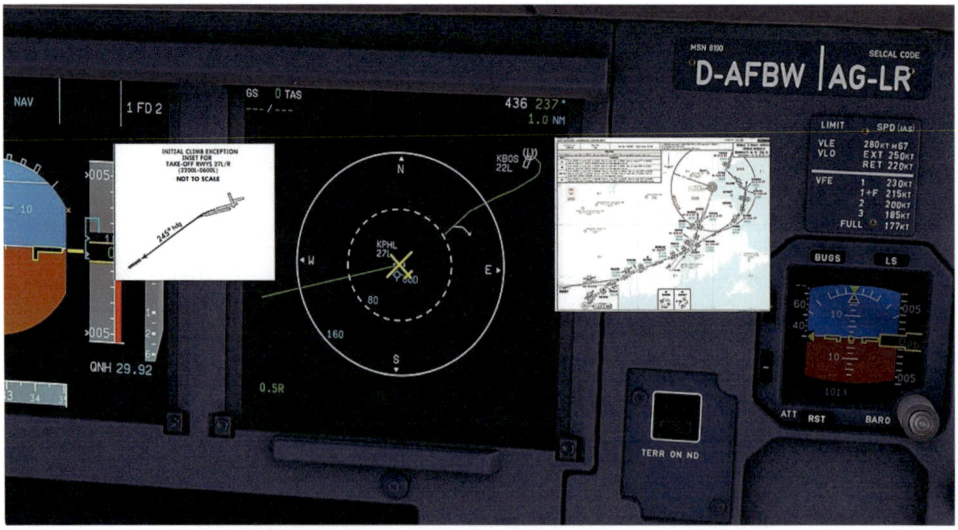

With both departure and arrival set, it's time to fill in the en-route section.

Adding En-Route Waypoints

The first waypoint after departure is **DITCH**. Enter DITCH in the scratchpad and insert it just **before JFK**.

Repeat the same process to add **LUIGI** and **HNNAH**.

Adding an Airway

At **HNNAH**, we'll join **airway Q450** toward **JFK**.

To add an airway in the A320:

1. Select the **starting waypoint** (HNNAH).

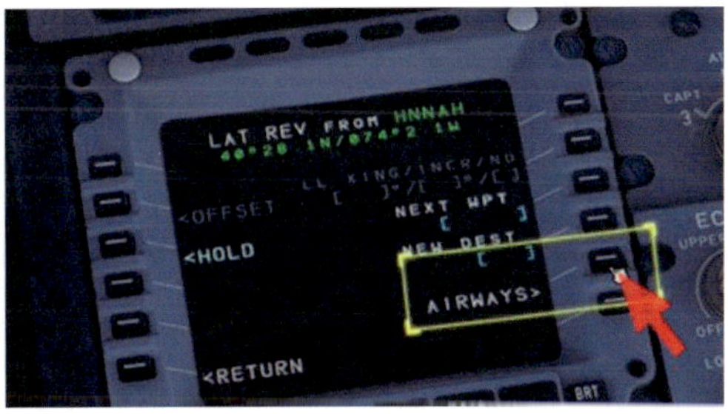

2. Press **Airways**.
3. Enter **Q450** on the left.
4. Enter **JFK** as the exit point on the right.
5. Press **Insert**.

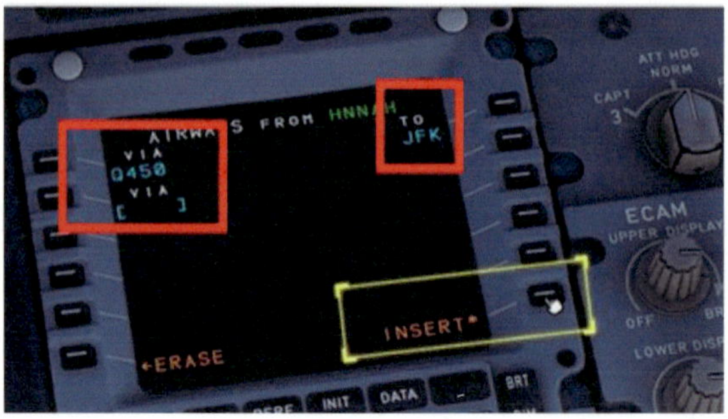

Reviewing the Flight Plan

For a clearer overview:

1. Press **PLAN** mode on the EFIS control panel.

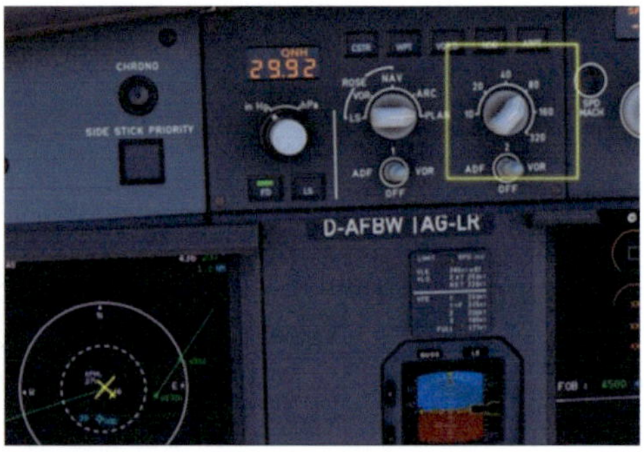

2. Adjust the **zoom knob** on the right side.

In PLAN mode, the display centers on the currently selected waypoint. You can scroll through each waypoint using the **up or down arrows** on the flight plan page.

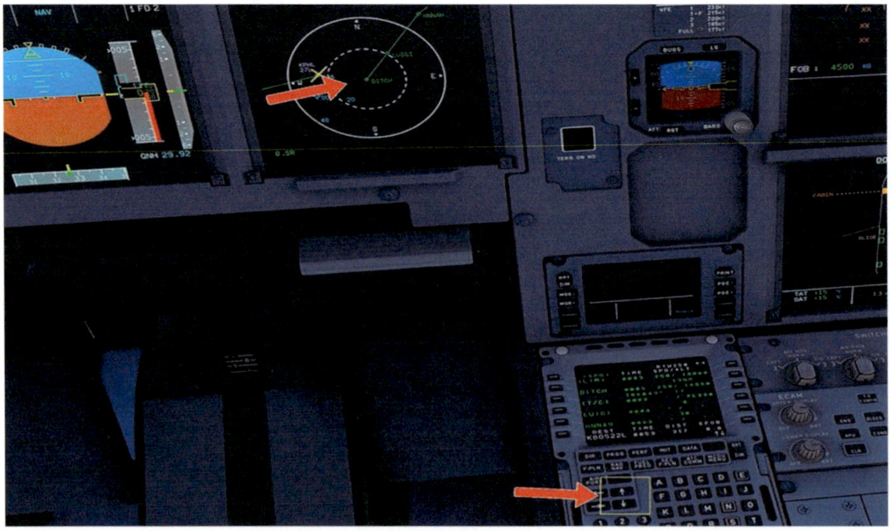

You may notice **discontinuities** at the beginning and end of the route. This is normal—these are points where **ATC will provide vectors. Do not delete them.**

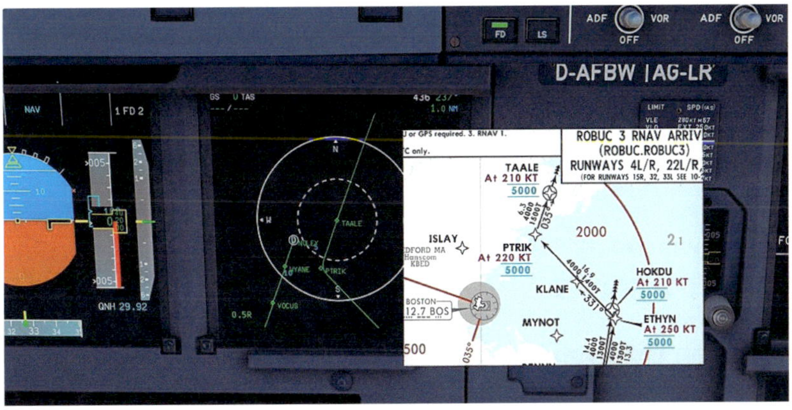

Configuring the Performance Page in the A320 MCDU

Next, we'll finalize the **Performance (Perf) page**, which is similar to the **N1 Limit page** on Boeing aircraft. Here, you define **takeoff and climb thrust**.

In real-world operations, pilots **do not use full engine power for takeoff**. Full power shortens engine life and wastes fuel. Instead, an **optimal takeoff thrust** is calculated—enough to ensure safety while limiting engine wear and fuel burn.

Step 1: Pre-Fill Basic Configuration

1. On the Perf page, click **"Fill from OFP"** to load the aircraft's configuration and weight information.

2. This will automatically populate some fields, like takeoff weight and center of gravity.

Step 2: Use an External Takeoff Calculator

While the tablet has a built-in calculator, it's not perfectly accurate. For precise numbers, use an **external website**:

1. Select **aircraft type** (A320-251N).
2. Enter **gross weight** from the OFP or payload page.
3. Set **flaps 1** for takeoff.
4. Disable **anti-ice**, but leave **air conditioning on**.
5. Input **departure airport, runway length, heading, elevation, QNH 1014 hPa, outside temperature 26°C**, and **wind from the southwest**.
6. Click **Calculate**.

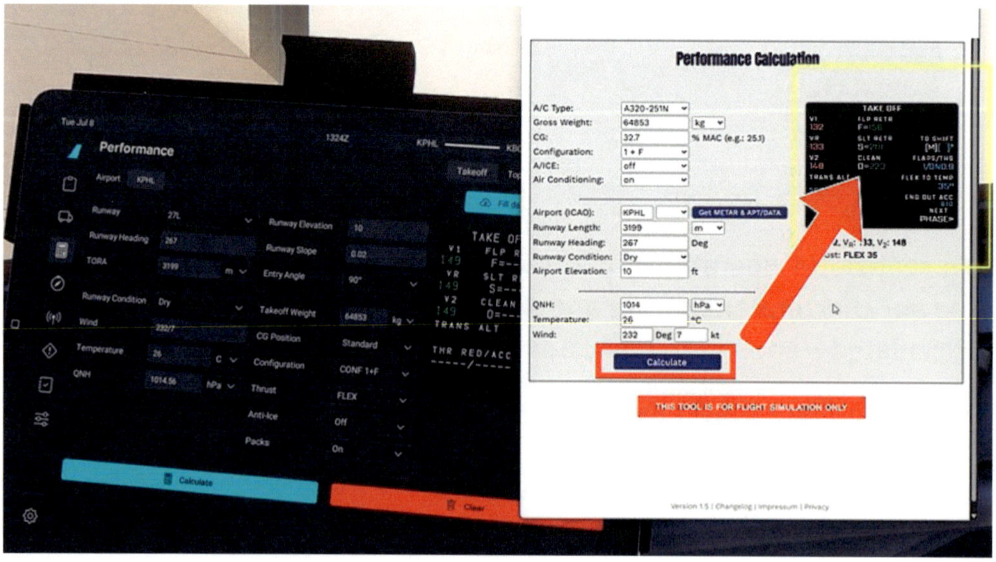

The calculator will generate key takeoff values.

Step 3: Input Performance Data

Enter the following into the MCDU's Perf page:

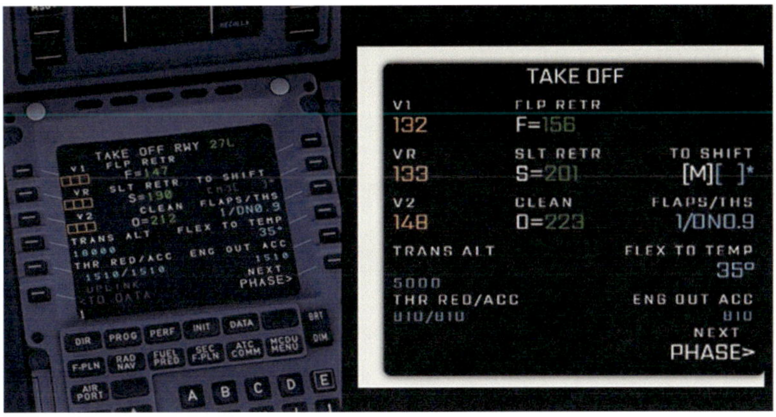

- **Rotation speed (Vr):** 133 knots
- **Takeoff safety speed (V2):** 148 knots
- **Trim setting:** 0.9° nose down

Note: We won't use trim now since engines are off.

Once configured, the **autopilot airspeed display** will show **three dashed lines** instead of numeric values. This indicates that the flight computer has all necessary information for a **flex takeoff** (optimal thrust takeoff). The system will manage engine power automatically while you focus on flying.

If you still see numbers instead of dashed lines, double-check the Perf page—something was likely missed during the setup.

MCDU Setup Complete

You now have a fully configured A320, ready for pushback and taxi. The flight computer will handle the takeoff thrust and airspeed, making your first moments off the ground smoother and more realistic.

STARTING UP THE FLYBYWIRE A320 IN MSFS 2024

Now that everything is configured, it's time to **power up and start the aircraft**. We're currently parked at the gate, and the aircraft is completely powered down.

Step 1: Powering the Aircraft

Begin by switching on the **two battery buttons** on the overhead panel.

The batteries only supply **essential systems**, so they're not enough on their own.

Next, connect **external power** by pressing the External Power button.

The aircraft is now connected to the airport's power grid, and you should hear the **ventilation system** come alive.

Step 2: Initializing the Navigation Systems (IRS)

Now, initialize the **Inertial Reference Systems (IRS)**:

- Turn all **three IRS knobs to NAV**.

The IRS determines the aircraft's position by calculating movement from a fixed GPS reference point using accelerations and rotations. This alignment process takes **about 5–10 minutes**, and **the aircraft must not move** during this time.

On the cockpit displays:

- All screens will appear **red**, which is normal.
- A **countdown timer** on the central display shows when alignment is complete.

This waiting period is ideal for **boarding passengers and final aircraft setup**.

Step 3: Preparing for Engine Start – APU Setup

Assume passengers are boarded, doors are closed, and the **MCDU is fully configured**. Now we're ready to start the engines.

First, we need to start the **APU (Auxiliary Power Unit)**—a small onboard turbine that provides electricity and compressed air.

1. Turn on **all six fuel pump switches**.

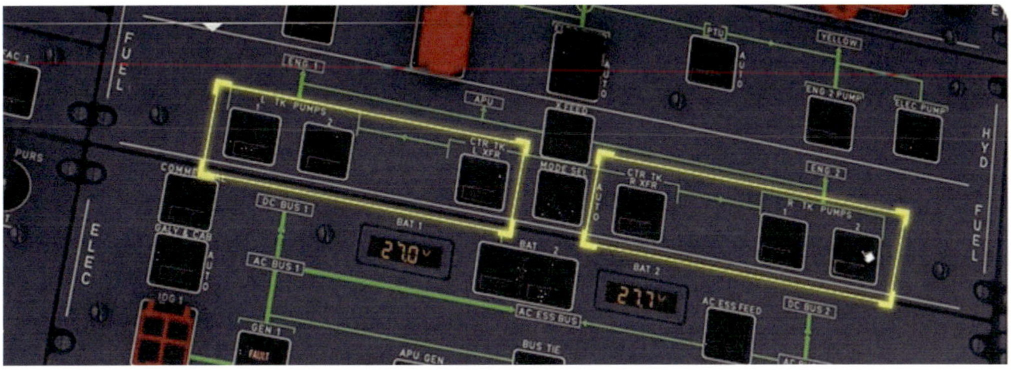

2. In the APU section of the overhead panel:
   - Press **APU Master Switch**
   - Then press **APU Start**

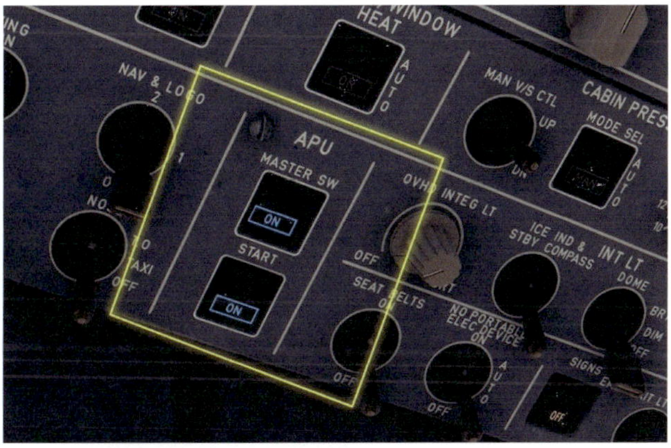

The APU will begin spooling up.

On the center display, monitor the APU status. Once it reaches **100%**, it's fully operational.

At this point, disconnect **External Power**.

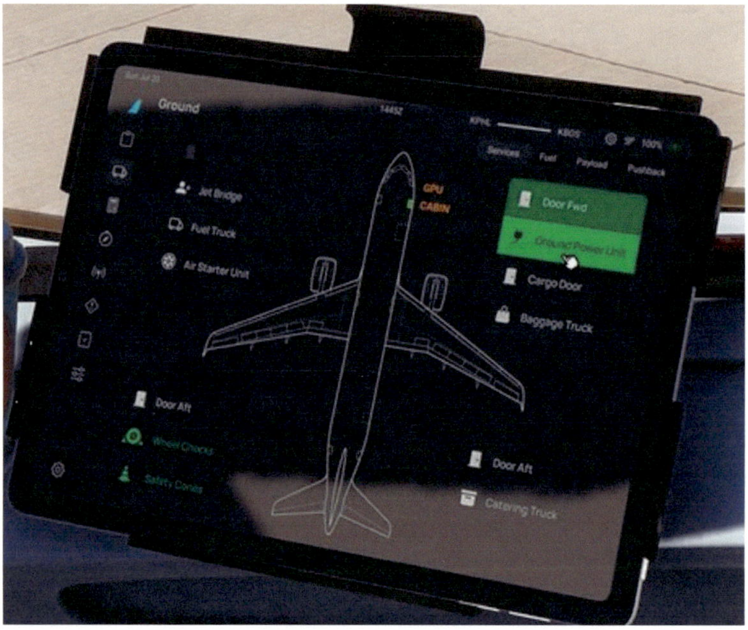

The aircraft is now **self-powered by the APU**.

Understanding Aircraft Power Sources (Quick Explanation)

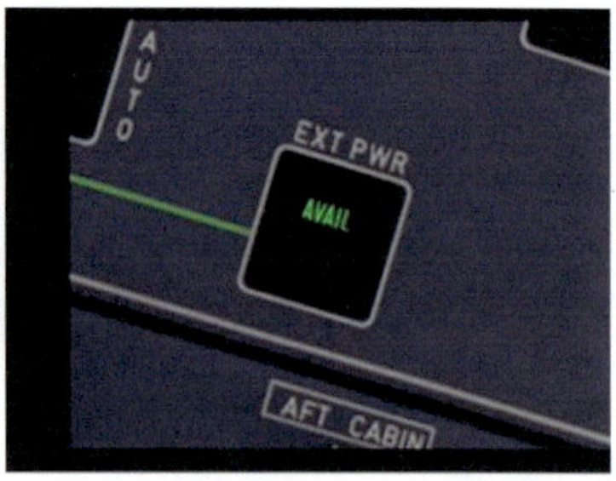

You may be wondering why aircraft use **multiple power sources**. Here's how they work together:

- **Battery:** Powers only essential systems. Like a car battery, it drains quickly if used alone.

- **External Power (GPU):** Supplied by the airport. Ideal during long ground operations such as boarding and preflight setup.

- **APU:** A small jet-powered generator inside the aircraft. It provides electricity and compressed air when external power isn't available—especially during pushback and engine start.

Using the APU instead of the battery prevents power drain, but since it burns fuel, it's used **only when necessary**.

Once the engines are running, they each drive large generators, making the APU unnecessary.

Step 4: Preparing for Pushback

We're now ready for **pushback**.

During pushback, the engines need **compressed air** to start, and at this stage, **only the APU can provide it**.

- Press the **APU Bleed** button to enable compressed air flow.

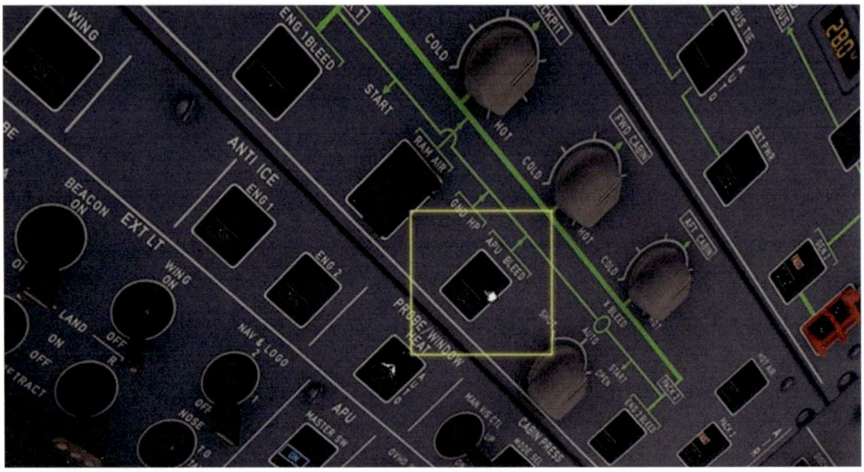

With that done, the aircraft is fully prepared for pushback and engine start.

Pushback and Engine Start – FlyByWire A320 (MSFS 2024)

With everything ready, let's begin the **pushback**.

Release the **parking brake** using the lever on the center console. The aircraft will start moving backward as the tug pushes us away from the gate.

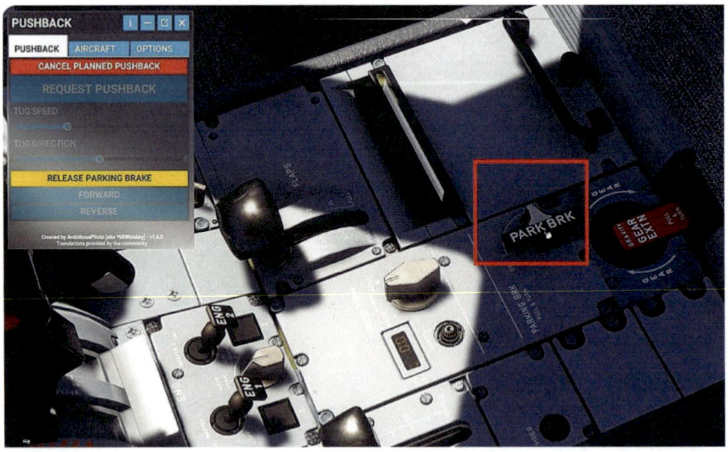

Engine Start Procedure

Once the aircraft is in motion, it's time to start the engines.

1. **Set Engine Mode Selector to IGN/START**

This switch is located just below the thrust levers.

2. **Start Engine 2 (Standard Airbus Procedure)**

- Move **Engine 2 master switch from OFF to ON**.
- Engine startup begins automatically.
- Monitor the engine parameters on the center display.

- N1 will gradually increase and stabilize around **20%**, indicating the engine is running normally.

(Yes, pushback can look a little strange sometimes—but as long as we're back on the ground safely, all is good.)

3. **Start Engine 1**

- Move **Engine 1 master switch from OFF to ON**.

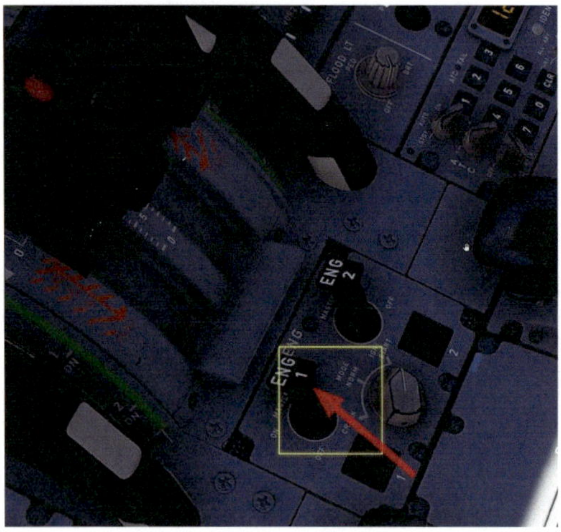

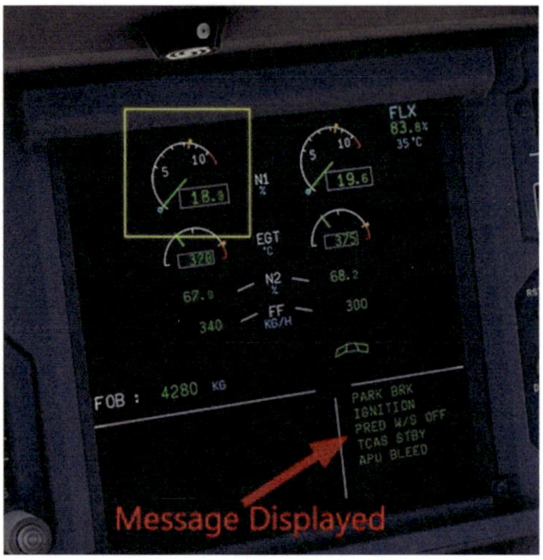

- Monitor the display again.
- Wait until N1 stabilizes around **20%** and the engine shows **AVAIL**.

At this point, **both engines are running and stable**.

After-Start Checklist

Now let's clean up the configuration.

- **Engine Mode Selector**

  Set it back to **NORM**, as ignition is no longer required.

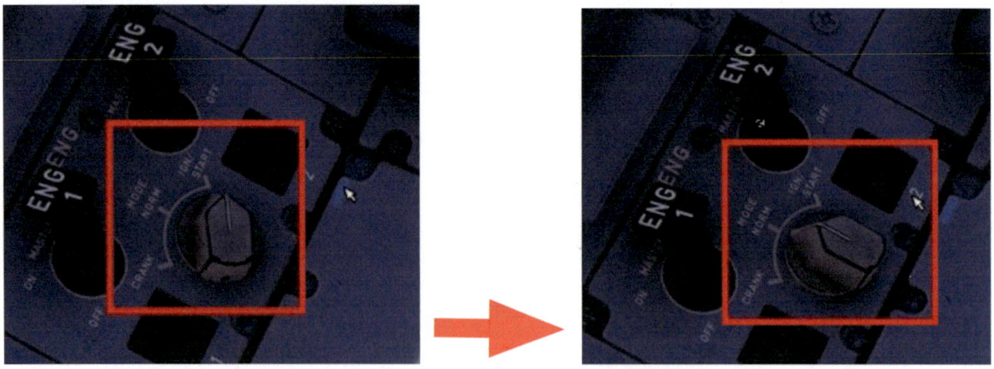

- **APU**

  The APU is no longer needed because electrical power and bleed air are now supplied by the engines.

  Turn **APU Bleed OFF**, then **APU OFF**.

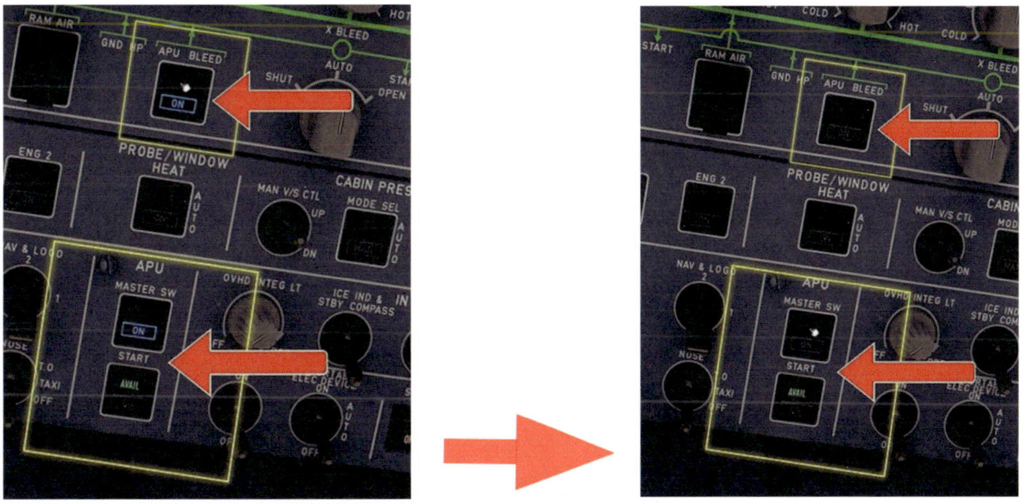

- **Predictive Windshear System**

  Activate the windshear warning system.

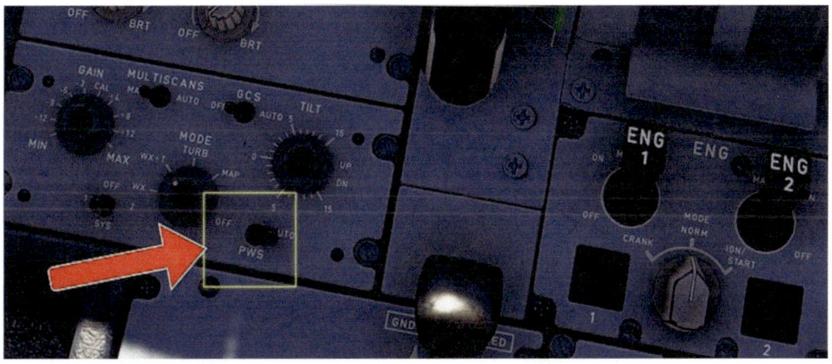

- **TCAS / Transponder Setup**
  - Turn the **transponder ON**.

- Set **TCAS to TA/RA (Traffic Advisory / Resolution Advisory)** to enable full traffic awareness.

Final Notes

You may still see a few messages on the display:

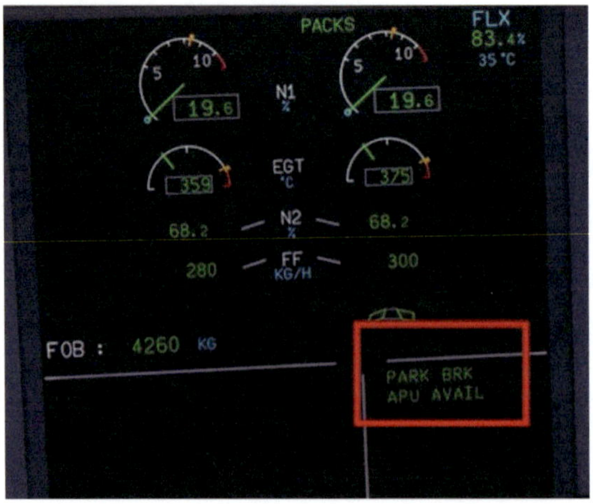

- **Parking Brake** warning — normal if the aircraft is stopped.
- **APU Available** — normal, as the APU takes a few minutes to fully shut down.

Once those clear, your aircraft is fully configured and ready for taxi.

TAKEOFF PROCEDURE – FLYBYWIRE A320 (MSFS 2024)

We are now **holding short of Runway 27L at Philadelphia**, ready for departure. For this phase, focus on the **Takeoff Checklist** displayed on the center screen and complete each item step by step.

Before Takeoff Checklist

1. **Autobrake – MAX:**

   Set the autobrake to **MAX**.

   This ensures maximum braking force in case of a **rejected takeoff**. The autobrake selector is located on the center pedestal.

2. **Cabin Crew – Advised**

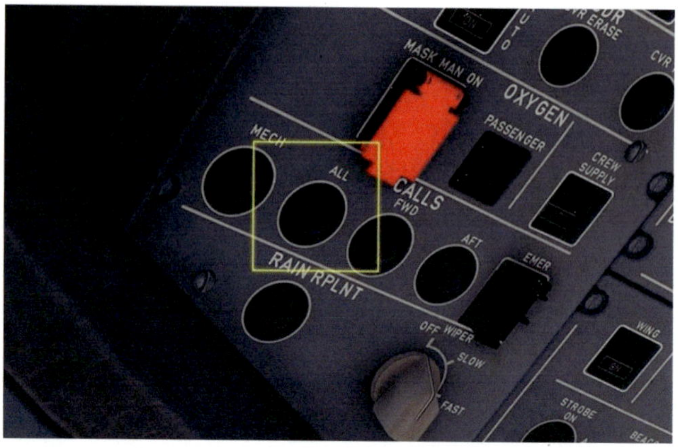

Inform the cabin crew that the aircraft is ready for departure. Use the **PA/cabin call button** on the overhead panel.

3. **Spoilers (Speed Brakes) – ARMED**

Arm the spoilers by lifting the speed brake lever.

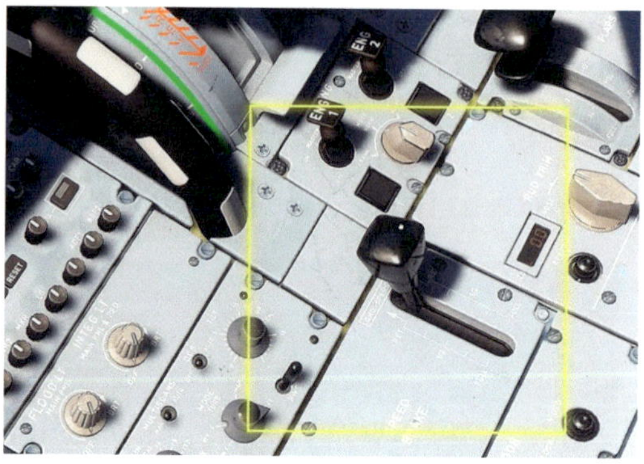

You should hear a **click**, confirming they are armed.

This allows automatic spoiler deployment during a rejected takeoff or after landing.

4. **Flaps – SET FOR TAKEOFF**

Set **Flaps 1** for takeoff, as planned in the performance calculations.

5. **Seat Belt Signs – ON / AUTO**

   Set the passenger seat belt sign to **AUTO** to secure the cabin.

At this point, the checklist should show **green across the board**, indicating readiness for departure.

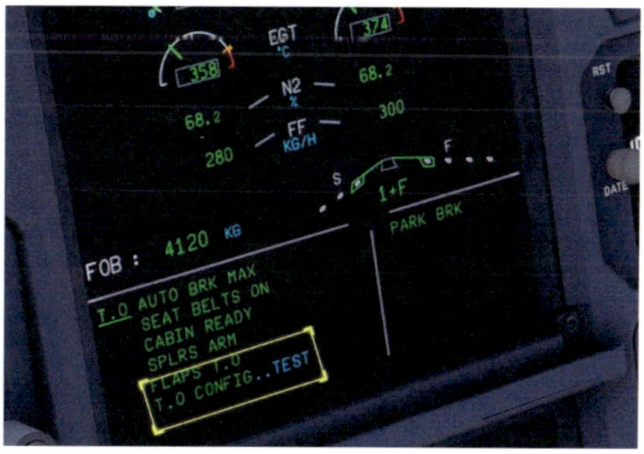

Takeoff Configuration Check

Before entering the runway, perform the **Takeoff Config Test**.

- Press the **T.O. CONFIG** button.

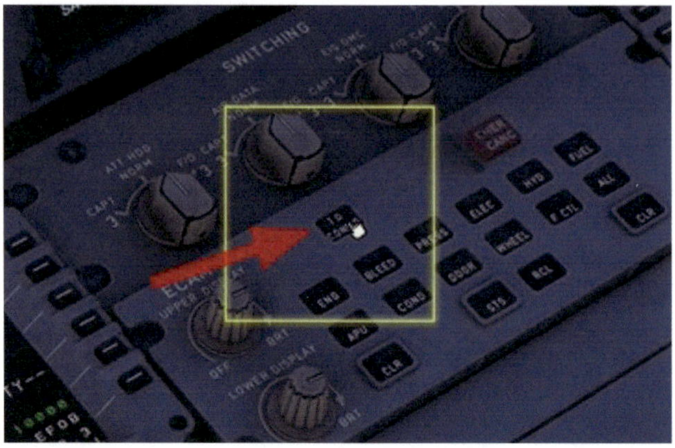

- If you hear a warning tone, something is incorrectly set.

In this case, the warning indicates that the **pitch trim** is not set correctly.

Based on our performance calculations, set the **pitch trim to DOWN 0.9**.

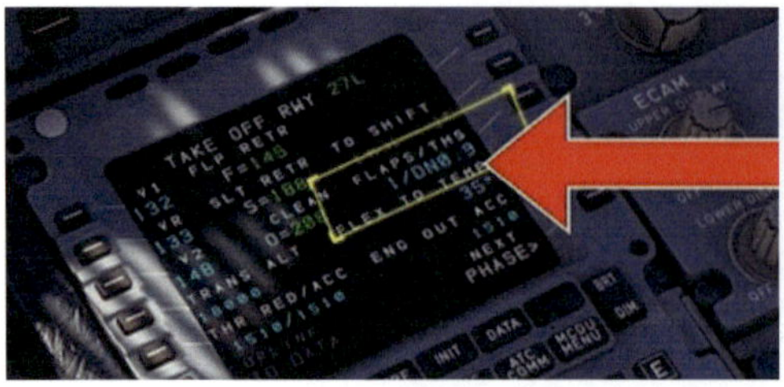

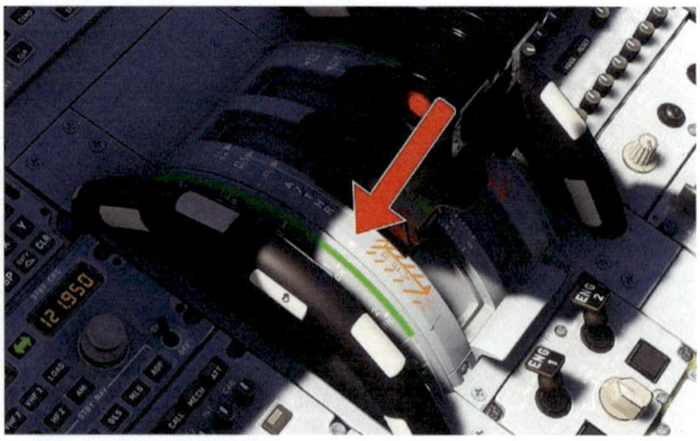

Once adjusted, repeat the check—everything should now be green.

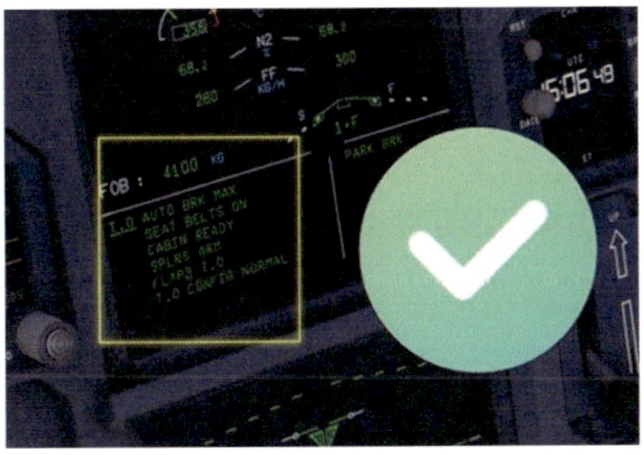

Line Up and Takeoff

Taxi onto the runway and **align the aircraft with the centerline**.

- Apply light thrust to roll forward.
- Press the brakes and come to a **complete stop**.

At this stage, your full attention should be on the **thrust levers**.

Thrust Lever Positions Explained

The A320 thrust levers have several detents:

- **TOGA** – Maximum thrust (Takeoff/Go-Around)
- **FLEX/MCT** – Reduced, optimized takeoff thrust
- **CL** – Climb power (used shortly after takeoff)

If you skipped all configuration steps, you could technically push the levers to **TOGA** and rotate around **130 knots**, but that's not how the aircraft is meant to be flown.

Earlier, we entered a **FLEX temperature of 35°C** in the performance page. This value allows the flight computer to calculate **optimal takeoff thrust**, reducing engine wear while maintaining safe performance.

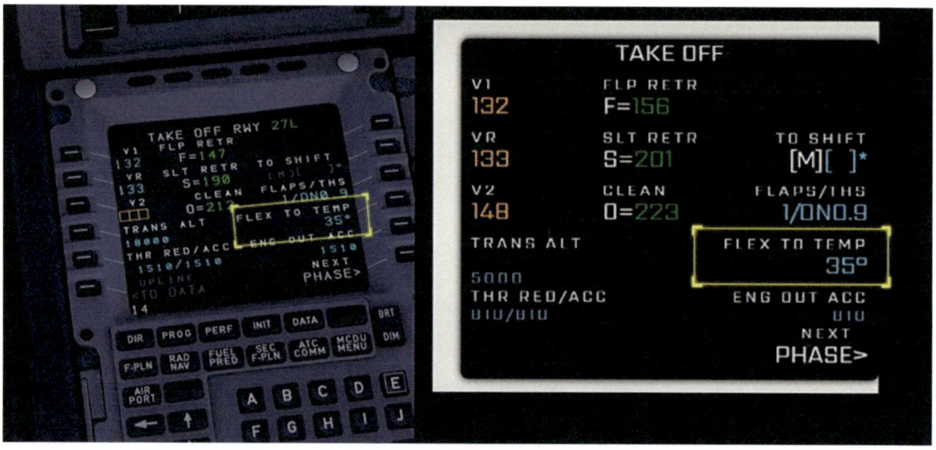

Takeoff and Initial Climb – FLEX Mode (A320 FBW)

Since a **FLEX temperature** has been entered, we will perform a **flex takeoff**.

Takeoff Roll

- **Release the parking brake.**

- Smoothly move the **thrust levers to the FLEX detent.**

- The engines will spool up automatically.
  On the **Flight Mode Annunciator (FMA)**, you should see **FLEX 35**, confirming that optimal takeoff thrust is set.

Maintain the **runway centerline** using gentle rudder inputs while closely monitoring airspeed.

- **V1** – Decision speed.
- **Rotate** – Gently pull back on the sidestick and pitch up to **approximately 20°**.

Initial Climb

- Follow the **Flight Director**, shown by the **two green bars on the PFD**:
  - The **horizontal bar** indicates target pitch.
  - The **vertical bar** indicates target roll.
- Keep the aircraft symbol centered on the flight director cues.

Once airborne:

- **Positive rate of climb → Gear up**.

Flight Director Explained (Quick Pause)

The flight director provides precise guidance to follow the programmed flight path:

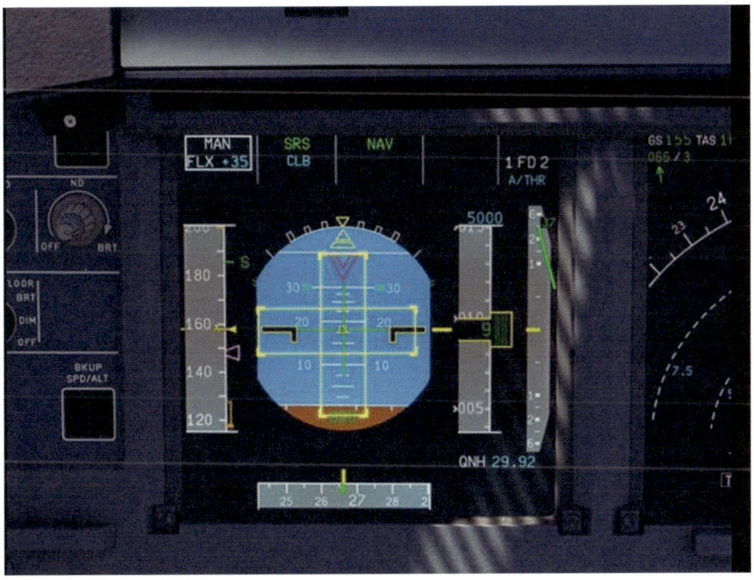

- Pitch guidance ensures the correct climb angle.
- Roll guidance keeps the aircraft aligned laterally.

  Your goal is to smoothly match both cues.

Automation and Profile Change

Once the aircraft is stabilized:

- **Engage the autopilot**.

During the initial climb, the aircraft maintains **V2 speed** with a steep climb profile. This phase prioritizes **obstacle clearance and safety**.

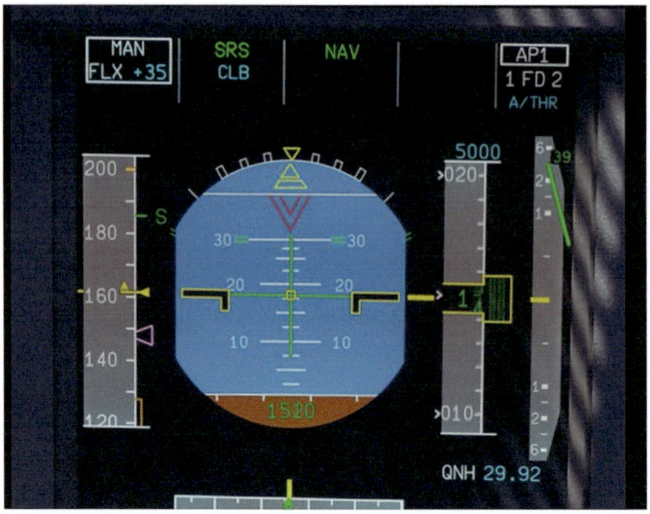

At approximately **1,500 feet AGL**:

- The aircraft automatically transitions to a **climb profile**.

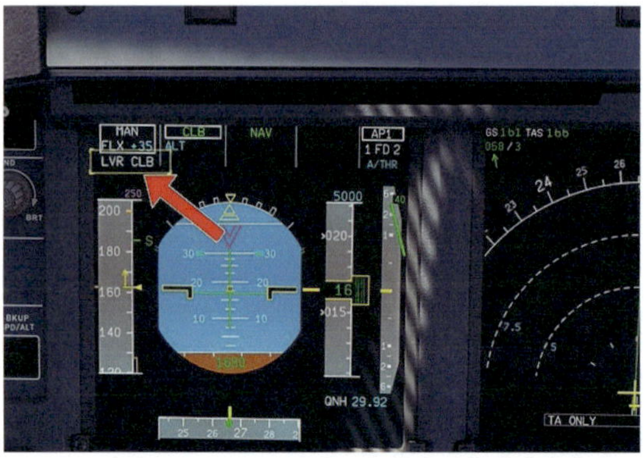

- Thrust is reduced, and pitch becomes less aggressive.
- The **FMA now indicates "THR CLB"**, instructing you to set **climb power**.

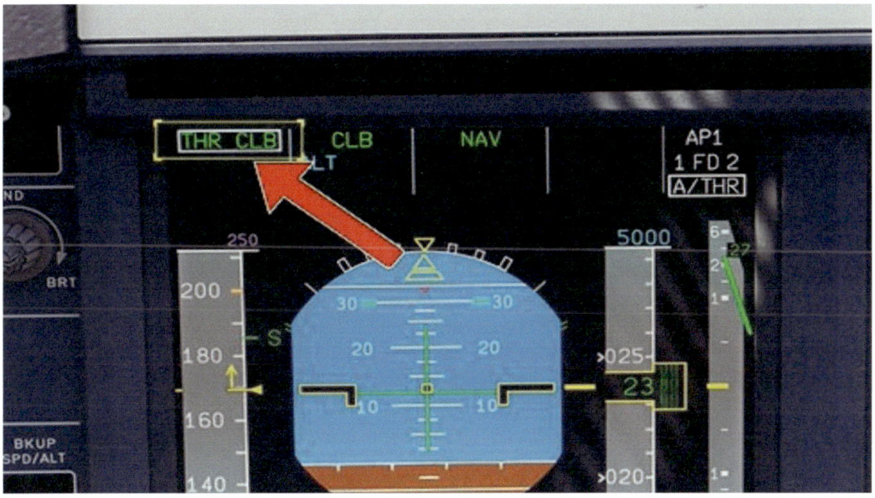

At the same time:

- Managed speed increases from **V2 to 250 knots**.
- The aircraft lowers pitch to accelerate.

Cleanup After Takeoff

- As speed increases, **retract flaps** once passing the **slats retraction marker** on the airspeed tape.

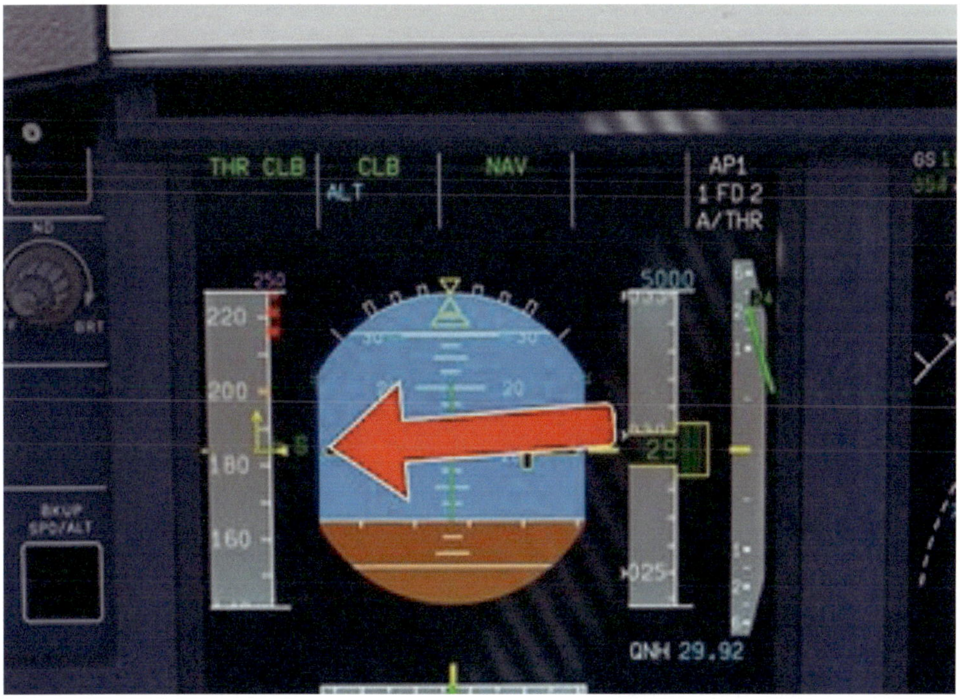

- Monitor the **FMA** to confirm:

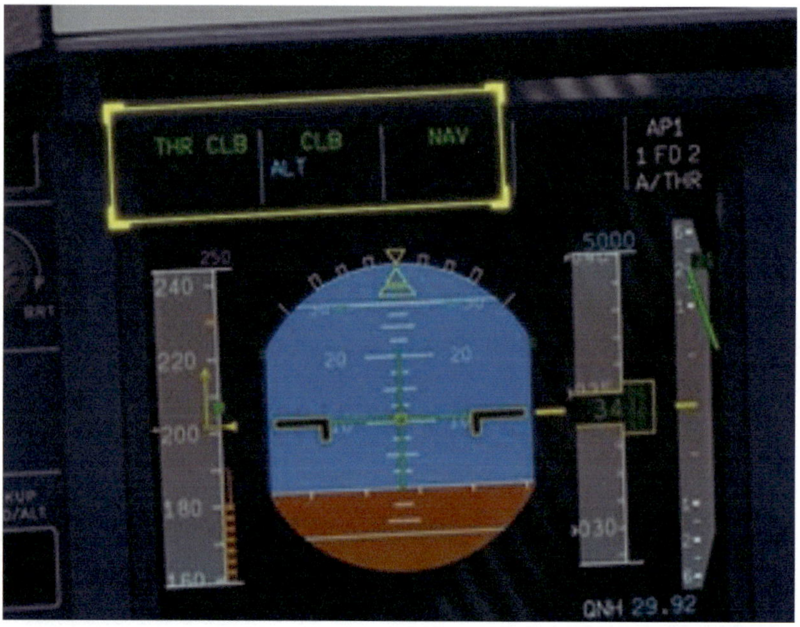

  - **THR CLB** for power
  - **CLB** profile for pitch
  - **NAV** for lateral guidance

Once stabilized:

- **Disarm spoilers**
- **Disarm autobrake**

CHAPTER FIFTEEN

MASTER EVERY LANDING IN MICROSOFT FLIGHT SIMULATOR 2024

We've all been there. Every pilot starts somewhere—confused, frustrated, and wondering why the aircraft simply refuses to touch down. Even the NPCs seem to be judging. If that sounds familiar, you're in the right place. And even if you already land smoothly, a quick refresher never hurts.

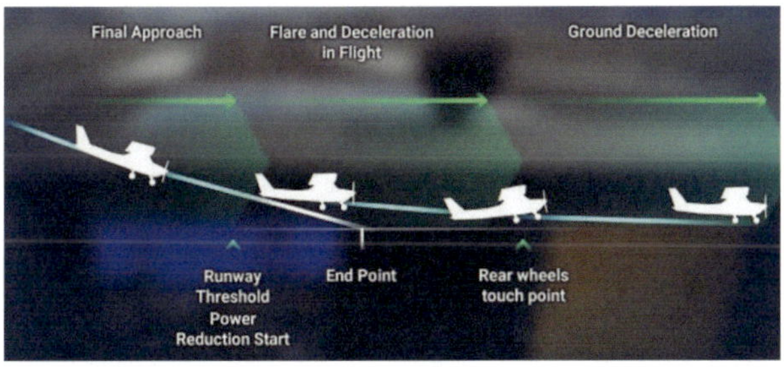

In this section, you'll learn the essential principles needed to go from chaotic landings to smooth, controlled touchdowns.

THE GOLDEN RULE OF LANDING: AIRSPEED IS EVERYTHING

Ask any pilot, and you'll hear the same phrase: **"Speed is life."**

Airspeed is the single most important factor during landing.

- **Too slow**, and the aircraft stalls and drops.
- **Too fast**, and the aircraft floats or bounces down the runway.

So how do you find the correct landing speed?

Finding the Correct Approach Speed

Look at your **airspeed indicator**. On most aircraft, you'll see colored arcs:

Step 1: Identify Stall Speed (VS_0)

- Focus on the **beginning of the white arc**
- This represents **VS_0**, the stall speed with **full flaps**

Step 2: Multiply by 1.3

This gives you your **optimal approach and landing speed (Vref)**.

Example:

- Stall speed (VS_0): 40 knots
- 40 × 1.3 = **52 knots**

That means your ideal landing speed with full flaps is **52 knots**.

For landings **without flaps**, use the beginning of the **green arc** instead and apply the same calculation.

LANDING SPEEDS IN LARGER AIRCRAFT

In airliners, landing speed depends heavily on:

- Aircraft weight

- Fuel load
- Weather conditions
- Configuration

Because of this, landing speeds are **calculated automatically by onboard computers** and will vary from flight to flight.

Where to Find Landing Speed:

- **Airbus**:
  Open *Performance* → Cycle to *Approach Phase* → Look for **Vapp**

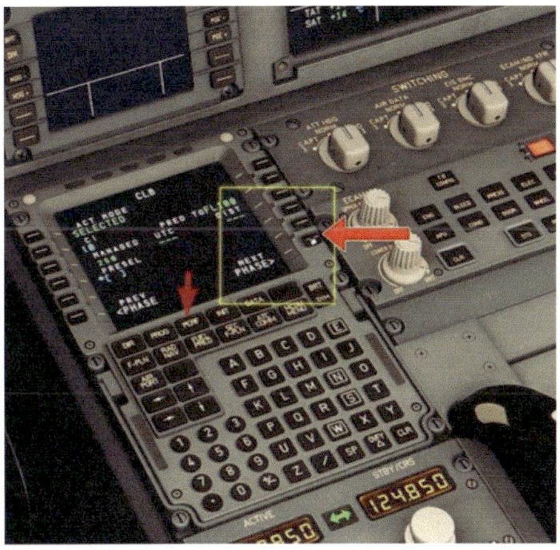

- **Boeing**:
  Open *INIT REF* → *INDEX* → *APPROACH* → Select flap setting (e.g., Flaps 30)

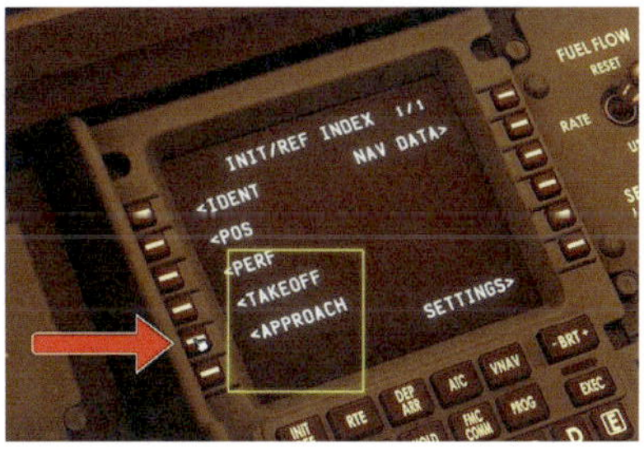

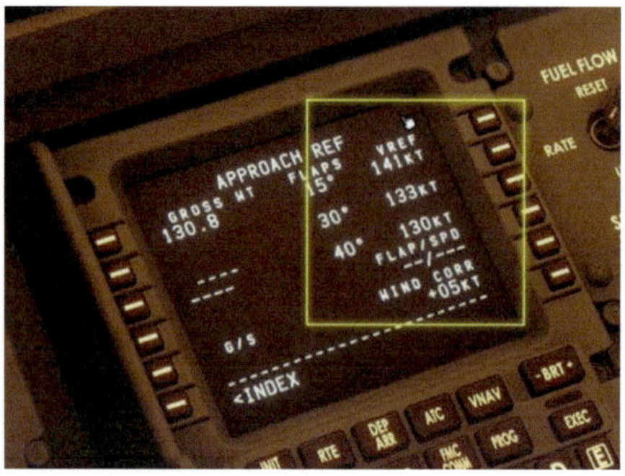

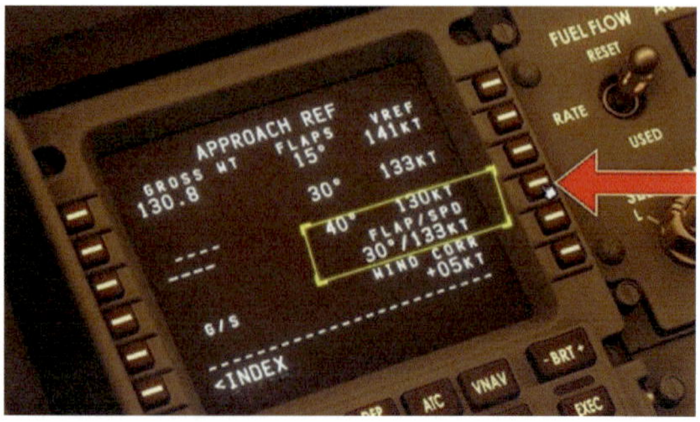

Once selected, input the speed into the flight computer.

WHY FLAPS MATTER

Flaps are not optional during landing.

Think of flaps as **a lift multiplier**:

- They allow the aircraft to stay airborne at lower speeds
- Without flaps, maintaining landing speed becomes difficult—and dangerous

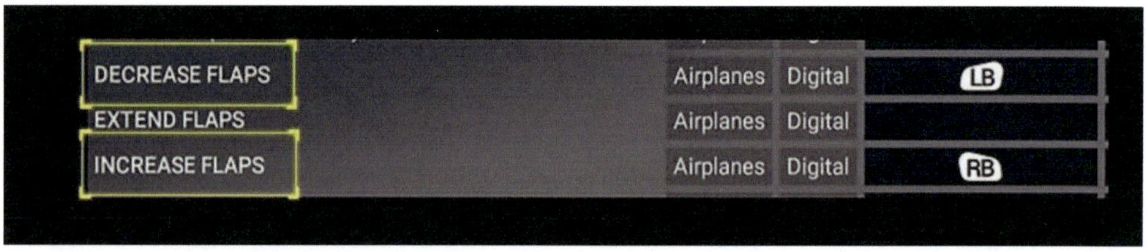

Lower flaps progressively to stay stable and on speed.

MASTERING THE VISUAL APPROACH

The MSFS 2024 tutorials can be confusing—one lesson teaches engine-off landings, another asks for constant power like a carrier landing. Ignore the noise.

Instead, remember **one simple rule**:

Aim at the target point using pitch and power

UNDERSTANDING THE TARGET POINT

Your **target point** is where you visually aim during approach. This is usually:

- The **runway aiming point markers** (the two white rectangles)

- Or, on short-field landings, the **runway threshold**

For this section, we'll use the aiming point markers.

Imagine the aiming point as a **fixed portal** you must fly through. Do not anticipate the flare or touchdown yet—just fly the approach.

PITCH AND POWER COORDINATION

Pitch controls **where you're going**

Power controls **how fast you get there**

If You're Too Low:

If the aircraft is too low on the glide path, gently pull back on the yoke. This reduces the rate of descent, but it also causes your airspeed to drop, so you must add power to maintain your target speed.

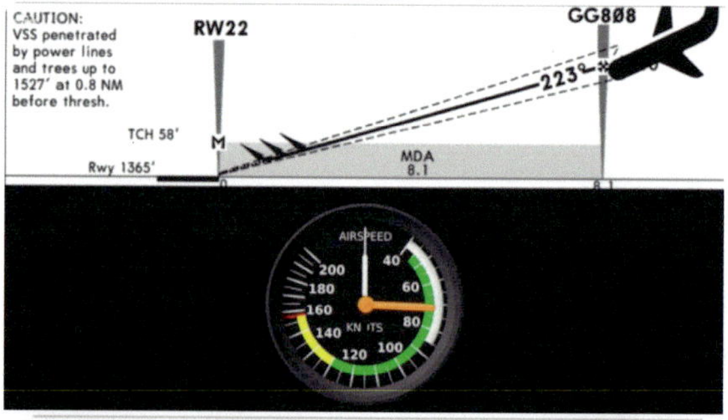

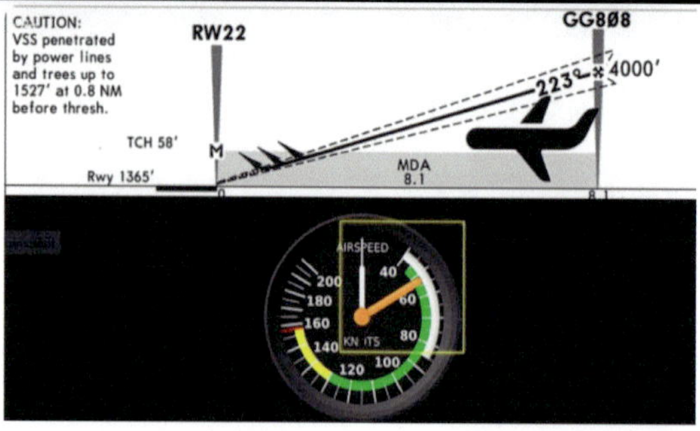

If You're Too High:

If the aircraft is too high, push forward slightly on the yoke to increase the descent rate. This will naturally cause the **airspeed to increase**, so you need to **reduce power** to stay within the correct approach speed.

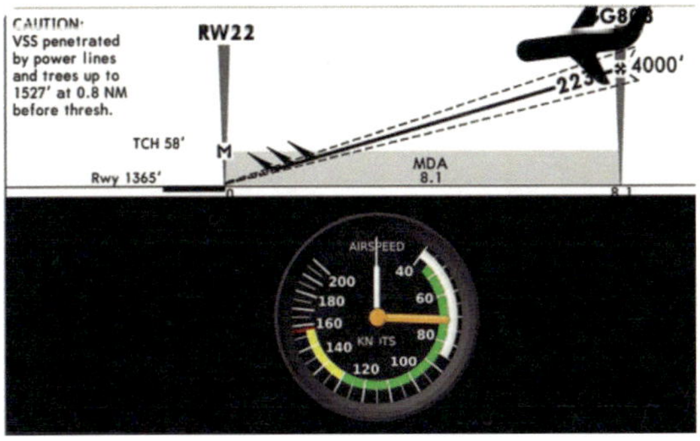

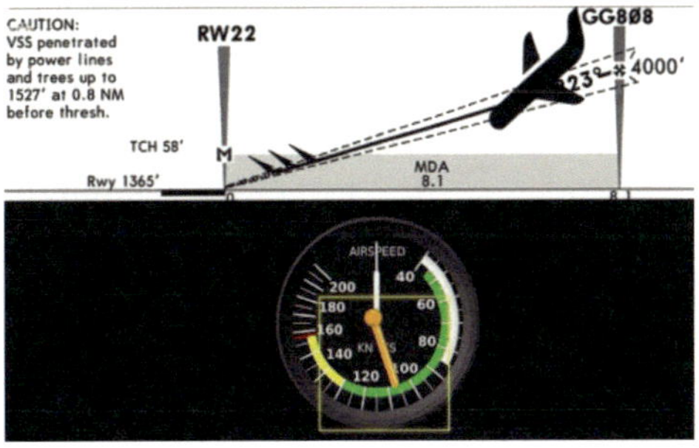

The goal is simple:

- Maintain the aiming point
- Hold your reference speed
- Make small, smooth corrections

Key Takeaways

- Always calculate and fly the correct approach speed
- Use flaps to maintain lift at low speed
- Aim at a fixed target point—don't overthink the flare
- Control glide path with **pitch**
- Control speed with **power**

Master these fundamentals, and consistent, smooth landings will follow.

CASE EXAMPLE: VISUAL LANDING IN THE CESSNA 172

Let's return to the **Cessna 172** and walk through a practical landing example.

- **Vref (approach speed):** 52 knots
- **Target:** Runway aiming point
- **Condition:** Stabilized on final approach

Managing the Descent Path

As we approach the runway, we notice that the aircraft is **slightly below the ideal glide path**.

Too Low

To correct this:

1. **Pitch up slightly** to reduce the descent rate
2. Airspeed immediately begins to drop
3. **Add a small amount of power** to maintain 52 knots

After a moment, we're back on the correct descent path.

Too High (Short Final)

Now, on short final, we notice we're **too high**.

To fix this:

1. **Pitch down slightly** to increase the descent rate
2. Airspeed naturally increases
3. **Reduce power** to maintain reference speed

Once again, we're back on the proper glide path.

Key Rule to Remember

- **Pitch controls your glide path**
- **Power controls your airspeed**

Keep your eyes locked on the **aiming point**.

Do **not** think about the flare yet.

PRACTICE THE HARDEST PART FIRST

At this stage, **do not flare**. Instead, deliberately touch down at the aiming point—even if it feels firm.

Repeat this process until you can:

- Hit the aiming point consistently
- Maintain the correct approach speed

If you can do that, you've already completed **90% of a successful landing**. The approach phase is by far the most challenging part.

HOW DO YOU KNOW IF YOU'RE TOO HIGH OR TOO LOW?

There's no shortcut—**experience is the real teacher**. Repetition builds the instinct.

However, there are useful **visual cues**:

Cockpit Reference

- If the runway appears to **move upward toward the top of the cockpit**, you're too high and will overshoot.

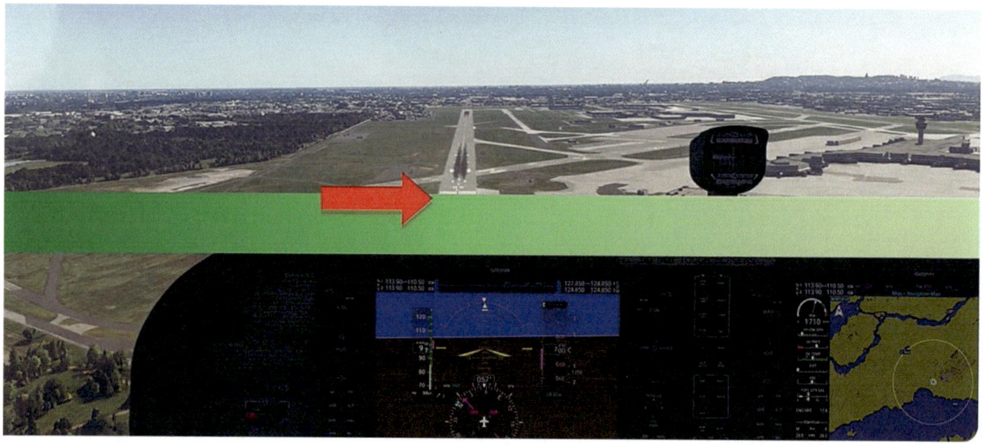

- If the runway appears to **drop away from the top of the cockpit**, you're too low and may land short.

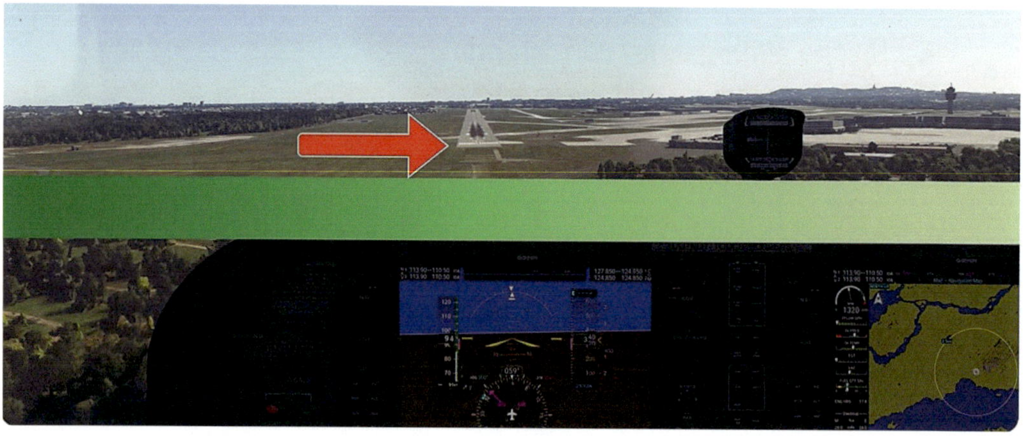

USING PAPI LIGHTS (IF AVAILABLE)

Many airports are equipped with **PAPI (Precision Approach Path Indicator)** lights:

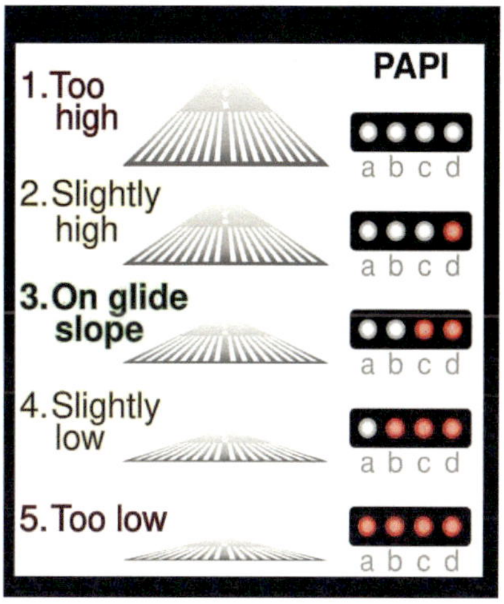

- **4 red:** Too low

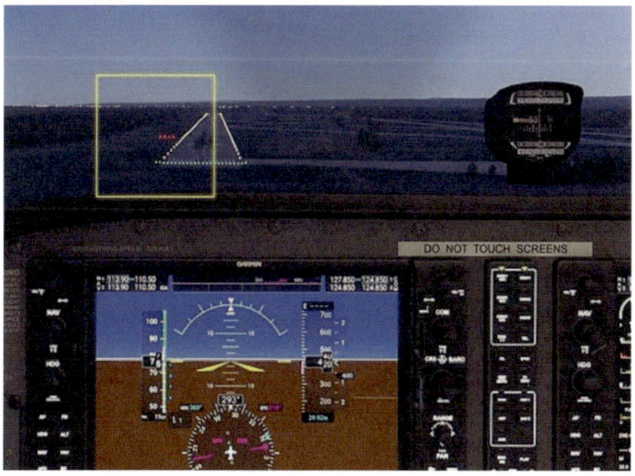

- **4 white:** Too high

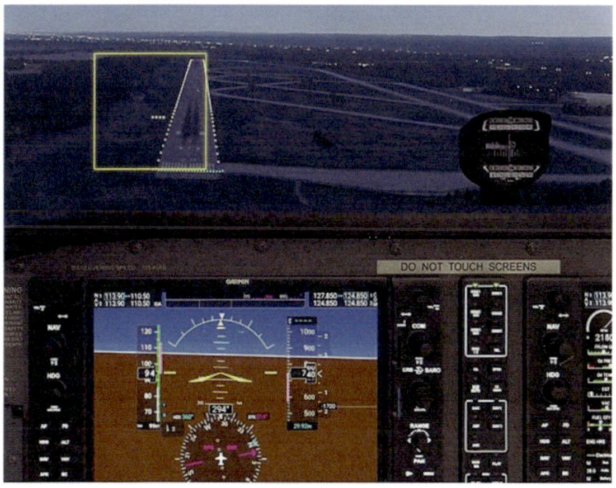

- **2 red / 2 white:** Perfect glide path

These lights are extremely helpful when learning visual approaches.

The Final Step: The Flare

As you approach the aiming point:

1. When a few feet above the runway, **gently pull back on the yoke**
2. **Reduce throttle to idle**
3. As airspeed decays, the aircraft will naturally settle
4. Continue pulling back until the **main landing gear touches first**

A smooth landing is nice—but **a controlled landing is what matters**.

After Touchdown

- Keep pulling back slightly on the yoke
- Lower the nose gear gently
- Once all wheels are down, apply brakes as needed

BONUS TIP

Here's a bonus tip that helped me a lot when I first started flight simming.

If you're using a monitor, check its built-in settings and see if it has an **on-screen aim point** or **crosshair** option. This feature simply places a small marker in the center of your screen.

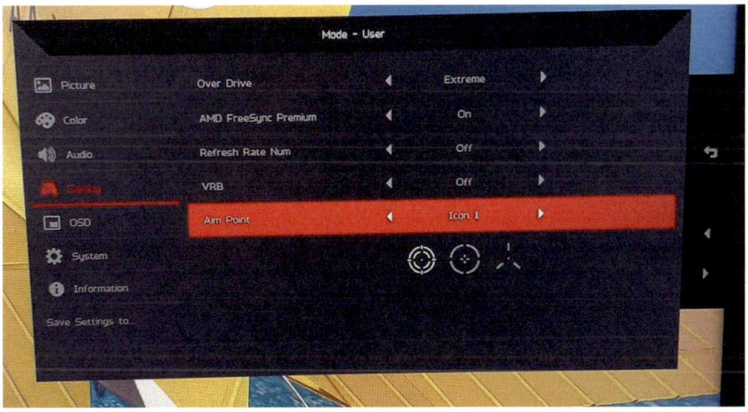

You can use that marker to **line yourself up with the center of the runway** during approach. Keep the aim point aligned with the runway centerline, and it will help you stay straight on final. If you place it over the **runway landing markers**, it can also help you maintain a more consistent aiming point.

It's a simple visual aid, but it can make a big difference—especially when you're still learning how to fly stable approaches.

HOW TO PERFORM A PERFECT CROSSWIND TAKEOFF

A crosswind during takeoff may not seem like a major challenge, but without proper control inputs, it can quickly push your aircraft off the runway—or worse. Correct technique ensures a smooth, safe departure while protecting your landing gear and maintaining runway alignment.

Wind Correction Basics

Crosswind takeoff technique begins the same way as crosswind taxiing: **deflect the ailerons fully into the wind**.

Without this correction, the upwind wing can lift prematurely, allowing the wind to push the aircraft sideways toward the runway edge.

Initial Takeoff Roll

Before applying power, **check the windsock** near the runway threshold to confirm wind direction and strength.

As you begin the roll, keep the ailerons fully deflected into the wind. Visually, the **raised aileron should be on the side the wind is coming from**.

Be prepared to use **rudder** as well. In stronger winds, the aircraft will naturally try to turn into the wind (weathervaning). Apply enough rudder to maintain alignment with the runway centerline and keep the aircraft tracking straight.

In this situation, apply right rudder input to counteract the aircraft's tendency to weathervane into the wind and maintain runway alignment.

Acceleration Down the Runway

As airspeed increases, your control surfaces become more effective. Gradually **reduce aileron deflection**, but only enough to keep the wings level and the aircraft aligned with the centerline. Too much deflection can cause a wingtip to contact the runway.

Throughout the roll, your goal is to **keep the wings level**. If the upwind wing lifts first, the aircraft may begin skipping sideways, increasing side-load stress on the landing gear and raising the risk of a runway excursion or wing strike.

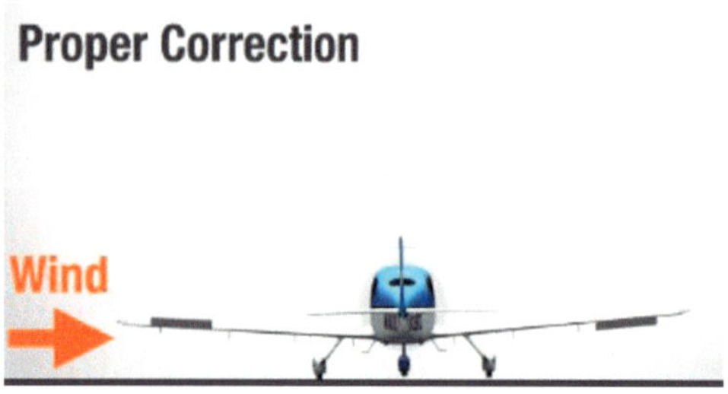

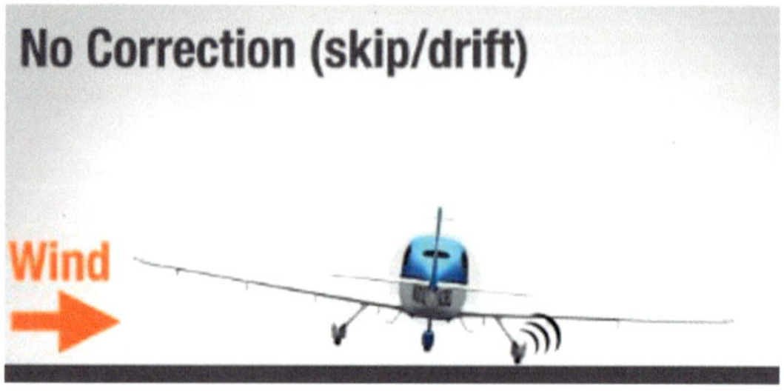

Lift-Off Technique

During rotation, **maintain aileron pressure into the wind** so the **downwind wheel lifts off first**, followed by the upwind wheel. This sequence prevents lateral drift and side-skipping.

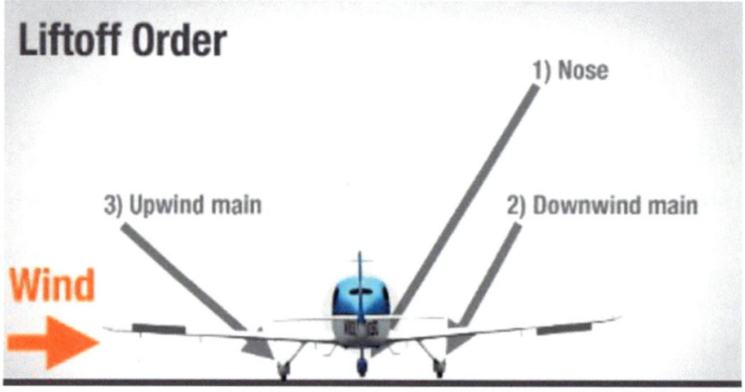

Ideal crosswind lift-off order:

1. Nosewheel
2. Downwind main wheel
3. Upwind main wheel

In stronger crosswinds, delay rotation slightly to allow the aircraft to reach a higher airspeed. This produces a more positive, controlled lift-off and improves stability as you transition into the climb.

Initial Climb

After liftoff, **gradually neutralize aileron input** to keep the wings level. You'll immediately notice the aircraft drifting sideways due to the wind.

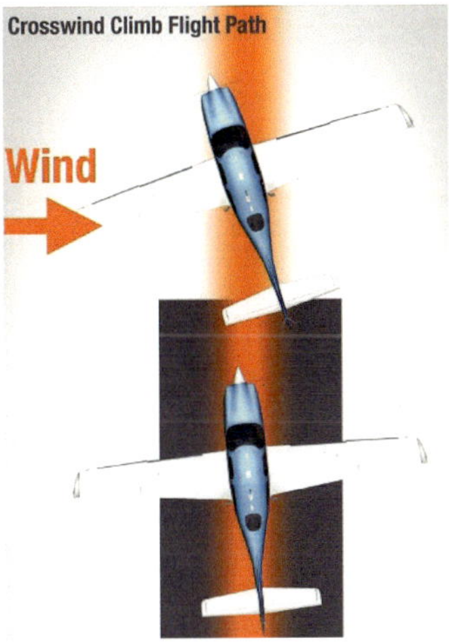

To maintain the extended runway centerline, **turn slightly into the wind**, establishing a crab angle that counters drift. Once the correct crab angle is set, the aircraft will track straight ahead during the climb.

TAMING THE WIND: CROSSWIND LANDINGS EXPLAINED

For many student pilots, crosswind landings are among the most challenging—and most essential—skills to master during flight training. Even with a strong understanding of flight theory, it's common to feel like everything just isn't clicking yet. That's because crosswind landings demand more than technical knowledge; they test a pilot's judgment, coordination, and adaptability in constantly changing conditions.

This guide breaks the process down with practical insights, actionable tips, and training-focused explanations to help you build confidence and sharpen your technique. With consistent practice and the right mindset, mastering crosswind landings brings you one step closer to that all-important first solo flight.

Did You Know?

- The strongest documented crosswind landing was performed by a Boeing 747 in a **35-knot crosswind**.
- Many airports use **angled runway layouts** to reduce crosswind exposure.
- Crosswind landings are **rigorously evaluated** in commercial pilot training and check rides.
- The **crab technique** mirrors how birds naturally align themselves when landing in strong winds.

What Is a Crosswind Landing?

In an ideal world, pilots would always land directly into a headwind. A headwind reduces ground speed, improves control, and makes touchdowns smoother and safer. In reality, however, the wind rarely aligns perfectly with the runway.

When wind approaches the aircraft from an angle during landing, the result is a **crosswind landing**. Unlike takeoff—where an aircraft can briefly yaw into the wind after liftoff—landing requires precise alignment. Touching down while the aircraft is yawed introduces significant **side-load stress** on the landing gear, which can lead to structural damage or loss of directional control.

The Core Challenges of Crosswind Landings

Crosswinds introduce two primary challenges that pilots must manage simultaneously:

1. **Maintaining alignment with the runway's extended centerline during approach**
2. **Ensuring the aircraft's longitudinal axis is aligned with the runway at touchdown**

Failure in either area increases the risk of instability, gear damage, or runway excursion.

Understanding the Aerodynamics

Crosswinds apply a lateral force to the aircraft's fuselage, causing it to yaw around its vertical axis. To counteract this, pilots must use **coordinated control inputs**:

- **Ailerons** to bank the aircraft into the wind
- **Rudder** to control yaw and maintain alignment

Wind gusts add another layer of complexity. Sudden increases in wind speed can momentarily boost lift, leading to floating, overshooting, or an unstable approach. Pilots must anticipate and correct for these changes smoothly to maintain a stable descent profile.

Mastering the aerodynamics of crosswind landings allows pilots to stay aligned, remain in control, and achieve safe, confident touchdowns—even in challenging conditions.

Crosswind Landing Techniques

Mastering crosswind landings requires understanding several proven techniques. Each method has its strengths and is best suited to specific wind conditions. Skilled pilots choose and adapt these techniques based on wind strength, runway conditions, and aircraft type.

The Crab Method

The crab method offers excellent stability during the approach and is especially effective in strong, steady crosswinds. It is typically used on final approach and transitioned out of just before touchdown.

In this technique, the aircraft's nose is pointed into the wind to counteract drift while the wings remain level. The sideways alignment resembles a crab's movement—hence the name.

How to Use the Crab Method

- Fly the approach with the aircraft yawed into the wind using rudder input.
- Maintain this crab angle to stay aligned with the runway centerline.
- Just before touchdown, apply rudder to straighten the nose and align the aircraft with the runway.

The Wing-Low (Sideslip) Method

The wing-low method corrects drift and alignment at the same time and is commonly preferred for light aircraft and during touchdown.

In this technique, the aircraft is slightly banked into the wind while opposite rudder is applied to keep the nose aligned with the runway.

How to Use the Wing-Low Method

- Apply aileron into the wind to bank the aircraft.
- Use opposite rudder to keep the nose pointed straight down the runway.
- Maintain coordinated inputs through the approach, flare, and touchdown.
- Make small, smooth adjustments to avoid overcorrection as wind conditions change.

Combination Technique

In stronger or more variable crosswinds, pilots often combine both methods to take advantage of their strengths.

How It Works

- Use the crab method during the approach for stability and reduced workload.
- Transition smoothly to the wing-low method just before touchdown to ensure proper alignment and eliminate drift.

This hybrid approach provides excellent control and precision in challenging conditions.

Go-Around: A Smart and Safe Choice

Not every landing needs to be completed. When conditions become unstable—such as sudden gusts, shifting winds, or poor alignment—a **go-around is always a valid and professional decision**.

Executing a go-around allows you to:

- Reassess wind conditions
- Re-stabilize the aircraft
- Set up a safer, more controlled approach

Good judgment is just as important as good technique, and choosing to go around is a sign of skill—not failure.

12 Common Crosswind Landing Mistakes — and How to Avoid Them

Crosswind landings are among the most demanding manoeuvres in aviation. Even experienced pilots can slip into bad habits when conditions deteriorate. Understanding these common mistakes—and how to correct them—will dramatically improve safety and confidence.

1. Failing to Anticipate the Crosswind

Not assessing wind direction and strength before the approach leads to rushed decisions and poor setup.

Avoid it: Review ATIS/ASOS, check windsocks, and brief your crosswind plan before entering the circuit.

2. Exceeding Personal Limits

Pressure to "get it on the ground" can override good judgment.

Avoid it: Know your limits. If the crosswind exceeds your comfort or aircraft capability, divert or go around. Safety always comes first.

3. Overcontrolling the Aircraft

Aggressive inputs cause instability, ballooning, or hard touchdowns. **Avoid it:** Use small, smooth corrections. If gusts or oscillations develop, go around early.

4. Landing in a Crab

Touching down with the nose misaligned creates dangerous side loads on the landing gear.

Avoid it: Use rudder to align the aircraft with the runway just before touchdown. Look far down the runway and anticipate increasing rudder input as speed decreases.

5. Failing to Touch Down on the Upwind Wheel

Levelling the wings too early allows the wind to push the aircraft sideways. **Avoid it:** Keep aileron into the wind through roundout and touchdown. The upwind main wheel should touch first.

6. Relaxing Controls After Touchdown

Reducing control inputs as speed decreases leads to loss of directional control. **Avoid it:** Increase aileron into the wind and maintain rudder as the aircraft slows. Fly the aircraft all the way to the parking stand.

7. Flying Too Fast on Final

Excess speed causes floating, bouncing, and poor control at touchdown.

Avoid it: Fly the correct approach speed. Practise low-speed handling to improve confidence and precision.

8. Misjudging Wind Speed or Angle

Underestimating the crosswind results in insufficient correction. **Avoid it:** Cross-check reported winds with visual cues such as windsocks, smoke, or surface movement.

9. Fixating on Instruments

Over-reliance on instruments reduces visual alignment and runway awareness. **Avoid it:** Look outside on short final. Use instruments to confirm airspeed—not to fly the landing visually blind.

10. Poor Rudder and Aileron Coordination

Unbalanced inputs cause drift or misalignment.

Avoid it: Practise coordinated control: rudder for alignment, aileron for drift. Smooth, simultaneous inputs are key.

11. Failing to Commit to a Go-Around

Pressing on with an unstable approach increases accident risk.

Avoid it: If alignment or drift becomes unmanageable, go around immediately and reset.

12. Losing Control During Rollout

Many runway excursions happen after touchdown.

Avoid it: Maintain crosswind controls throughout rollout and taxi. Only relax controls once parked.

Control Basics and Power Management

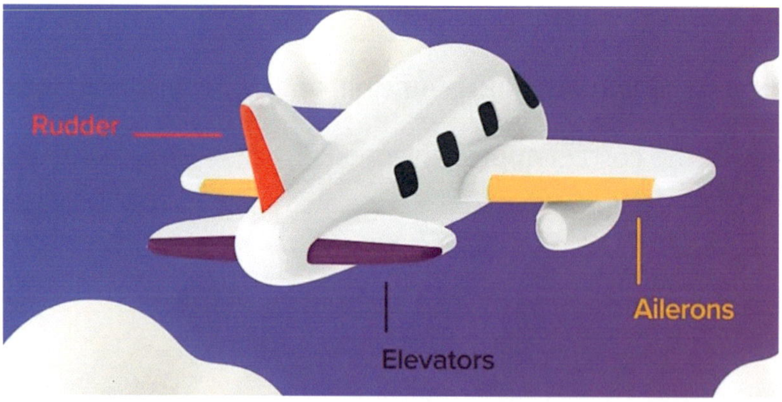

Forget overthinking crosswind theory. Focus on simple cause-and-effect corrections:

Rudder — Controls Alignment

- Nose left of centreline → **Right rudder**
- Nose right of centreline → **Left rudder**

Ailerons — Control Drift

- Drifting left → **Right aileron**
- Drifting right → **Left aileron**

In a crosswind, this naturally results in cross-controlled inputs: **aileron into the wind, rudder away from it**. Focus on what the aircraft is doing—not on memorised control combinations.

Maintain airspeed with **appropriate power or slight nose-down pitch** while crosswind controls are applied.

10 Steps to a Perfect Crosswind Landing

1. Analyse the Wind

Study windsocks, ATIS, and ASOS reports to determine wind direction and strength. Practise estimating crosswind components for different runways. Strong pre-flight wind awareness builds confidence and leads to better decision-making.

2. Practise in a Simulator

Use a flight simulator or train with an instructor to practise crosswind landings in a controlled environment. Focus on alignment, drift correction, and gust management without real-world pressure.

3. Train Progressively

Start with light crosswinds and gradually increase difficulty as your skills improve. This steady progression builds competence without overwhelming you.

4. Use Touch-and-Go Drills

Perform repeated touch-and-go landings to refine approach alignment and drift correction. Immediate repetition reinforces learning and highlights what needs improvement.

5. Mentally Rehearse the Landing

Before flight, visualise each phase—from final approach to flare and touchdown. Mentally practise control inputs for gusts and power changes to reduce hesitation in the air.

6. Practise Low Approaches: On long runways, practise flying 10–30 feet above the surface while maintaining centreline alignment. Once control feels natural, transition to full landings.

7. Establish a Centreline Reference: Choose a fixed reference point on the cowling (such as a screw or marking) that aligns with the taxiway centreline. Use this same reference in flight to maintain precise runway alignment and avoid parallax errors.

8. Correct Alignment and Drift: Use rudder to keep the nose aligned with the runway and ailerons to counter lateral drift. Reduce power smoothly as you approach touchdown.

9. Touch Down Properly: Allow the **upwind main wheel** to touch first, then gently lower the remaining wheels. This ensures stability and prevents sideways movement.

10. Maintain Control After Touchdown: Continue flying the aircraft during rollout. Increase aileron into the wind as speed decreases. At taxi speed, the yoke should be fully deflected into the wind.

Three Key Reminders

- **Happy Feet:** Expect constant rudder work. Small, continuous pedal inputs keep the aircraft aligned.
- **Small Corrections:** Use gentle, precise control inputs. Overcorrection leads to instability.
- **Don't Rush:** If the landing feels unstable or rushed, go around. A second attempt is always the safer option.

CHAPTER SIXTEEN

NIGHT FLYING AND LOW VISIBILITY OPERATION IN MICROSOFT FLIGHT SIMULATOR 2024

In **Microsoft Flight Simulator 2024**, night flying and low visibility operations have been enhanced with a new lighting engine and improved atmospheric effects.

Night Flying Improvements

- **Volumetric Lighting:** The 2024 engine introduces a more realistic "bloom" effect for airport lights, including runway and taxiway edge lighting, which provides a greater sense of depth compared to previous versions.
- **Cockpit Management:** To preserve night vision, pilots can now more effectively dim instrument panels and radio displays. High-fidelity aircraft like the **Airbus A321** and **H125** have received specific updates to their emissive lighting values for better night readability.
- **External Visibility:** Aircraft lights now reflect realistically off the fuselage and ground surfaces. However, some users have reported a "hazy" look or light shafts in clear night conditions, which may require adjustment of in-game exposure settings.

Low Visibility Operations

- **ILS Categories:** The sim supports advanced Instrument Landing Systems (ILS) for low-visibility landings:
  - **CAT II:** Requires redundant systems and allows landing with a decision height (DH) as low as 100 feet.
  - **CAT III:** Enables fully automated landings (Autoland) in near-zero visibility conditions.
- **Enhanced Fog and Haze:** The simulation features more accurate volumetric fog and heavy cloud cover, which now affects "screen exposure" to mimic how a pilot's eyes adjust to changing light levels in thick weather.
- **Visual Aids:** High-intensity approach lighting systems (ALSF-2) and touchdown zone markers are included to assist in identifying the runway in foggy conditions.

New Features and Tools

- **Night Vision Goggles (NVG):** Certain military and utility aircraft, such as the **F-117 Nighthawk**, now include native support for Night Vision Goggles for tactical or search-and-rescue missions.
- **Advanced Weather Planning:** The native flight planner now provides detailed **NOTAMS** and real-time weather information to help pilots identify airports with suitable lighting and ILS capabilities before departure.
- **Third-Party Enhancements:** Add-ons like MSFS DarkStreets help improve realism by removing unrealistic street lights in rural areas.

TAKING OFF AT NIGHT IN LOW VISIBILITY

Taking off at night in low visibility within MSFS 2024 requires a heavy reliance on instruments (IFR) rather than visual references, as runway lighting can sometimes appear over-bloomed or, conversely, hard to locate due to bugs in light rendering. In MSFS 2024, lighting at night has been updated to be more immersive, but it can be challenging, as airports may not be as brightly lit as expected.

Here is a guide for handling low-visibility night takeoffs in MSFS 2024:

1. Preparation and Setup

- **Lights On:** Turn on all lights (Nav, Beacon, Taxi, Landing, Strobe, Wing, Logo) before entering the runway to maximize visibility.
- **Instrument Check:** Ensure your Primary Flight Display (PFD) and Navigation instruments (G1000 NXi, G3000, etc.) are functional and set to the correct frequency.
- **Set View:** Adjust your cockpit view (Shift + W/S or Shift + Q/E) to ensure you can see both the runway lights and your flight instruments clearly.
- **Cockpit Lighting:** Adjust instrument lighting to avoid blinding yourself, as some planes have very bright panels, making the exterior look darker.

2. Takeoff Procedure

- **Align and Hold:** Line up with the runway center line, focusing on the center white lights, which may shift to red near the end of the runway.
- **Instruments over Visuals:** Do not rely on visual cues for pitch or roll. Use the Attitude Indicator (Artificial Horizon) on your PFD to maintain a straight, wings-level attitude.

- **Rotate:** Upon reaching rotation speed (V_r) smoothly pull back on the yoke. Maintain a steady climb rate, watching your vertical speed indicator.
- **Keep Straight:** In extremely low visibility, use the heading indicator to maintain runway heading.

3. Challenges and Tips

- **Lighting Issues:** In MSFS 2024, taxi and landing lights can be ineffective in moderate darkness, only working well in total darkness.
- **Low Visibility/Fog:** If the weather has fog, the runway lights might be obscured until you are very close.
- **Performance Setting:** If you experience poor performance (stutters) during takeoff, reduce the **Terrain Level of Detail (LOD)** setting in the options menu, as high settings can heavily impact CPU performance.
- **Camera Angle:** If you are having trouble seeing the runway, use Shift + E to move your head position higher for a better view over the dashboard.

4. Safety

- **Maintain Control:** In the event of disorientation, immediately trust your instruments (IFR) rather than trying to look outside.
- **Go-Around:** If the takeoff feels unsafe or you lose control of your orientation, abort the takeoff if safe to do so, or immediately begin an instrument-guided climb to a safe altitude.

APPROACHING AND LANDING IN LOW VISIBILITY

In **Microsoft Flight Simulator 2024**, approaching and landing in low visibility requires heavy reliance on onboard technology, such as the Instrument Landing System (ILS) and Synthetic Vision Systems (SVS).

1. Preparation and Setup

- **Tune the ILS Frequency**: Before your descent, enter the localizer frequency for your arrival runway into your Nav radio (NAV1).
- **Set the Final Approach Course**: Input the runway heading on your Course (CRS) selector to align your instruments with the physical runway.
- **Identify Minimums**: Determine the decision altitude (DA) or decision height (DH) for the approach. If you cannot see the runway at this altitude, you must execute a missed approach.

2. The Approach Phase

- **Capture the Localizer and Glideslope**: Fly toward the approach path at an angle (usually 30 degrees). Once the localizer (lateral) and glideslope (vertical) diamonds appear on your Primary Flight Display (PFD), engage **Approach Mode (APR)** on your autopilot.
- **Capture from Below**: Always intercept the glideslope from beneath the magenta diamond to ensure the autopilot locks onto the correct signal.
- **Configure the Aircraft**: Gradually lower flaps and landing gear as you slow to your target approach speed (Vref) to maintain stability on the glide path.

3. Landing Techniques

- **Synthetic Vision (SVS)**: For aircraft equipped with modern Garmin G1000 or G3000 suites, use the synthetic vision display to "see" the digital terrain and runway through the fog.
- **Autoland (CAT III)**: Large airliners like the Airbus A320 or Boeing 737 can perform a fully automated landing. To use this, engage both autopilots (AP1 and AP2) after capturing the ILS to enable **CAT III Dual Channel** mode.
- **Visual Cues**: Keep an eye out for high-intensity approach lighting systems (ALS) and touchdown zone lights (TDZL) that become visible at very low altitudes.
- **Manual Transition**: If not using Autoland, disconnect the autopilot once you have the runway lights in sight (usually around 100–200 feet) to perform the final flare and touchdown.

4. Critical Systems to Monitor

- **PAPI Lights**: Use the Precision Approach Path Indicator lights (two red, two white) to verify your vertical position once the ground is visible.
- **Radio Altimeter**: Monitor your height above ground level (AGL) for the final flare callouts ("Fifty, Forty, Thirty...").

CHAPTER SEVENTEEN

EXPLORING CROSS COUNTRY AND LONG HAUL FLIGHT

Exploring cross-country and long-haul flights involves considering different planning, booking, and comfort strategies for each type of journey.

CROSS-COUNTRY FLIGHTS

Cross-country flights are typically domestic journeys (e.g., within the US) that cover significant distances, potentially involving light aircraft for private pilots, or standard commercial airliners for public travel.

- **Planning and Logistics**: For private pilots, planning is detailed, focusing on weather analysis, terrain (avoiding mountains or controlled airspaces), fuel management, and filing a comprehensive flight plan. For commercial travel, these flights are a standard part of airline schedules.
- **Aircraft**: Various aircraft are suitable, from single-engine pistons like the **Cessna 206** and **Cirrus SR22** to private jets like the **Challenger 300**, with options for commercial airlines also being widely available.
- **Booking Tips**: Booking around one to two months in advance is often ideal for domestic trips. Look into options from both major carriers and budget airlines, and consider flying mid-week for potential savings.

LONG-HAUL FLIGHTS

Long-haul flights are generally international flights with a journey time of 6-12 hours, and ultra-long-haul flights can exceed 16 hours, often crossing continents.

- **Airlines & Aircraft**: Airlines like **Singapore Airlines** and **Qatar Airways** consistently rank high for long-haul service due to their comfort and amenities. These flights typically use wide-body aircraft such as the **Airbus A350**, **Boeing 787**, and **Boeing 777**.
- **Booking Tips**: For international flights, booking three to five months in advance is usually best for securing good prices. You may find value in booking two one-way tickets on different airlines or leveraging frequent flyer miles for upgrades to Premium Economy or Business Class.
- **Comfort & Health**:
    - **Wear loose, comfortable clothing** and compression socks to aid blood circulation.
    - **Stay hydrated** and avoid alcohol and excessive caffeine.

- **Walk around every 2-3 hours** or perform seated exercises to prevent stiffness.
- **Pack essentials** like a travel pillow, eye mask, and noise-canceling headphones.

ENROUTE NAVIGATION AND WAYPOINT MANAGEMENT

In 2026, enroute navigation for cross-country and long-haul flights centers on **Performance-Based Navigation (PBN)** and digital integration between the cockpit and air traffic control (ATC).

1. Enroute Navigation Techniques

Modern long-haul and cross-country flights utilize several overlapping methods to ensure precision:

- **Performance-Based Navigation (PBN):** Relies on satellite-based systems (GPS/GNSS) rather than ground-based beacons.
  - **RNAV 10:** Standard for oceanic and remote long-haul phases.
  - **RNAV 5/2/1:** Used for continental enroute and arrival segments.
- **Future Air Navigation System (FANS):** Crucial for long-haul routes beyond radar coverage (e.g., oceanic tracks). It uses **ADS-C** (Automatic Dependent Surveillance-Contract) to automatically report positions to ATC via satellite.
- **Digital Communication:** Systems like **DataComm** and **CPDLC** (Controller-Pilot Data Link Communication) allow pilots to receive clearances and route changes as text messages directly into the Flight Management System (FMS), reducing voice-readback errors.

2. Waypoint Management Procedures

Managing waypoints involves verifying the intended path against real-time operational data:

- **Cross-Verification:** Pilots independently check FMS-loaded waypoints against their master flight plan. For oceanic crossings, crews verify the latitude and longitude of each waypoint before entry.
- **Handling "Direct To" Clears:** If ATC clears a flight to a waypoint not on the original plan, pilots must input the new waypoint and resolve any "discontinuities" in the FMS to ensure the route remains logical.

- **Waypoint Callouts:** During long-haul cruises, standard procedures include calling out the next waypoint, track, and distance to the other pilot as the aircraft crosses its current position.
- **Vertical Management:** Long-haul flights use **step climbs**. As fuel is burned and the aircraft becomes lighter, pilots update the FMS to climb to more efficient altitudes at designated waypoints.

3. Flight Planning & Strategic Tools (2026 Context)

- **Dynamic Optimization:** Advanced airline route planning software now integrates real-time weather and traffic flow data to optimize fuel efficiency.
- **NextGen Modernization:** Under the FAA's Flight Plan 2026, there is an increased push toward satellite-based tracking (ADS-B) and digitized certification to improve safety and reduce near-miss incidents.
- **Electronic Flight Bags (EFBs):** Tools like SkyDemon or SimBrief are used to generate detailed navigation logs, including calculated groundspeeds, headings, and fuel burns based on current wind forecasts.

USING REAL WORLD TOOLS AND ADD-ONS

Real-world cross-country and long-haul flight planning in 2026 relies on integrated Electronic Flight Bags (EFBs), real-time weather data, and sophisticated dispatch systems.

Primary Flight Planning Tools (EFBs)

EFBs have replaced traditional paper charts, offering integrated route planning, performance calculations, and in-flight navigation.

- **ForeFlight Mobile**: The industry standard for iOS, widely used by general aviation and business pilots. It features a web interface for desk planning that syncs automatically with mobile devices.
- Garmin Pilot: The top choice for pilots using Garmin avionics, offering deep integration with cockpit hardware and a data-driven map layout similar to panel-mount systems.
- **SkyVector**: A popular free web-based tool for initial route plotting and viewing aeronautical charts worldwide.

Essential Planning Add-ons & Resources

- **Weather Analysis**:

  - **AviationWeather.gov**: The primary source for official METARs, TAFs, and winds aloft.
  - **Skew-T Charts**: Used by advanced pilots to check cloud tops, freezing levels, and atmospheric stability.
- **Airport & FBO Information**:
  - AirNav: Critical for finding fuel prices and FBO (Fixed-Base Operator) services at stopover airports.
- **Filing & NOTAMs**:
  - **FltPlan.com**: A robust web-based system often preferred for IFR (Instrument Flight Rules) filing due to its extensive library of ATC-cleared routes.
  - **FAA NOTAM Search**: Essential for checking temporary flight restrictions (TFRs) or runway closures.

Long-Haul & Simulation Specifics

For ultra-long-haul or professional airline simulation, specialized dispatch tools are used:

- SimBrief by Navigraph: A free, comprehensive virtual dispatch system used for realistic long-haul planning, featuring ETOPS (Extended-range Twin-engine Operational Performance Standards) calculations and detailed fuel planning.
- **Lido Flight 4D**: Professional-grade software used by major airlines to compute the most fuel-efficient routes based on real-time weather and ATC restrictions.
- Microsoft Flight Simulator 2024 Planner: A modern tool for simulation enthusiasts to sync complex flight plans directly into the sim environment.

Key Planning Steps for 2026

1. **Weather "Go/No-Go"**: Check current and forecast weather at departure, enroute, and arrival.
2. **Weight & Balance**: Use apps like **WnB Pro** or integrated EFB tools to ensure the aircraft is within safe limits.
3. **Fuel Management**: Plan legs based on personal fuel minimums; for long-haul, use progressive planning to adjust for changing winds.
4. **NOTAM Review**: Legally required review of all notices affecting the planned route.

TIPS AND TRICKS

MSFS 2024 SIM RATE GUIDE: HOW TO FAST-FORWARD TIME

Watching the world pass by from the cockpit in *Microsoft Flight Simulator 2024* is part of the experience—until you're hours into a long-haul flight. When cruise becomes repetitive and you just want to reach the approach phase, **Sim Rate** allows you to speed up time and effectively "fast-forward" your flight.

Unlike *MSFS 2020*, older shortcuts such as **Ctrl + R** no longer work. In MSFS 2024, Sim Rate must be manually configured before it can be used.

How to Speed Up Time in MSFS 2024

Sim Rate is not assigned to any controls by default on **PC, Xbox, or PS5**, so setup is required.

1. Open **Settings**.
2. Navigate to the **Controls** menu.
3. Use the search bar and type **Sim Rate**.
4. Assign a key or button to **Sim Rate Toggle** (for example, *Alt + R*).
5. Assign separate bindings for:
   - **Increase Sim Rate**
   - **Decrease Sim Rate**
6. Use these key bindings during a flight to accelerate or slow down time.

Console Tip

On Xbox (and controller setups), selecting a Sim Rate command will display a **"Scanning"** prompt. Press the button combination you want to assign. Choose inputs that won't interfere with critical flight controls, especially during takeoff or landing.

Using Sim Rate as a Fast-Travel Alternative

MSFS 2024 does not include a traditional fast-travel feature, but Sim Rate can be used as an effective workaround—especially for long flights.

1. Ensure Sim Rate controls are assigned.
2. Activate the aircraft's **Autopilot**.
3. Set Autopilot to **NAV mode** so it follows your flight plan.
4. Increase the Sim Rate to accelerate time and reach your destination faster.

This method is ideal for cruising phases and can significantly reduce flight time while still allowing you to earn **Credits** during Career Mode.

Important Things to Know About Sim Rate

Before using Sim Rate, keep the following in mind:

- **No EXP Penalty**

  Fast-forwarding time does **not** reduce Experience Points. Unlike skipping flight segments, Sim Rate preserves full mission rewards.

- **Career Mode Risks**

  At higher simulation speeds, reaction time is drastically reduced. Unexpected weather, traffic conflicts, or system failures can result in crashes if you're not attentive. Use Sim Rate cautiously in Career Mode and only on stable, predictable routes.

- **No Visual Speed Indicator**

  MSFS 2024 does not display how fast time is moving. As a general guideline:

  - Pressing **Increase Sim Rate** about four times usually reaches maximum speed.
  - Press **Decrease Sim Rate** the same number of times to return to normal time.
- **Performance Impact**

  Higher Sim Rates can cause frame drops or instability, especially on systems already struggling with performance. If you experience stuttering or crashes, reduce Sim Rate or return to real-time speed.

BASIC CONTROLS: UNDERSTANDING AIRCRAFT MOVEMENT

To fly a light aircraft such as the **Cessna 172**, you must understand the three fundamental movements that control how the aircraft behaves in the air.

Roll: Roll is the aircraft's rotation around its **longitudinal axis** (nose to tail). Moving the joystick left or right controls the **ailerons**, causing the aircraft to bank in that direction.

Pitch: Pitch is movement around the **lateral axis** (wing to wing). Pushing the joystick forward lowers the nose, while pulling it back raises the nose. This controls climbs and descents.

Yaw: Yaw is rotation around the **vertical axis**. Using the joystick's third axis or rudder pedals moves the **rudder**, swinging the aircraft's nose left or right. Yaw is essential for coordinated turns and directional control.

Power Management: Using the Throttle

Speed is critical in aviation, and it's managed with the **throttle**:

- Pushing the throttle **increases engine power and speed**.
- Pulling the throttle **reduces power and speed**.

Power works together with pitch—more power without pitch change increases speed; more pitch without power reduces it.

Essential Flight Instruments

Once you understand the controls, focus on the core cockpit instruments that keep the aircraft safe and stable.

Airspeed Indicator

Located on the left, this shows the aircraft's speed relative to the surrounding air (not ground speed).

- **Green arc**: Normal operating range
- **Yellow zone, then red**: Overspeed danger
- **White zone, then red**: Too slow—risk of stall

Attitude Indicator

Positioned in the center, this shows the aircraft's orientation relative to the horizon. It's vital for maintaining stable flight, especially in poor visibility.

Altimeter

Found on the right, this displays altitude above sea level using air pressure. As altitude increases, air pressure decreases.

Mastering these three instruments prepares you for safe flight in good weather conditions.

Choosing the Right Aircraft to Learn

Beginners should start with simple, forgiving aircraft that make learning easier:

- **Cessna 172** – The gold standard for training aircraft
- **Flight Design CTSL** – Light, responsive, and easy to control
- **CubCrafters NX Cub** – Ideal for low-speed and low-altitude flying
- **Robin DR-400-100 Cadet** – Excellent for progressive skill development

These aircraft provide stable handling and clear feedback, making them ideal for mastering flight fundamentals without unnecessary complexity.

INDEX

A

B

C

D

E

F

G

H

I

J

K

L

M

T

V

W

X

Y

This book has been produced in line with the EU GPSR guidelines about the safety of products.

The General Product Safety Regulation is the European Union's updated framework for ensuring that all consumer products, including books, are safe for consumers.

This book has been printed by Amazon. The printer has issued safety certificates for the materials - like ink, paper and glue - being used.

The product identifier is: 9789403878126

The author is responsible for the content of the book and had it produced by Bookmundo.

Should there be any questions in regard to the safety of the product, please contact us.

Bookmundo
Delftsestraat 33
3013AE Rotterdam
The Netherlands
info@bookmundo.com